D1569059

PROFILES IN QUALITY

Learning from the Masters

PROFILES IN QUALITY

Learning from the Masters

Louis E. Schultz

Contributing Editors
Tom Cothran
Margaret Kaeter
Dick Schaaf

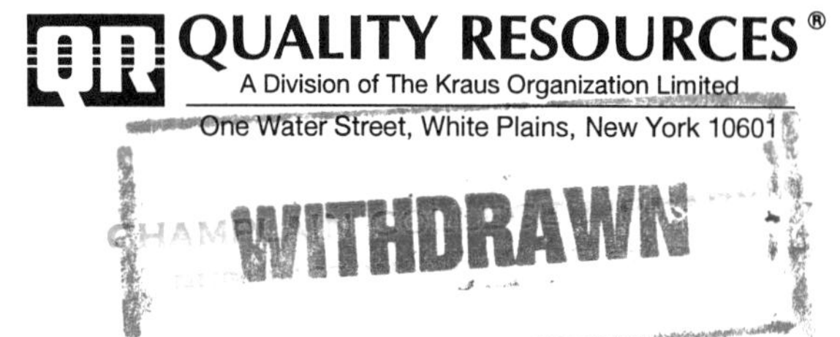

QUALITY RESOURCES®
A Division of The Kraus Organization Limited
One Water Street, White Plains, New York 10601

Most Quality Resources books are available at quantity discounts when purchased in bulk. For more information contact:

Special Sales Department
Quality Resources
A Division of The Kraus Organization Limited
One Water Street
White Plains, New York 10601
800-247-8519 914-761-9600

Printed in the United States of America

97 96 95 94 10 9 8 7 6 5 4 3 2 1

Quality Resources
A Division of The Kraus Organization Limited
One Water Street
White Plains, New York 10601
914-761-9600
800-247-8519

The paper used in this publication meets the minimum requirements of American National Standard for Information Sciences—Performance of Paper for Printed Library Materials, ANSI Z39.48-1984.

ISBN 0-527-76238-5

Library of Congress Cataloging-in-Publication Data

Schultz, Louis E.
Profiles in quality : learning from the masters / Louis E. Schultz.
p. cm.
Includes bibliographical references and index.
ISBN 0-527-76238-5
1. Total quality management—History.
HD62.15.S385 1994
658.5′62—dc20 94-32836
CIP

Contents

List of Figures

Preface

There is, arrayed across a wall in my office, a set of photographs. Most of the so-called gurus of quality are represented there—W. Edwards Deming, Joseph M. Juran, Kaoru Ishikawa. My wife Kay calls it my Ego Wall. I also am in each photograph. After all, my business is training and consulting in the field of quality, and I'm proud to have known so many brilliant people, including most of the ones portrayed in this book.

These personal contacts, of course, influenced my decision to include various individuals in the book. Also, the time required to study each expert's work and write a synthesis had a bearing on the selection. Each of the experts cited here contributed to my education. Someone else writing a book like this might pick different people, but a few would probably be common to us. The ones included here are the ones I have come to know and admire, whose thoughts make the most sense to me. It is from their contributions that I have synthesized my own ideas about quality, which, in this book, are reflected in the last section.

There are some whose names are not here. Charlie Bicking, a colleague of Deming, had a unique knack for asking insightful questions of the corporate managers he helped. The answers he inspired led to clear, informative flowcharts that launched many an enterprise on a strong quality transformation. C. I. Lewis, the Harvard University professor who contributed enormously to the theory of knowledge, might also be here. Yoshinori Iizuka, the prominent Japanese quality master, has generated many excellent theories. Hiroshi Osada, who helped and encouraged me to study Japanese methods, might have been included. But, again, the limits of the enterprise necessitate making difficult choices.

Without doubt, the most influential was W. Edwards Deming.

I often think of Deming as the general who fought on both sides of the economic war. In another kind of war, of course, that would have been unacceptable, but economic wars today are different: they are more civilized. Consultants travel all over the world helping organizations and whole nations to improve quality. Deming did that and more. Although trained as a physicist, he understood and cared about *people*—more than anyone else I have known or studied. Deming's understanding of poverty, born of his own experience, helped him give hope to a demoralized people in post-war Japan. Thirty years later, he gave Americans hope as we began to think we could no longer compete internationally. Thousands of Western organizations crossed the bridge to quality once Deming's theories began to spread in the early 1980s. Deming died in December 1993, leaving a legacy of tenacity and imagination aimed at making things better. He left no formal institute to carry on his work, instead depending on the intrinsic desire of people and organizations to improve themselves.

Sustaining that desire in the West is crucial. The American dream includes the assumption that hardworking people will be able to pass to their children a life that is better than the one they had; but today we are witnessing the first generation that is not able to pass along the belief in a better life. It is more difficult for young people to buy a first home, to get started, to save for the education of their children. Only in the past few years has a sense of national alarm risen to challenge this pessimistic outlook.

There are ample reasons to believe instead in a philosophy of unending personal, professional, and national growth. I, for one, believe we are in the most exciting period in world history. Changes are occurring so rapidly that one can have no concept of what business and society are going to be like 10 years from now. Business must be ready for the changes to come, and to do that, it must shift to a new, better way of thinking. Many people and organizations have done this, but many others still have not. It is my hope that the ideas and principles contained in this book will help them as they strive to get there. Dr. Deming laid the most comprehensive foundation for this, and others helped immeasurably. I think Deming lived just long enough to see business in this country begin to reverse its downward spiral. Now, of course, it's up to us to continue the trend.

Introduction
The Roots of Quality

Seven hundred years ago, people thought the world was flat. Even the most adventuresome explorers believed the storm-tossed Atlantic and Pacific oceans to be one continuous body of water. When people began to think that the world might be round, the old flat maps were simply rolled around a log to show a mass of land—Europe and Asia—and a single body of water. That's why Columbus figured he had to be in India when he made landfall in the Caribbean.

Seventy years ago, it was thought that the world of business was flat. Following the lead of management theorist Frederick Winslow Taylor and his contemporaries, business professionals plotted business on a flat plane. Flowcharts, organizational diagrams, and the whole understanding of manufacturing-driven business in the early years of the Industrial Age, was a variation on the "flat earth" theme—finite beginnings and endings with a series of well-defined steps in between. To Taylor and the generations of business executives who have since cut their management eye-teeth on his teachings, business is a simple, straightline process, beginning with specification of the product, continuing to production, and ending with inspection.

But in 1918, Western Electric—a subsidiary of AT&T—hired a young physicist named Walter A. Shewhart. During the next few years, this soft-spoken, scholarly mathematician began to develop statistical techniques to bring his company's manufacturing processes under control. The result was a distinctly nonlinear approach to business encompassing circular action plans and pinpoint statistical processes.

In Shewhart's case, necessity was indeed the mother of invention. In the early years of this century, Western Electric was one of the pioneer companies on the cutting edge of advancing technology. Its products—truly "new-fangled inventions"—struggled to harness the genie of electricity that transformed the face of the planet in a matter of decades. Not only did they have to work on their own merits, the products had to be able to work when connected to fledgling new electrical power systems that were often unreliable and prone to voltage fluctuations and faulty wiring. Product reliability, ease of use, compatibility with existing and emerging systems, and lasting value were all part of a primary challenge for Western Electric.

And the word for the answer to that challenge? Quality—the supposedly new Holy Grail of American business in the 1990s.

QUANTIFYING QUALITY

The quest for quality is not new. Its roots are firmly anchored in the bedrock of American business. Ironically, though foreign nations, particularly Japan, have taken quality theories and implemented them most effectively, the most renowned theorists are Americans, led by W. Edwards Deming and Joseph M. Juran.

Before these two, however, is another generation of quality trailblazers, most of whom made their primary contributions in the U.S.. Typically overlooked today (though Taylor's legacy lives on), Shewhart was far from alone in his early quality control and improvement efforts.

Although now applied so thoroughly to manufacturing, the use of statistics in general grew out of agricultural research. Prior to the development of statistics, crop experiments were painfully slow, limited to one shot a year because of growing cycles. Ronald A. Fisher, a Briton who was knighted for his efforts, developed shortcuts for sorting data to spot important cause-and-effect relationships. Fisher devised a way to reorganize experiments so that a relatively small number of tests can reveal crucial interactions among a large number of factors, such as planting times, seed depths, fertilizer formulas, and irrigation.[1]

In 1921, G. S. Radford extended this work to the world of

industry with his book, *The Control of Quality in Manufacturing*, which described the duties of management in developing quality early in the design of a product.

Shewhart, having studied the works of both Fisher and Radford, expanded them by developing the control chart, a standard way of plotting the variables that combine to make up product quality, and by distinguishing between two major types of quality problems. Today, he is finally being acknowledged as the father of statistical process control (SPC), the foundation on which virtually all modern quality theory and practices are built.

SHEWHART'S CONTRIBUTIONS

Shewhart's work, however, really represents more. His mathematical methods of 70 years ago were accompanied by a philosophy so advanced that many managers still do not understand it. Shewhart effectively debunked the "scientific" management theory of Taylor and those who, like him, saw the manufacturing process as a straight line. He saw the manufacturing process as a continuous cycle, with inspection leading to new specifications and each process and product intimately linked to past and successive generations.

He also introduced the idea that product defects should rarely be blamed on the worker—that the process, established and controlled by managers, was more often to blame. Finally, Shewhart echoed Radford's refrain that management had to buy in to the culture of quality for it to have any chance of surviving and energizing the organization. To manage the process rather than be managed by it, he identified four steps familiar to anyone who has spent an hour with the current literature of quality: Plan, Do, Check (now more commonly labeled Study), Act—a never-ending quality cycle.

THE CHALLENGE FOR THE U.S.

Alas, how much we have forgotten! Today, newly minted consultants preaching top-down management commitment to "total quality" (as if there were a range of options from "total" through "occasional") are regarded with the awe accorded to Biblical prophets. The continuous cycle approach to quality comes as a revelation to "flat earth" managers, though in reality the world has been round all along. The idea of driving fear out of the workplace in order to empower employees at every level of the organization to work toward quality goals is routinely hailed as management's equivalent to manna from heaven—never mind that W. Edwards Deming has been hammering home this exact point for more than 50 years.

Small wonder then that quality efforts so often fail in America today. In recent years, whether spurred by global competition, bleated common sense, or a sudden urge to bring home a Malcolm Baldrige National Quality Award for the corporate trophy case, company after company has professed to have seen the quality light. Yet, in company after company, "quality improvement" efforts predictably peak fast, plateau for a while, then fall off and fail. In those companies, it turns out, only the rhetoric has changed. In the quest for the All-American quick fix, we reach for the newest, shiniest, easiest-to-grab-onto patent nostrum being peddled in our neighborhood.

Instead of a new corporate religion or little green pill, the real answer to the quality challenge lies in a renewed understanding of the cyclical nature of business operations and a management-driven focus on the kind of day-to-day and long-term quality championed by Radford, Shewhart, and their successors. Not rhetoric but work can effectively bridge the chasm between theory and practice.

The theory is sound. The practice generates profits. Getting from one to the other, constructing and then crossing the bridge to quality, requires rethinking some of the most basic assumptions in American business—and then remaking the business itself. To figure out where to go and how to get there, it's worth understanding more about the most prominent thinkers and their philosophies.

PIECES OF THE QUALITY PUZZLE

Before examining the influence of the ideas of Deming and Juran in post-World War II Japan, a brief look at the world of quality today is in order. On Shewhart's original foundation, other major quality figures have built various parts of a richly detailed quality mosaic—parts that sometimes interlock, overlap, and approach similar ideas from very different vantage points.

Figure 0.1 illustrates the changes that have taken place in the quality control movement since Deming, who was influenced by Shewhart, began to teach it widely. This graphic helps place each thinker in his respective place:

Shewhart developed the first control chart, but his quietly stated theories went far beyond that. He also persuaded many that the highest executives in any company had to be personally involved in efforts to improve quality. Ultimately, Shewhart believed, quality is what the customer believes it is.

Deming's initial training focused on the continuous improve-

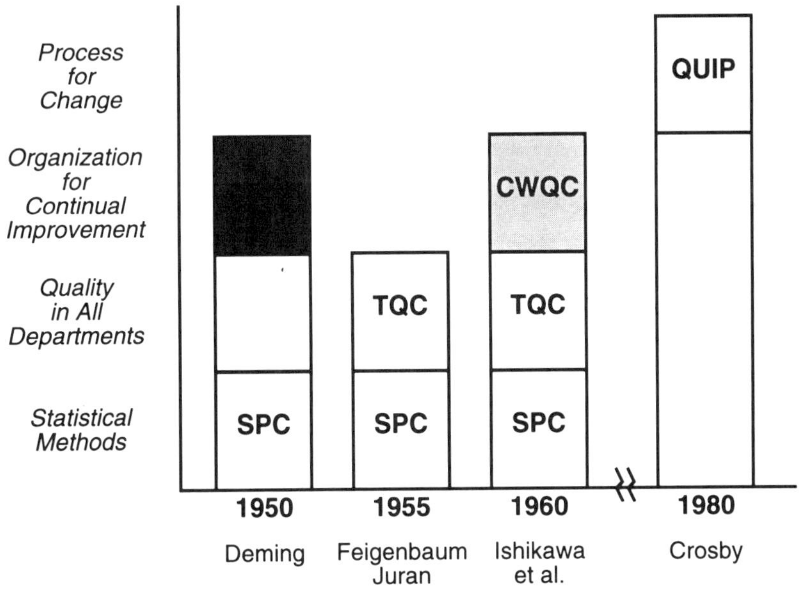

FIGURE 0.1. Evolution of Quality Improvement.

ment cycle, thc importance of knowledge and dispersion in statistics, and how to use control charts. His demand for a higher level of performance by leaders in every endeavor from public education to business management, made him legendary. Deming advocated unflagging efforts to improve and learn, [which he pursued] well into his 90s.

Homer Sarasohn sowed the seeds of participative management in post World War II Japan by insisting all communications from management be extensively transmitted to all subordinates. He also prepared the new generation of Japanese managers for learning statistical quality control and other concepts by first giving them a solid foundation in basic business concepts.

Juran, who with Deming helped Japanese managers develop new principles and practices, introduced the concept of getting every department involved in a commitment to Total Quality Control (TQC) within a company.

Allan Mogensen is especially known for his work in the area of work simplification, developing techniques and methods for ensuring that any job—from clerical work to large production processes—is completed as efficiently as possible. Seen as the father of the concept, he is credited with the slogan, "Work smarter, not harder."

Armand Feigenbaum coined the term *Total* in Total Quality Control and popularized the concept of the "hidden factory" to illustrate the cost of quality shortfalls and, along with Juran, supported the concept of a strong quality control organization. Building on the statistical base laid by Deming, Feigenbaum and Juran focused on elimination of waste and rework.

Philip Crosby's contributions in the 1980s gave companies a well-defined program to create awareness and change attitudes toward the importance of quality. His theory challenges organizations and individuals to achieve Zero Defects (ZD), which brought to renewed prominence the far-reaching quality initiatives of American manufacturing in the Sputnik era.

Myron Tribus has developed a four-system theory that shows which factors must be considered when introducing quality management into any enterprise, whether it is industry, service, government or education. To be successful, the effort must take into account the know-how of the company, the social system in the organization, the managerial system, and preconceived ideas that have been created from the employees' formal education.

Kaoru Ishikawa in the late 1950s and early 1960s was prominent among Japan's first generation of home-grown quality leaders, which developed quality control circles and other organizational activities. His work emphasized Total Quality Control enabling managers to work with production employees in order to jointly solve problems. Taking Deming's statistical base and Juran's and Feigenbaum's theories further, Ishikawa and his contemporaries demonstrated that when the responsibility for quality was placed with each worker, only a smaller quality control department was needed for guidance.

Shigeru Mizuno detailed the techniques and processes for spreading the concepts of Feigenbaum and Ishikawa to the entire organization. His ideas became known as *Company-Wide Quality Control.* They epitomize the Japanese view of quality, with everyone working in harmony to achieve the best results for the whole organization.

Yoji Akao, recognizing the need for additional means to understand customer needs and desires and communicate them during the design phase, developed the concepts that became Quality Function Deployment (QFD). Now highly popular with many U.S. companies practicing quality theories, Akao's matrices and diagrams allow organizations to illustrate and evaluate customer wishes, engineering considerations.

Genichi Taguchi became famous for his ability to help companies develop what he called "robust products" that would stand up to variability in manufacturing and use. Taguchi also won acclaim for his descriptions of how companies view their quality target values.

Noriaki Kano defined the structure of organizational efforts to achieve quality with his House of Total Quality Control (or Management) graphic and theory. His reminder that knowing quality is not enough, but willingness to sweat for it equally necessary, rings an alarm for any company struggling to instill quality concepts and techniques.

OVER THERE

Uncomfortable as it may be for a nation accustomed to seeing itself as the world's foremost promoter of progress, we must nonetheless concede that the impetus for the second coming of quality in America today comes from the United States' primary economic competitor—and partner—during the past 40 years: Japan. To understand quality, Japanese style, we must return to the postwar nation Deming, and later Juran, were brought to.

Japan was in turmoil after World War II. The country's industry was almost nonexistent. Factories were dirt-floor shacks and had to produce without experienced managers, few resources, and little experience producing consumer goods. It's not surprising that, under these circumstances, quality was the last goal of Japanese industrialists. Meeting basic needs was far more important.

However, that need to manufacture the basic necessities of post-war life is exactly why the quality movement was able to take root in Japan. While the U.S. was struggling to meet the demands of an expanding and demanding society with turn-of-the-century manufacturing plants, Japan had to start from scratch. It literally had the opportunity to build a modern production economy from the ground up. Japanese manufacturers had little time to pay deference to old-fashioned methods just because someone remembered doing something that way years earlier. Getting the job done the best way possible was the key.

It was this effort that opened the door to a set of principles that today make up the quality movement—employee involvement, process management, and statistical analysis. These concepts will be presented in the following chapters. The biographies of the people who created these concepts reveal how these ideas were products of their time as well as how they have evolved and are applied today. This book also shows how these varied concepts can be unified by a theory called "The Rings of Management," which culls the best from the world's best quality theories.

I

THE AMERICANS

The industrial revolution brought the first interchangeable parts for machinery. Once mass production began, it took manufacturing out of the hands of the individual craftsman and put it in the hands of large organizations. Those who led the organizations realized that assembly-line manufacturing was a process to be studied, and people with certain skills were required to study it.

At the same time, scholars such as Britain's Fisher were using statistics to study agricultural cycles. These techniques were soon adapted to the manufacturing process, which also could be studied through numbers. Walter Shewhart was the first to devise a way to use numbers to examine processes; but others, such as Deming and Juran, soon followed. All three worked during the 1920s at Western Electric's Hawthorne Plant in Chicago, where the company sought to create new ways to make its equipment—then, the most high-tech products in the world—more reliable. Once the effort was initiated, however, it became clear that quality and reliability could be increased in almost any industry. Thus, the search for higher quality was launched.

1
Walter A. Shewhart

The telephone was the space program of its day. In the decades after its invention, the telephone spawned a vast, broadening circle of new technology, requiring and creating a level of quality and dependability previously unknown in manufacturing. Each component of the telephone system had to meet precise specifications and tolerances for the system to work. Western Electric, the manufacturing arm of American Telephone & Telegraph (AT&T), hired the brightest engineers and scientists it could find to develop the new communications equipment. The company's research and development facilities provided an atmosphere in which new ideas were embraced with fervor, and creative minds were working to overcome challenges never before confronted. One of those minds belonged to Walter Shewhart, who was assigned to study the carbon microphone and to develop experimental techniques for measuring its properties. While doing that, Shewhart became involved in the development and application of statistical methods then new to engineering.

Shewhart's probing mind and close examination of manufacturing problems quickly earned him the respect of both his colleagues and superiors. Asked to apply statistical theory in the development of inspection sampling plans, Shewhart treated the problem as an opportunity for innovation. One of the central problems he tackled was how large a sample was required to justify the acceptance or rejection of a lot of products.

In May 1924, Shewhart and R. L. Jones, then director of inspection, discussed the need for a printed form that inspectors might use in their work. On May 16, Shewhart sent Jones a memorandum suggesting how such a chart might work and a sample copy of the chart (see Figures 1.1 and 1.2). It was, to borrow a phrase, one of those days that the universe changed.

"That diagram, and the short text that preceded and followed it, set forth all of the essential principles and considerations that are involved in what we know today as process quality control," writes George Edwards, Shewhart's boss and also a recipient of the memo and chart.[1]

Shewhart's relatively simple looking device calculated upper and lower control limits for a product, tracked the production process over time, calculated upper and lower control limits for the process, and identified when the process was in trouble. The control chart later became the chief tool in thousands of companies for building quality into products. Shewhart, who became known to thousands of statisticians, engineers, scientists, and managers as the father of the control chart, was 33 years old when he invented the chart.

Shewhart's subsequent work in statistical theory showed that techniques could be devised to study, discover, and measure the effects of unknown causes on a system. He also suggested ways of modifying such a system to reduce variation, successfully showing that a system operating closer to nominal limits produced fewer rejections.

The purpose of inspection was—and still is—to find and remove faulty products or lots of products, but Shewhart showed that statistical methods could be used to improve the product when it was still in the production stage. The focus then became one of "building in" good quality instead of "inspecting out" poor quality.

"Quality control meant to him use of statistical methods all the way from raw material to consumer and back again, through redesign of product, reworking of specifications of raw materials, in a continuous cycle as results come in from consumer research and from other tests," said W. Edwards Deming, Shewhart's friend and protege.[2]

It was the beginning of a revolution that would take the rest of the century to play itself out. When it was done, many long-held and accepted management beliefs would be disproved.

Born in Canton, Illinois, on March 18, 1891, Shewhart re-

Case 18013

WAS-724-5-16-24-FQ

MR. R. L. JONES:

A few days ago, you mentioned some of the problems connected with the development of an acceptable form of inspection report which might be modified from time to time, in order to give at a glance the greatest amount of accurate information.

The attached form of report is designed to indicate whether or not the observed variations in the percent of defective apparatus of a given type are significant; that is, to indicate whether or not the product is satisfactory. The theory underlying the method of determining the significance of the variations in the value of p is somewhat involved when considered in such a form as to cover practically all types of problems. I have already started the preparation of a series of memoranda covering these points in detail. Should it be found desirable, however, to make use of this form of chart in any of the studies now being conducted within the Inspection Department, it will be possible to indicate the method to be followed in the particular examples.

W. A. SHEWHART.

Enc.:
Form of Report.

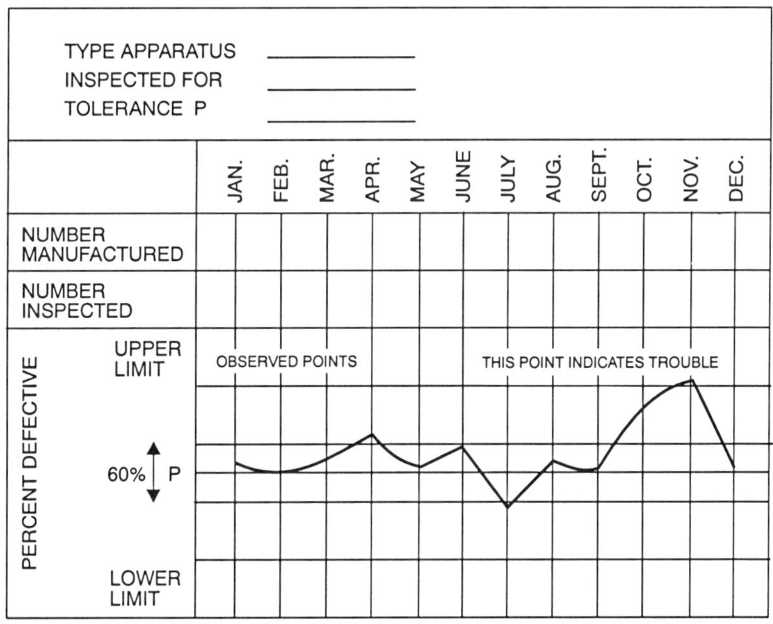

FIGURE 1.1. Shewhart's First Control Chart and Accompanying Memo. (Courtesy of AT&T Archives.)

ceived his bachelors and masters degrees from the University of Illinois. He joined Western Electric after receiving his doctorate in physics at the University of California at Berkeley in 1917.

Shewhart moved in late 1924 from Western Electric's Hawthorne plant in Chicago to Bell Telephone Laboratories in New Jersey. He continued his research into statistical process control, and in 1931 published his first book, *Economic Control of Quality of Manufactured Product*. Greeted enthusiastically on publication, the book has since been hailed as a monumental work by statisticians and engineers worldwide. It touched virtually all aspects of quality control—specifications, inspection of incoming materials and of the production line, process improvement, operational definitions and problems in the definition of quality.[3]

Shewhart defined the state of control as one when a phenomenon could be predicted to behave—approximately—in a certain way, on the basis of past experience. Using control charts, parabolas and detailed explanations, he demonstrated the role that statistical theory plays in the control of variation and in the reduction of the cost of inspecting and rejecting faulty products. Quality, Shewhart noted, comes from the Latin word *qualis*, meaning "how constituted." Objectively, an organization should define a product or service as a particular set of characteristics. He added, however, that it was "impossible to think of a thing as having goodness independent of some human want."[4] The subjective side of quality poses serious difficulties, because there are four kinds of value: use, cost, esteem, and exchange—the last three of which are relative and subject to wide variation, Shewhart said.

The elusive nature of subjective views of quality, though of primary interest for commercial purposes, he maintained, make it necessary to establish quantitative measures for quality. It is the engineer's job to translate the wishes of consumers into quantifiable information as well as possible and to set up means of making a product that would differ from arbitrarily set standards as little as possible.

Shewhart's landmark work covers the spectrum from very simple methods to very complex ones for understanding variation and its effects on quality. One may view random variation, for example, by repeatedly writing the letter 'a' and observing that all the letters are not written the same.

Shewhart used simple graphical methods such as run charts, histograms and scatter diagrams to help the reader visualize variation. For instance, he presented a brilliant table/scatter diagram[5] that allows the user to form a scatter diagram between the two variables, thus illustrating the relationship between them and to summarize the data for each variable into categories to make histograms. His use of empirical histograms and theoretical distribution functions helps the reader see variation. Simulated data from various distributions is used to show the sampling distribution of averages,[6] medians, standard deviations, skewness, and other statistical information. The results are presented on histograms. These graphical representations display Shewhart's basic statistical concepts.

Economic Control of Quality of Manufactured Product also tackles more complicated statistical methods. Applications of correlations coefficients, both useful and whimsical, are provided. On the more complex side, there are theoretical distributions of a correlation coefficient, skewness, and flatness. The book examines these control charts with data from various theoretical distributions and demonstrates the use of bivariate control charts and probability plots.

Sampling and the measurement process are crucial to gathering information. Shewhart highlights four kinds of measurement efforts and how to handle them as well as such specific problem measurements as errors in measuring temperature. Again, Shewhart covers the topic by moving from the simple (e.g., visual displays that explain how people can make measurement errors through optical illusions) to the more complex. In addition to statistical tools, Shewhart describes specific applications in detail, with examples from economics to tensile strength and creosoting telephone poles.

Statisticians in recent decades have veered away from Shewhart's approach to their field. When asked, many professionals experienced in statistical process control say they have not read it, perhaps because of the time required to study and absorb the information. Those who do, however, often come away with a new point of view. If schools for the last 50 years had taught statistics as Shewhart presents it, "we would understand it much better," commented Jason Jones, a statistician and professional consultant. Statistician Donald J. Wheeler, one of the leading modern advocates of Shewhart's charts and other methods, says statisticians who came after Shewhart sought to strengthen his charts by filling in what they perceived as gaps. They actually weakened the charts, Wheeler says in a paper presented in June 1993. "Shewhart's charts are unsurpassed in simplicity," he adds. "They are unsurpassed in statistical validity, and they are essentially unsurpassed in sensitivity to process changes. This combination of simplicity, validity and sensitivity is not seen in any other statistical technique."[7]

Shewhart's second book, *Statistical Method From the Viewpoint of Quality Control*, is as famous as his first. It is made up of his 1939 lectures to the U.S. Department of Agriculture Graduate School. Deming, who invited him to deliver the lectures, later edited them into book form.

In *Statistical Method*, Shewhart traces the history of quality control from prehistoric times to the present, noting that the first attempt to manufacture interchangeable parts was made by Eli Whitney in 1787. Whitney and his colleagues eventually understood, however, that no two parts could be fabricated to be exactly the same. This led to the introduction of specification limits, or tolerances. Destructive testing, which requires that small samples be taken from the product lot for testing, can only share or infer the properties of the entire lot if the manufacturing process is in a state of statistical control, Shewhart notes.

The act of control has three parts: specifying what is required, trying to produce what is specified, and judging whether the requirements have been met. The first part is achieved through statistical control, setting numerical values for what is required.

Specification limits provide a way to judge a product that is already manufactured. Control limits, however, provide ways to take action to remove what Shewhart termed *assignable causes* of variation so the product would have less variation. Assignable causes are external to the system. Control limits become, therefore, a way to identify when assignable causes of variation may be prevented rather than corrected after the fact.

Shewhart also identified what he called *chance causes* of variation as those that occur consistently over time and are part of the system. These are relatively small causes of variation and do not mean that the process is out of statistical control. *Assignable causes* of variation are external and sporadic, and must be identified and removed.

To achieve a state of statistical control, Shewhart observes in *Statistical Method*, five steps must be taken:

- Specifying in a general way how data is to be examined for clues to the existence of assignable causes of variability.
- Specifying how original data is to be gathered and divided into subsamples, based on judgements about whether conditions were essentially the same.
- Specifying a criterion of control.
- Specifying what is to be done when an observed statistic falls outside its control limits.
- Specifying how much data is to be gathered to satisfy the criterion of control.

Prior to the introduction of the control chart, the three elements of control—specification, production and inspection—were viewed as independent acts. Shewhart displayed three steps moving in a straight line. When control limits were introduced through use of statistics, however, a new concept of variation was born. The new concept, Shewhart said, should be demonstrated by a circle showing the three steps in continuous revolution. "Specification, production and inspection correspond respectively to making a hypothesis, carrying out an experiment and testing the hypothesis. The three steps constitute a dynamic scientific process of acquiring knowledge,"[8] he added.

Shewhart's ideas continued to evolve, and were developed further by W. Edwards Deming, who named the concept the *Shewhart Cycle*. Usually referred to nowadays as the *PDSA* (Plan-Do-Study-Act) *Cycle*, it is still a mainstay of quality improvement efforts.

Known to colleagues for his warm and insightful conversation, Shewhart constantly encouraged others to join or form committees and societies for the study of engineering, statistics, standardization, and manufacturing processes. Communicating by letter to colleagues and fellow committee members, he often pushed professional committees in what he believed was the right direction while remaining out of the spotlight. "He made his points not so much by giving his own point of view, but by asking questions—embarrassing questions," Deming once wrote.[9]

Between his work for Bell Labs, Shewhart served as a lecturer in statistical theory at Stevens Institute of Technology, the University of London, the University of Calcutta and other Indian scientific organizations. He consulted for the War Department on ammunition specifications from 1936 to 1944.

The daunting nature of Shewhart's books and papers was—and still is—famous. "Although his explanations could be simple and clear in a face-to-face discussion, his greatest papers remain as difficult for the reader as they were for him to write," Deming wrote of Shewhart on his death in 1967.[10] "As he told me once, when he writes, he must make it foolproof. I replied in a particular instance that he had made it so foolproof that no one would understand it."[11]

A similar story was told by U.S. Army Gen. Leslie E. Simon, who reported that he once congratulated Shewhart on a magazine article, adding, "But Walter, it took me four hours to read it thoroughly."

"Cheer up," replied Shewhart. "It took me four years to write it."[12]

Although Shewhart's writings pertain to technical matters, colleagues recalled that discussions often centered on other important concepts, including the need for top management to accept responsibility for quality and the necessity of measuring consumer interests. "One of Walter Shewhart's major contributions to the control of quality of consumer products was the realization that human wants and preferences were an indispensable part of what needed to be specified," John E. Karlin, a colleague at Bell Telephone Laboratories, once wrote. "The type of interest in human factors stimulated by Walter has today become pervasive" at the company.[13]

Shewhart pushed for the establishment of the Joint Committee on Measurement of Opinions, Attitudes and Consumer Wants of the Social Science Research Council and National Research Council. In 1947, he was selected to head a newly formed User Preference Department in Bell's Research Division. The department's job was to learn whether the company could develop more valid methods of determining and measuring human wants and needs to guide the development of new telephone services.

Just as he brought managers and engineers a better understanding of the vast possibilities of statistics in manufacturing, Shewhart performed the critical role in bringing human factors into equipment and system designs.

Today, his ideas still permeate the quality movement, influencing the now growing American interest in statistical control, management, and the need to focus on the customer's needs and desires. Some of what Shewhart taught came to him from others, such as Fisher. History will remember him, however, not just for originating the control chart but for understanding and teaching a management philosophy that stressed leadership and customer satisfaction long before those terms were buzzwords.

2
W. Edwards Deming

Shewhart started it all, and legions of others continued the work, but no one casts so large a shadow across the quality movement as W. Edwards Deming. Often called the man who taught quality to the Japanese, Deming persisted throughout his career in going where few others dared—from an unchallenged mastery of statistics to a crusade for greater understanding of the new role of management.

As we will see, other quality masters shared the workload in Japan. It was Deming, however, who sought the attention of Japan's chiefs of industry in 1950 as he began lecturing on statistical quality control. It also was Deming whose name first was offered 30 years later when befuddled Americans began asking how Japan had managed to dominate markets long considered American domains.

Deming first visited Japan in 1947, summoned there by the occupation government to help Japan with its census. He was invited back in 1950 by the Union of Japanese Scientists and Engineers (JUSE) to teach quality control. He accepted the invitation but refused a fee. Deming's lectures were translated into Japanese and published as a booklet titled *Elementary Principles of the Statistical Control of Quality*. Deming refused the royalties also and asked JUSE Managing Director Ken-Ichi Koyanagi to use them instead for any purpose he wanted. Out of gratitude, Koyanagi devised a plan for the creation of a quality award and named it after Deming.[1] The Deming Prize is now the most revered quality award in the world.

Deming's generosity to and understanding of the people of postwar Japan also accounts for their reverence of him. "Most of the Japanese were in a servile spirit as the vanquished, and among Allied personnel there were not a few with an air of importance," Koyanagi wrote later. "In striking contrast, Dr. Deming showed his warm cordiality to every Japanese whom he met . . . He loved Japan and the Japanese from his own heart."[2]

THE EARLY DAYS

Deming understood what it meant to be poor and struggling. He spent part of his childhood living in a tar paper shack on the windswept plains of northern Wyoming, where hard work and deprivation built into his psyche a lifelong love of work and desire to excel. He was born October 14, 1900 in Sioux City, Iowa, and moved west at the age of seven. His father, William Deming, had a variety of jobs, including legal work, farming, insurance, and real estate. His mother, Pluma, gave music lessons. They lived in Cody for two years, and then moved to Camp Coulter (later renamed Powell) where Deming's father bought a 40-acre farm. The water from the shack's pump was so hard that Deming would ride his bicycle a half-mile to fetch soft water from a canal. He earned $1.25 a week bringing kindling and coal to a local eating establishment and at times helped pay for family necessities. There was no electricity in Powell, and at the age of 14, Deming took the job of lighting the town's gas street lamps at night for $10 a month.

Deming recounts his years at the University of Wyoming as good ones, filled with study, friends, and a series of odd jobs: cutting ice from a frozen pond, shoveling snow, working at a soda fountain, painting, cleaning boilers at a refinery, cutting railroad ties by hand. He also found time to play in the school band and credits the band with helping him find his first job, teaching physics at the Colorado School of Mines, to which the band leader, A. E. Bellis, had moved. He also received his masters degree in mathematics and physics from the University of Colorado in 1925.

In 1928, Deming got his doctorate from Yale, but in 1926 and 1927, he had summer jobs at Western Electric's Hawthorne plant in Chicago. There were approximately 46,000 employees at the plant, assembling telephone equipment in what was then a progressive atmosphere and good pay. But to Deming, fresh from the plains of Wyoming, the assembly work seemed monotonous and the conditions hot and dirty. Although he was only there a few months, lessons learned at the Hawthorne plant had a lasting effect on Deming and influenced his ideas about managerial responsibility to workers.

Western Electric later offered him a job, but he went to work instead at the U.S. Department of Agriculture's Fixed Nitrogen Laboratory. His boss at the laboratory introduced Deming to Walter Shewhart, whose work Deming heard of when he was at the Hawthorne plant. Deming and Shewhart became fast friends, and spent hours together discussing statistical theory at Shewhart's home in Mountain Lakes, New Jersey. Deming took a year's leave of absence in the mid-1930s to study in England under Sir Ronald A. Fisher.

The Department of Agriculture established its own graduate school, and Deming was asked to arrange for lectures by statistical experts, including Fisher and Shewhart. Deming then took over the project of sampling for the 1940 census, the first time sampling had been approved. In that effort, Deming demonstrated that statistical tools and controls could be used accurately in clerical as well as industrial applications.[3] When World War II broke out, Deming was asked to teach statistical quality control to companies supplying the war effort. Deming and other instructors taught the methods to approximately 31,000 people, both in government and the private sector. The training of so many people in statistical quality control led to the creation, after the war, of the American Society of Quality Control (ASQC).

Deming then began his private practice as a statistical consultant specializing in transportation and also began to teach at New York University. The call to Japan came soon after, and Deming, long viewed as a respected statistician in his own country, was en route to *sensei* (master) status in Japan.

Deming's compassion for ordinary working class people surfaced in postwar Japan. For example, he made a habit of visiting the U.S. Army Post Exchanges to stock up on candy bars and canned goods as gifts to the Japanese he met.

THE PDSA CYCLE

In his 1950 lectures, Deming taught Japanese engineers and statisticians to use a control chart and other tools during eight-day courses in Tokyo and Fukuoka. A meeting was arranged for 21 industrial leaders representing 80 percent of the wealth in the nation. "The meeting went off well," Deming wrote. "That was the birth of the New Japan, if a date can be put on it."[4] The 21 leaders and others attended subsequent training sessions. During those lectures Deming drew Shewhart's scheme of Plan, Do, Check, and Act on a chalkboard as a cycle to be perpetually repeated.[5] Deming called it the Shewhart Cycle; the Japanese referred to it as the Deming Cycle. He later refined it by replacing the word *check* with the word *study*, and today it continues to be referred to as the PDCA or PDSA cycle (see Figure 2.1).

The cycle has four components:

Plan. Planning a change or a test in a product or service, listing the obstacles to overcome, and beginning determining what new information is needed.

Do. Carrying it out, preferably on a small-scale.

Study. Testing and analyzing the results. What was learned?

Act. Adopting the change, abandoning it or running through the cycle again, and possibly taking the product and what was learned to market. Sampling how the product is received by those who buy it, and those who do not. Determining from these reactions the risks of proceeding further.

Deming also gave lectures to top Japanese business leaders regarding the importance of management's understanding statistical methods. He emphasized that information gathering tools should be used for every activity.[6] He also stressed using research to learn what consumers wanted and then designing products accordingly.

At the same time, Deming was disappointed that the statistical

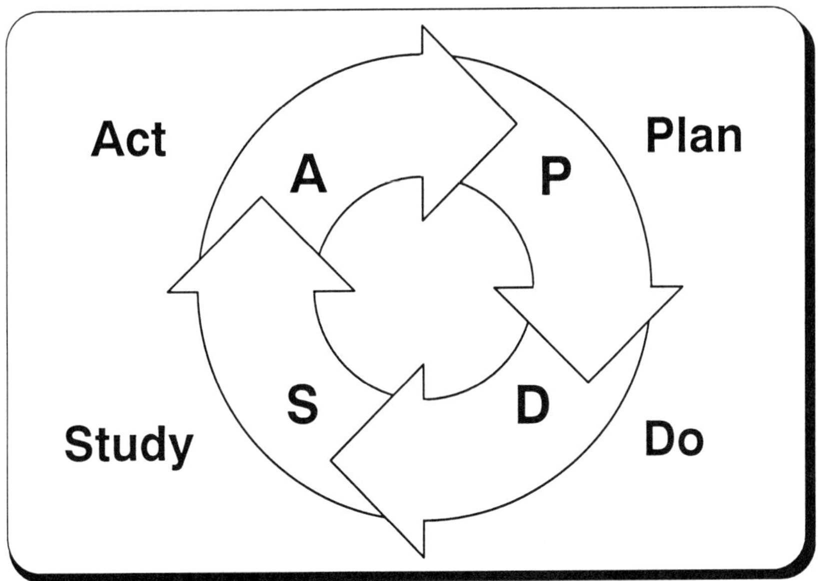

FIGURE 2.1. Plan, Do, Study, and Act Cycle.

methods taught to so many Americans during the war were de-emphasized as U.S. manufacturing, with its production facilities intact after the war, changed its orientation to one of quantity, with waste and rework covered by ample profits. Industries in other nations were just recovering from the war, and America had the world for a market. Deming's disappointment partially prompted his requests for sessions with Japan's top industrialists. Some of them would later tell him they initially considered his optimism crazy but decided there was nothing to lose.[7] Their subsequent adherence to Deming's teachings would prove they had everything to gain.

Deming revisited Japan often in following years but most of his work there was completed by the 1960s. By then he had developed the quality management theories that became the foundation of his consulting and teaching. His finely honed philosophy, however, was largely ignored in his own nation until June 1980, by which time the Japanese had captured major market shares in everything from such highly engineered products as automobiles and televisions to such basic items as coffee mugs and ballpoint pens.

On June 24, 1980 NBC aired a documentary titled "If Japan Can . . . Why Can't We?" which revealed that Deming was one of the foremost Americans who taught the Japanese statistical quality control. It included a segment on how his philosophy was being put to use by the Nashua Corp. in Nashua, New Hampshire, with enormous success.

The next day, Deming's telephone rang off the hook. At the age of 79, he started his career anew; this time at home. Deming threw himself into a schedule of seminars and high-level consulting that would have exhausted people half his age. With the help of a growing number of followers, he developed his famous four-day seminars. The seminars changed over the years, but certain elements, such as the red bead experiment, remain virtually the same.

A SYSTEM OF PROFOUND KNOWLEDGE

According to Deming, management, as developed in the 19th century and continued during the 20th century, is the major cause of waste, rework, and untold losses. Emphasis on short-term results, outdated personnel ranking practices, and failure to understand a system are responsible for losses of both human and financial resources so great that the total amount will never be known. "The prevailing style of management has led us into decline," Deming says. "Transformation into a new style of management is required. The route to take is what I call profound knowledge. It is not automatic. It must be learned; it must be led."[8]

Profound knowledge begins with an appreciation for a system, which can be achieved through a flow diagram, such as the one Deming used in 1950 in Japan (see Figure 2.2).

The consumer is the most important part of the production line. "To make the flow diagram work, the flow of material and

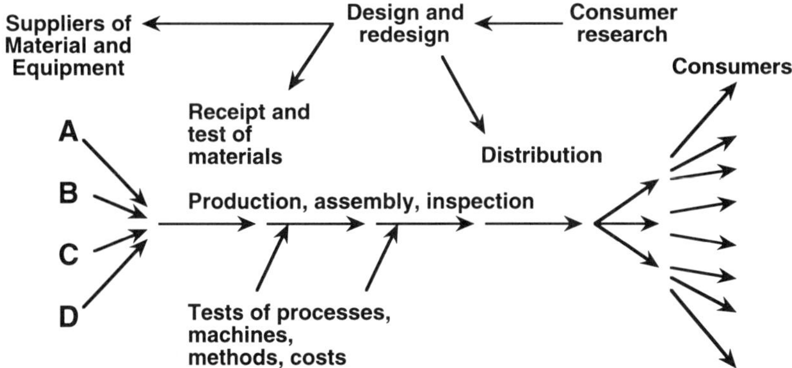

FIGURE 2.2. Deming's Flow Diagram Showing the Enterprise as a System. (Reprinted from *Out of Crisis* by W. Edwards Deming by permission of MIT and W. Edwards Deming. Published by MIT, Center for Advanced Engineering Study, Cambridge MA 02139. Copyright 1986 by W. Edwards Deming.)

information from any part of the system must match the input requirements of the next stages," offers Deming.[9] The flow chart may also be viewed as an organization chart, showing people within the organization what their jobs are and how they should interact with each other. Managers must understand their system and how it works before they can make any recommendations for improvement.

Along with appreciation for a system, a system of profound knowledge must entail understanding of the theory of variation, theory of knowledge, and psychology. The system of profound knowledge cannot be separated into pieces. The parts must be seen as interacting with each other.

THEORY OF KNOWLEDGE

"Experience by itself teaches you nothing," insists Deming. "You must have a theory. A statement devoid of rational prediction does not convey knowledge."[10] A theory can never be proved—it can only be supported or disproved. By comparing experience with theory, lessons that provide guidance can be learned.

To manage effectively, leaders must have theories applicable to their businesses today. Without theory, nothing can be learned and there is no improvement.

A theory is based on certain premises, including:

- A plan is a prediction or expression of a theory. Management is prediction.
- Measurements or observations are the basis for prediction and theory.
- There are no absolute truths, only data from measurement or observation.
- Theory is essential for understanding results.
- Learning requires comparison of results with the original prediction or theory.
- From the comparison comes knowledge, based partly on past observations and predictions regarding what might happen in the future.
- Operational definitions are the basis for communicating plans.

Deming defined an operational definition as an understanding by which employees may work or people may do business with each other. An operational definition is only an attempt for people to understand each other. It conceptualizes communicable meaning.

Relying on experience is no help unless that experience is first understood in light of a theory. Copying a successful venture without first understanding the theory behind the success could lead to failure. "People are trying to do their best," Deming notes. "What they need is a theory. There is no knowledge without theory."[11]

The word *theory* comes from the same Greek root word as theater and means "to get a view of, to understand," Deming says. "Knowledge gives us a basis for planning. A theory of management discloses faulty operations."[12]

Deming was fond of quoting Julian Huxley's comment that a practical man is one who practices the errors of his forefathers.

APPRECIATION FOR A SYSTEM

A manager's role is to understand how the organization works as a system and to know when and how to optimize the system. The manager must recognize the roles people play as part of the system and how to help them perform those roles. Instead of managing each part separately or breaking things down to the lowest common denominator, managers should focus on ways to improve the whole system. One of Deming's first steps with any organization is to draw a flow chart, or diagram of the organization viewed as a system. "Until you draw a flow diagram, you do not understand your business," he declares.[13]

Deming defines a system as "a series of functions or activities within an organization that work together for the aim of the organization."[14] For instance, a ski team is a system. It has coaches, trainers, managers, skiers and equipment. The actual competition is an individual effort, with the times tabulated to determine which team has won. There is a low degree of interdependence. A football team, on the other hand, has a higher degree of interdependence among the players, coaches, and trainers. If the trainer does not properly treat the guard's sprained ankle, the guard will be slow on the field, resulting in a ball carrier being tackled in the backfield. Likewise, an orchestra is an example of a well optimized system, where the players are there to support each other. They must be very proficient with their instruments but individually need not be the very best players.

Industry requires the highest degree of interdependence, creating such products as automobiles with thousands of pieces designed to work together.

Almost any system has interdependent components, and the performance of any component must be evaluated as it relates to the system. Managers must know and understand the interrelationships of the components and continually seek ways to optimize the system. They must gather the information to decide which components should operate at a loss for the system as a whole to achieve its greatest optimization. The aim of management is for everyone—customers, stockholders, employees, suppliers, community, environment—to gain. All are part of the system, and all may contribute to its improvement. Although management's job is to optimize the system so the parts work well together, some outside guidance is essential. "A system cannot understand itself," notes Deming. Managers also must know the boundaries of a system and be ready to change a boundary to better serve its aim.[15]

Management must state a system's aim so that everyone can understand and be guided by it. "Without an aim, there is no system," Deming states. "The components of a system are necessary but not sufficient of themselves to accomplish the aim. They must be managed."[16]

According to Deming, focusing on part of a system while ignoring its connections to the other parts will, at best, provide less improvement than is possible. At worst, the entire system may be damaged. Changing the aim, size or boundary of a system affects how the components ought to be combined for best performance. Any changes in a system should be considered against the aim of the system. Performance of any components should be judged against their contribution to the overall aim; some components may appear to operate at a loss when viewed in isolation. Managers must seek to optimize the whole system not the components individually, which may cause a suboptimization of the system. They must seek to create win-win situations within the system and for the system.

It is poor management, Deming always said, to purchase materials or services at the lowest price or to otherwise minimize cost of manufacture or design without considering the effect on other components of a system. All represent suboptimization, as does any system that results in a win-lose situation.

For example, Deming cited a small company that decided to make pianos. The owners purchased a Steinway piano and dismantled it to study its parts. They meticulously made parts identical to those in the Steinway and put their piano together, but it didn't play like a Steinway. Having failed, they decided to reassemble the Steinway and sell it to recover their investment. Unfortunately, the reassembled Steinway didn't play either. They had failed to understand the theory behind the manufacturing of a Steinway.

KNOWLEDGE OF VARIATION

Managers also must have a knowledge of variation, which exists in everything—systems, services, people and, of course, nature. Understanding what a system can do—and what it cannot do—depends on having statistical data and knowing how the data was obtained. Deming's statement, "the past is helpful to us only if it helps in the future, if it predicts,"[17] provides a clue as to why he focuses his statistical efforts on control charts. Other statistical methods using enumerative data can be used to explain what happened in a certain population but cannot be used to predict what will happen in another population. Control charts points are more analytical.

Deming often used the speed of light as an example of variation. Over the years, various texts have used different values for the speed of light as scientists have developed different ways of measuring it. To emphasize the point, he attributed a statement to Galileo in 1606: "If the speed of light is not infinite, it's awful damn fast."[18]

Like Shewhart, Deming identified two ways to improve work processes: eliminating "special" causes of variation and reducing "common" causes of variation. Managers must know the difference.[19] Special causes of variation appear on a control chart as a point lying outside the calculated control limits or as other nonrandom patterns. A manager should ask: "Is the process performing in a dependable, predictable way over time, with no evidence of assignable causes of variation?"

If the answer is no, the process is not stable; that is, there are sources of variation that are not part of the process. These are called special causes of variation, which must be identified and eliminated before the process can become stable.

The elimination of special causes is often the responsibility of someone working directly with the operation. The appearance (and detection) of variation is the way that the process indicates that something unusual has happened and should be checked and corrected. At times, management assistance or intervention may be required.

If the answer is yes, the system is in a state of statistical control and any variation is due to common causes. The manager then can make predictions regarding the performance of the process in the near future. The manager must conscientiously work to reduce common causes of variation.

Common causes, or problems with the overall system, are management's responsibility. Common causes of variation are those inherent in a system (i.e., a characteristic of the existing system). Managers must determine whether the variation is acceptable and, if not, seek ways to reduce normal variation or shift the mean in a desired direction. Management's efforts to do this must be unceasing and must be consistently communicated to the workers. Management must know when not to alter a stable process.

PSYCHOLOGY

Management too often operates under the supposition that people are all alike, Deming proposed. In fact, of course, they are all quite different from each other, having different ways of learning and different values.

Consequently, a manager must have some knowledge of psychology to better understand people, and how they react to circumstances, other people, and any system of management. The leader needs to understand the differences between people and use them to optimize each employee's abilities, including the different ways that people learn, whether by reading, watching, listening, or by observing others.

Deming believed in the value of a person's intrinsic motivation, that is, the person's innate desire to perform well at tasks and to learn new skills and concepts.[20] The traditional system of management has stamped out those virtues in many people, whether they are workers or pupils.

Everyone, said Deming, "is born with a natural inclination to learn and to be innovative. One inherits a right to enjoy his work. Psychology helps us to nurture and preserve these positive innate attributes of people."[21]

Psychology helps people to understand each other and, thereby, guides the interactions between them. Greater understanding fosters greater cooperation and mutual respect. It improves the relationships between teacher and pupil or between a leader and employees and any system of management. "Ethics is important in quality. You have to have trust," said Deming.[22]

Likewise, knowing psychology helps management understand its obligation to make changes in the system to bring about improvements. It may boil down to simple things, such as "a pat on the back – dogs like it and so do people," stated Deming.[23]

Asked what legacy he would like to leave, Deming once replied, "A theory of systems and win-win."[24]

CHANGES IN THE PHILOSOPHY

Deming formulated his System of Profound Knowledge during the 1980s. Clare Crawford-Mason, producer of the famous NBC television documentary "If Japan Can, Why Can't We?", several other television shows, and the Deming Library educational videos, often heard Deming say that leaders should manage from a system of profound knowledge. Several times she asked him what he meant by profound knowledge but did not get a reply. The next week he sent her a memo about profound knowledge, which she used as voice over in a video presentation a few weeks later. Deming asked, "Where did you get that?"

"I got it from you, Dr. Deming," she replied.

"I can do better than that," he said.[25]

In June 1988, he outlined his System of Profound Knowledge as having five components, including:

- Knowledge of variation–statistical theory
- Knowledge of the distinction between common causes and special causes
- Statistical theory of interaction
- Knowledge about operational definitions and communication
- Knowledge of psychology

In 1989, the theory evolved further to include:

- Understanding variation. There will always be variation, in people, performance, services, and products. What is the variation trying to tell?
- Knowledge of variation helps to understand the losses from tampering:
  - Treating a fault, complaint, mistake, accident, as if it came from a special cause when in fact it came from a common cause of random variation
  - The converse
- Knowledge of procedures aimed at minimum net economic loss from both of the above mistakes
- Losses from demands that are beyond the capability of the system.
- Knowledge about loss functions, in particular the Taguchi loss function.
- Knowledge of interaction of forces and effect of systems on performance of people
- Knowledge about the creation of chaos and loss resulting from successive applications of such random individually unimportant forces as:
  - Worker training worker
  - Executives meeting together to guide policy, without guidance of profound knowledge
  - Committees and government agencies working without guidance of profound knowledge
  - Competition for share of market (i.e., win-lose)
  - Trade barriers

- Some theory of knowledge:
  - There is no knowledge without theory
  - There is no knowledge without prediction
  - Experience and examples teaches nothing unless studied with the aid of theory
  - Any plan, however simple, requires prediction
  - Operational definitions and communication
  - No number of examples establishes a theory
- Knowledge of psychology, including:
  - Intrinsic motivation (e.g., for innovation, improvement, for joy in work, and in learning)
  - Extrinsic motivation (e.g., slogans and ratings)
  - Overjustification
  - Losses from demands placed on people beyond the capability of the system

Deming presented the final, four-part System of Profound Knowledge in a paper written for presentation to a conference in Japan in 1989.[26]

THE RED BEAD EXPERIMENT

The Red Bead experiment, which was a highlight of Deming's seminars, involved some role-playing. Deming played the role of owner-plant manager, and volunteers from the audience played his inspector, supervisor, and six workers. Deming typically showed the workers a box full of tiny beads, the vast majority of them white and a few red. Deming then gave the workers instructions to dip a paddle with 50 tiny holes into the beads and take the paddle to the inspectors. About five red beads—the number varied—will show up on the paddle. The exercise was intended to show how little control the workers have over the color of beads on the paddle. After three passes, Deming would fire three workers whose work contained the most red beads and tells the remaining three to work two shifts. There would still be too many red beads generated, so Deming would finally close the plant.

The red bead experiment demonstrates several points, including:

- Variation is natural and a part of any process.
- Half the workers are always above average; half are always below average.
- Workers perform in a system that is always beyond their ability to control; the system determines how they perform.
- Only management can change the system.

DEMING'S 14-POINT THEORY OF MANAGEMENT

Deming's 14-point Theory of Management basically encompass his thoughts in a sequential format. They are broad lines of action that management must take if the organization is to achieve a true quality transformation. "You cannot separate the 14 points," said Deming. "Number one is the foundation. Without it, there is no point in talking about the others."[27] The same is true for the other 13. The points are discussed in the following sections.

Constancy of Purpose

1. Create constancy of purpose toward improvement of product and service, with the aim to become competitive and stay in business and to provide jobs.

Management, suggests Deming, has two problems: those of today and those of tomorrow. Both must be addressed with short- and long-term mission statements regarding the company's quality expectations. The customer's expectations also must be addressed in the company's search for constancy, and all plans must be developed with the company's long-range mission in mind. The highest-level executives must state a clear definition of the mission and overall strategies and determine how to implement changes through communication and organization. They also must be visibly active and unwavering in their commitment to the purpose, including committing financial resources to innovation, research, and education as well as improving designs and aids to production.

Adopting the New Philosophy

> 2. *Adopt the new philosophy. In this new economic age, Western management must awaken to the challenge, learn their responsibilities, and take on leadership for change.*

One of Deming's broadest mandates, this point demands a comprehensive change in management's attitudes on everything from personnel to distribution. It means a whole new corporate culture, in which employees feel empowered to innovate, ask questions, and exercise leadership. High-level executives, middle management, and line employees and suppliers must contribute to a cooperative culture that is focused on delivering the finest products and services to the customer.

For many managers, this may mean a virtual self exile from accepted attitudes among their peers to halt the internecine competition that goes on in many companies. Managers especially must avoid adopting the tools of statistical process control without adopting the rest of Deming's holistic philosophy. This is difficult, because senior managers must change decades of business practices. Anything less, however, means adhering to the old ways of waste and rework, inadequate supervision, and a declining competitive position. "The first step in the transformation process is the transformation of the individual," states Deming.[28]

More than any other proponent of quality, Deming denounced traditional management practices and attitudes as undermining the very systems and people they should be serving. During the early 1980s, humiliating high-ranking managers seemed to be his forte. Private, four-day seminars conducted for special clients sometimes began with the question, "So, you want me to tell you how to run your company?" Then he would proceed to do just that. "Your problems are not the Japanese. They are not your competitors. They are yourselves," he would say. "Quality is made in the boardroom. It can be no better directed than that."[29]

Cease Dependence on Inspection

> 3. *Cease dependence on inspection to achieve quality. Eliminate the need for mass inspection by building quality into the product in the first place.*

Inspection is a sort of game of industrial hide-and-seek. Dependence on inspection means planning for defects, allowing the system to create defects, and then organizing teams to go find them. It means that the process is out of statistical control or the specifications are impractical. The quality of the product cannot be good until the quality of the process is good. Workers must be trained so they know how to collect statistical data on the process and how to interpret the data.

Inspection is not 100 percent effective in locating bad parts. Deming used to tell about the suit he purchased with an inspector's ticket in the pocket and five or six blatant defects in the jacket.

To get rid of inspection, companies must move backward in the production process and obtain information about its reliability. Japan began doing that in the early 1950s, and in the 1980s began moving further back into the system to achieve quality through such other tools as design and analysis of experiments. Some inspection is always necessary, but end-of-the-line inspection happens too late to improve quality.

Supplier Selection

4. The process of awarding business can no longer be based on the price tag alone. Instead, total cost should be minimized, and there should be a single supplier for any one item, on a long-term relationship of loyalty and trust.

Once one of Deming's more controversial points, this principle mandates that companies look at the total cost of products or services provided by others, and not just the purchase price. It is standard practice for American businesses—and a mandate of many government agencies—to award contracts to the lowest bidder. By working with a single supplier, the company ensures a consistent level of quality at a consistent price. The company must work closely with the chosen supplier to improve the quality of the supplier's product through joint training of employees on statistical process control, including the supplier in strategy and design meetings and having firm schedules. These actions also improve the relationship with the supplier.

Accepting the lowest bid does not guarantee that the purchasing company the lowest total cost. Indeed, the result of accepting the lowest bid may be faulty products, rework, and, when the dissatisfaction end users are figured into the bargain, a greater final cost. The best way to save money in the long run is to develop a close relationship with a vendor who is committed to quality and can provide statistical evidence of process control and a good history of performance, eliminating the need for a second vendor. After all, asked Deming, "Do you have a second wife?"

As long as suppliers have short-term contracts, they have little incentive to invest in equipment or training so they can do a better job.[30] Single suppliers should be selected on basis of their ability to work as a team with the customer. The results are continuous improvement and lower costs. Many companies may not be able to use only one supplier. Even so, they should reduce the number of suppliers as much as possible so they can work more closely with those that remain.

Deming often railed against the evils of pitting people against each other. Collaboration and cooperation get better results than competition. "We had the best telephone system in the world," he noted. "What happened? We got competition. Now we are the laughing stock of the world."[31]

Constant Improvement

> 5. *Improvement to the system of production and service must be continual to improve quality and productivity as well as to constantly decrease costs.*

Employees are assigned to produce a consistent product within the capability of the process. Management's role is constantly to strive to improve the process and to use the tools necessary to do so. Assuming the product has a market, the PDSA cycle is then repeated, with modifications based on the cusomters' reactions.

Deming always said quality must be built in at the design stage. Companies beginning quality programs often mistake putting out fires for improvements to the process, he said. They should be seen instead as removing special causes of deviation from the product control limits.

Training

> 6. *Training should be given on the job.*

Most companies need to change their attitude toward training. Conversations with workers often reveal concerns about new employees who come to the job with no training or about a busy worker being asked to train a new employee.

Training and retraining must be institutionalized in the company. They must become part of the company's routine functions and philosophy. Everyone should be trained in basic statistical methods, and training itself should be measured to determine when the training is adequate. Training and retraining, handled properly and coupled with measurements to know when the training is effective, helps workers understand their jobs and what their job procedures should be. It must include formal class work, experiential work, and instructional materials. The end result is higher quality.

Training boosts morale, because it provides the worker with a greater sense of security and value and a lower stress level. (Point 6 refers to the foundations of training for management and for new employees. Point 13 refers to continual education and self improvement for everyone on the job.)

Deming liked to tell a story about a conversation he had with a factory worker. "I don't know how to do my job," the worker said. "Why don't you go to your foreman? Can't he help you?" Deming asked. "Listen, if you want to learn something, do you go to someone just as dumb as you are?" the man replied.[32]

Leadership

> 7. *Leadership must be instituted (see point 12). The aim of leadership should be to help people and machines do a better job. Leadership of management as well as leadership of production workers needs an overhaul.*

As defined by Deming, a leader is someone whose job is to transform the organization from traditional flat-earth orientation to one of unending quality improvement. What makes a leader? Leaders must have a vision of what the organization will be after it is transformed. They must be practical enough to create a plan that is not too difficult for others, be able to guide and persuade people to accept plans, and must understand people and their limitations.

Like statistical tools, leadership must be encouraged at every level of the company, Deming said. It must move downward until employees feel empowered to lead, though they may not be managers or supervisors. The employees' brainpower has to be viewed as the company's most valuable asset. Management's responsibility is to create an organizational climate that welcomes and encourages employee recommendations. Supervisors should coach and counsel.

A leader also must understand variation, and what has to be done to help an employee whose work appears to be outside the job specifications. The leader's handling of special help for that employee should create trust and not fear. "A leader is someone who brings change," Deming said. "The new philosophy requires leadership. We need to think in terms of win-win. There was a time for rugged individualism. It was not wrong, (but) times have changed."[33]

Leaders today must discover who among their staff needs help to do a better job or is providing exceptionally good performance. They must also work to improve the system, which shrinks the differences between the people who work in the system. Leaders must have theories, enabling them to understand what a transformation would do for an organization and those who work there. Leaders should feel a sense of obligation to accomplish a transformation and have a plan for the transformation.

New education to develop leadership must be offered, with better selection. Teachers and leaders must become colleagues to those under them, educating and coaching but never pulling rank. Deming notes a Chinese Tao written 4,000 years ago that says, "Reward for merit brings strife and contention."[34]

According to Deming, the leader's job is to:

- Find out who is in need of special help and see that they get it.
- Coach and counsel.
- Understand variation.
- Remove obstacles.
- Focus on the customer.
- Understand the mission of the company (i.e., constancy of purpose).
- Improve the system.
- Create an atmosphere of trust.

- Know the job, how it fits the overall product.
- Forgive a mistake.

No Fear

> 8. *Drive out fear, so that everyone may work effectively for the company.*

Nothing crushes innovation and quality more effectively than fear. If employees fear they will be blamed for inadequacies in the system, they may go to great lengths to hide those problems. Deming used to tell a story about a supervisor who heard a rumor that the plant manager said he would close the plant if any product was found to be outside certain specifications. The supervisor then falsified reports to hide any problems. Other repercussions of fear include employees reporting to management only what they believe management wants to hear. Creativity is stifled because workers believe that management does not want to hear what they really think. The result is a reduction in the amount and quality of information received by management. Accurate information to management—positive and negative—is crucial if the company is to thrive.

Fear also can result in physical and emotional disorders among employees, which may result in substance abuse, absenteeism, poor morale, low productivity, and poor interpersonal relationships. "The economic loss from fear is appalling," Deming said.

Fear can result from such blatant causes as failure to meet quotas or receiving blame for faults in the system or from such more subtle causes as ignorance of company goals, lack of supervision or lack of operational definitions (i.e., a vague sense of anxiety).

Deming in the last years of his career used to draw a distinction between fear, the cause of which is known, and anxiety, the cause of which is unknown. Anxiety comes from not knowing what to do and is the worse of the two, Deming said, because the cause often cannot be expressed. "Fear is preferable," he said. "There is a chance to do something about it. Anxiety leads to paralysis."[35]

Breaking Down Barriers

> *9. Management must break down barriers between departments. People in research, design, sales, and production must work as a team, to foresee problems of production and in use of a product or service.*

Too frequently departments or divisions in a company see each other as competitors, and the ensuing rivalries hinder the company's long-range growth. Competition among departments is often fostered by setting up each as a profit center and by perhaps evaluating managers according to profitability. The idea is that maximizing the profit of each department is good for the profitability of the whole company. That proposition would be true if the departments were independent entities, but cannot be the case when they are working for the same company as departments for purchasing, engineering, assembly, and other business activities. Often, each department has its own goals, and sticks to them regardless of the impact on the others. "That's their problem," they might say. The result is mistrust, delays and subpar performance for the whole company.

Having the manager answer for the department's profitability has obvious ill effects, such as management job hopping, which is one of Deming's seven Deadly Obstacles to quality. "When it comes to a showdown under the present system and someone has to make a decision—his own rating or the company's—he will decide for himself," Deming said. "Can you blame him?"[36]

Instead of having independent goals, each department must be trained to see the other departments as its internal customers—individuals and organizations to be satisfied just as the consumer of the company's products must be satisfied. When all departments and employees begin to see each other as customers, the barriers begin to fall. This kind of teamwork can be promoted through the establishment of interdepartmental work teams, statistical methods implementation teams, and the identification of who the clients and suppliers are for each employee.

No Coercion

10. Management must eliminate slogans, exhortations, and targets asking for zero defects and new levels of productivity from the work force.

Such exhortations create adversarial relationships, because most causes of low quality and low productivity belong to the system and lie beyond the power of the employees, Deming said. Employees may resent some exhortations, because they often reveal that managers are unaware of the barriers to pride in workmanship.

Slogans arise from the management supposition that production workers can achieve perfection or some other goal management sets by putting their backs into the job a little more. Slogans imply that something more than the worker is doing now is desired or required. They are an indirect put-down. Furthermore, if the slogans ask the workers to accomplish tasks they are unable to accomplish, the effect is fear and mistrust of management.

Promoting Leadership

11a. Management should eliminate work standards (i.e., quotas) on the factory floor and replace it with leadership.

The intent of establishing a work standard, for the individual or the company, is usually good, but its impact is often to stifle pride in workmanship and even to raise costs of production. In fact, work standards, rates, and piece work are often the crutches of poor supervision. Some quotas are set to reach a productivity or profit number in mind, but many are set arbitrarily with no regard for quality. They are also limiting; workers learn that if the quota is met, a tougher one is set. Quotas pressure workers to produce poor quality to meet the goal, or to stop when the quota is reached. Either situation makes both workers and management unhappy.

> *11b. Eliminate management by objective. Eliminate management by numbers, numerical goals. Substitute leadership.*

Deming included management by objective (MBO) as an example of setting work standards, because it focuses on results rather than process. Freed from work quotas, ranking systems, and other short-term goals, he contended that individual workers work hard out of pride. The role of management is to encourage them and to preserve the intrinsic motivation and dignity with which people are born.

Promoting Pride

> *12a. Management must remove barriers that rob the hourly workers of their right to pride of workmanship. The responsibility of supervisors must be changed from sheer numbers to quality.*

The barriers to pride in workmanship include inadequate training, inconsistent standards, lack of adequate documentation of operating procedures, lack of direction, focusing on quantity, poor equipment, fear, and inadequate measures of the process. Deming often met with workers out of the presence of their managers and skillfully led them into conversations about their jobs. They frequently revealed frustration with all of the previously mentioned problems, plus a feeling of powerlessness to do anything about it.

The problems lie in the system, Deming noted, not with the workers. It is management's role to remove the barriers by seeking open communication with the workers. Unfortunately, this often has meant starting "employee involvement" groups or even groups labeled as quality control circles. Deming said these are a "smokescreen" to allow managers to appear to be doing something about the problem. The result is even greater disillusionment among workers when the program fades away or employees are never empowered to do something about the situation. Deming estimated that two people out of a hundred have a chance to perform their work with pride.[37]

> *12b. Management must remove barriers that rob people in management and in engineering of their right to pride in workmanship. This means, inter alia, abolishment of the annual or merit rating and of management by objective or by numbers.*

Abolishing the annual merit or rating system is Deming's most controversial principle, especially because he insists that grades in school be included. Most managers, educators, and parents are unable to conceive of anything that would effectively replace the practice of giving grades or assessing worker productivity. Yet, annual appraisals are "a weapon to hold people in line," Deming said. "They were created to hold people in conformance with the system, not to improve the system."[38]

Deming makes this point: If the work of any group of people is counted in any way showing what the average, half of the people's work will be above that average and half will be below it, even if there is little difference in each's work effort. Those in the lower half will be hurt, though they do not deserve it.

Instead of doing annual ratings, a leader should:

- Learn who, if any, of his employees is in need of individual help.
- Learn whose work processes show extra good performance.
- Improve the system. This improvement shrinks the differences between the people that belong to the system. The people that belong to the system all get the same raise. They must not be ranked top to bottom.

Rating people within a stable system only makes the system worse through excessive tweaking. Ratings alone are not so great a problem as is the way they are used, often nourishing rivalry and politics, Deming said. They also cause people to agree, to go along, anything to not miss a raise.

Deming used an algebraic equation to prove his point:

$$x + [yx] = 8$$

The *x* is the impact on the outcome by the individual, and the *yx* is the impact on the outcome by the process in which the individual works. He assigned the value of 8 as an arbitrary value used by a manager to evaluate the individual, but it ignores the impact of the process, which may be a much larger contributor. There is no way of establishing such a value because there are two unknowns and one equation, which cannot be solved, Deming said.

Education and Self Improvement

13. Institute a vigorous program of education and self-improvement.

Joy on the job and innovation come partly from self-improvement and self-confidence. Managers can foster these by offering opportunities for continuous education, Deming says.[39]

Rapid changes in technology are constantly requiring everyone—executives, supervisors, and workers—to learn new equipment and new terminology. Production workers need courses in basic statistical process control tools. Engineers need constant improvement in design techniques. All employees need education in consensus decision-making, conflict resolution, time management, and other interpersonal skills. Top management requires education in Deming's new management philosophy.[40]

The immediate results of providing a worker with more education are an improvement in the employee's morale and job perspective as well as new skills. Improving the skill level of the employees, Deming insisted, inevitably improves the overall quality of the company, thereby resulting in less variability in processes. With the decline in quality of public education in the United States, many companies find themselves forced to offer their employees continuing education.

Deming believed that many types of study serve to improve the organization. He used to tell the following story to underscore this belief: A company once approved as a business expense a course on ancient Egyptian culture for an employee, but the Internal Revenue Service disallowed it. Deming said the expense should be allowable, because the ancient Egyptians had an advanced culture and managerial system that might benefit the modern company. "Just wait till I catch up to those people at the IRS," he added.[41]

Participation of Everyone

> *14. Put everybody in the company to work to accomplish the transformation. The transformation is everybody's job.*

Once management understands what must be done, it faces the challenge of beginning the transformation. This happens when there is a critical mass of managers, supervisors, and workers who learn the new philosophy and want to change. They must be educated. Usually, this is accomplished by bringing in a trainer or consulting company to provide seminars or workshops in quality transformation. A statistical consultant is also required to teach every manager and employee how to improve quality. Then the company needs to follow the PDSA cycle and continually study and make improvements.

Top management must feel a burning desire to depart from its old ways of running the company and move to the Deming philosophy. Then it must take the necessary steps—some of them requiring both courage and a commitment to education—to move the transformation thinking downward, so that everyone is exposed to the new philosophy.

THE SEVEN DEADLY DISEASES AND OBSTACLES

Deming identified seven obstacles that prevent Western management from optimizing systems and achieving higher quality and productivity. The obstacles are characteristic of traditional management and Deming believed nothing less than "a complete shakeup"[42] of such management is essential to get rid of these obstacles.

1. Lack of Constancy of Purpose

Executives often state that their companies have a purpose, but there must be a wholesale transformation to the new philosophy to develop the tenacity to stick to it. Even boards of directors must adhere to the purpose, so the selection of a new chief executive does not derail a company on its path to the new philosophy. Managers must take such concrete actions as spending money on training and equipment to make clear that they are serious about the transformation.[43] They also must clearly define and communicate the purpose to their organizations and continuously check that decisions are in line with the purpose. Perhaps most importantly, managers must be role models for others in an organization.

2. Emphasis on Short-Term Profits

Short-term thinking by management is often fed by fear of an unfriendly takeover, or by a push from bankers and owners for dividends. Many managers have as their chief purpose the achievement of a good quarterly dividend for the company's owners or shareholders, regardless of the short-term viewpoint it requires and the long-term damage it does. It is not possible to have as dual purposes short-term profits and never-ending quality improvement. The latter, however, brings long-term growth and greater profitability and productivity, though the stock market often views a company's quarterly dividend as its chief sign of health. Sales quotas is also an example of a short-term result. To eliminate emphasis on short-term profits, management must focus on such investments for the future as research and development, new equipment, and education. It must strike a balance between long-term and short-term profits.

3. The Personal Review System

Personal review systems, evaluation of performance, merit rating, annual reviews, or annual appraisals for people in management are devastating. Management by objective on a go/no-go basis, without a method for accomplishment of the objective, is the same thing by another name. Management by fear is still a better name.

The annual review forces managers and supervisors to engage in managing people rather than process. Evaluations encourage short-term performances at the expense of long-term planning. They also foster fear, rivalry, and internecine politics while discouraging teamwork. The annual review increases reliance on a numbering system, because the evaluator must find some tangible means of measuring the individual's performance.

Understanding the role of leadership can help abolish the need for the annual appraisal. A more educated leader understands principles and methods, appreciates variability in a process, takes care in selecting someone for a job, and is willing and able to work as a counselor, leader, and team player with others.

4. Mobility of Management: Job Hopping

The professional executive whose training and experience apply to almost any industry is a given in American business. There is also a perception that managers who stay in one position too long become stale and are no longer upwardly mobile. The result for the manager is job-hopping and resume-building through frequent changes. The result for the organization is instability.

A short-term manager cannot create long-term changes. The lack of continuity leads to poor quality and low productivity. Programs, procedures, and goals may change with each managerial turnover, and employees put their momentum and creativity on hold while waiting to see what the new boss will do. Eliminating this obstacle is the responsibility of management, which must minimize it by being consistent, focusing on long-term goals, and providing for continual development of employees. The benefits are committed employees, better decisions by managers who know the business, and greater stability.

5. Use of Visible Figures Only

Managers often use only visible figures and pay little or no consideration to figures that are unknown or unknowable. Deming liked to talk about figures that are unknown and unknowable. These include the multiplicative effect of a happy or an unhappy customer. Management logically prefers to act according to such facts as sales numbers, budgets, and financial reports, but too often fails to consider hidden costs, which can result in poor quality, unhappy customers, frustrated and squabbling employees, and lack of brand loyalty. Eliminating this disease depends on management study and anticipation of the unknown.

6. Excessive Medical Costs

The United States spends the highest percentage of its gross national product on health care—currently about 15 percent and climbing. During the 1980s, health care costs went through an inflationary spiral; for example, a health care premiums rose from $100 in 1984 to $196 in 1991. The reasons for the sharp rise include expensive life support systems, increases in the number of expensive surgical operations, liability protection, and waste and rework in the medical profession. To eliminate this obstacle, management must focus on programs for preventive health care, efficient and effective safety programs, better management of existing health care programs, and hidden costs of absenteeism, low productivity and turnover.

7. Excessive Liability Costs

U.S. society is a litigious one, it is often said. Many believe it appropriate to spend time and money on lawsuits for personal injury, property damage, product liability, and malpractice. The question arises, however: Is it society, or is it the interplay and spiraling costs of insurance and our legal system? Liability laws are actually stricter in Japan than in the United States, but claims are settled more quickly and money goes to the victims more than to the courts or the lawyers. The result is that revenues, which might go into improving the competitive positions of private companies, are being channeled into legal fees. Lawyers do the best they can within the system, but management must challenge costs that do not contribute to producing a product or service. Management must use quality control tools to eliminate an unsafe or unhealthy work environment.

CHANGING WITH KNOWLEDGE

During the years, Deming's philosophy, including the content of his 14 Principles, has changed, largely because of his devotion to constant, never-ending learning. For instance, in 1985, the 14th point stated:

> Clearly define top management's permanent commitment to quality and productivity and its obligation to implement all these principles.[44]

Today, it states:

> Put everybody in the company to work to accomplish the transformation. The transformation is everybody's job.

Another example is the seventh point, which in 1985 stated:

> Focus supervision on helping people do a better job. Ensure that immediate action is taken on reports of defects, maintenance requirements, poor tools, inadequate operating definitions, or other conditions detrimental to quality.[45]

Today, it states:

> Institute leadership. The aim of leadership should be to help people and machines and gadgets do a better job. Leadership of management is in need of overhaul, as well as leadership of production workers.[50]

The wording of other points has changed as well, but the underlying philosophy has not changed: Management has the responsibility for the overall system. Managers must stop blaming workers for problems inherent in systems. They must set about fixing systems so workers can do their jobs better. They also should cease their preoccupation with this month, this quarter, or even this year, and start thinking about where their company will be in five years. Only with a strong vision of the future, solid information derived from statistical methods, and an understanding of human psychology can a company compete in the rapidly changing world market.

DEMING'S WORK

Although other quality experts founded institutes or consultancies to carry on their teachings, Deming chose a less formal route and attracted a cadre of consultants and academicians as disciples. Consultants, mostly statisticians, started their own companies to disseminate his teachings. In several communities, people whose lives changed when they learned his theories formed nonprofit clubs and other organizations to help each other learn more.[46]

Deming carried on his famous four-day seminars well into his 90s, intoning in his basso profondo, "Why are we here? To learn and have fun." Much of Deming's teaching, as outlined in previous sections, concerns understanding psychology, variation, systems, and theory of knowledge. These concerns, however, are only the tips of icebergs that must be viewed beneath the surface to be truly comprehended. "If you have not produced the data, you cannot understand (or use) it," Deming told audiences. "You need to understand the production of the data."

Deming's seminars made a powerful impact on those who attend. This is partially because Deming supported his behavioral theories with scientific proof, such as pointing to trade restrictions as tampering with a system and making it worse.

His seminars, in his words, were "education, not training. You will not pick up skills that will allow your fingers to do something differently on Monday morning, but you will pick up things that will haunt you the rest of your life."

"Are your top people here?" Deming asks, "If not, you are going to have to teach them. Desire is the first step—recognition that something is wrong. People need to know why. They need to understand the theory. They need guidance. It is more important for people to know why they are doing their job than it is to know how."[47]

Many quality experts offer their own definitions of quality, but Deming declined to do so, saying quality "is not easy to define. No few words can describe it. Quality has no meaning without reference to customers. Put yourself in the customer's shoes. What changes can you make to render the service more acceptable to the customer? If I have to define it, it would be meeting and exceeding the customer's needs and expectations, and then continuing to improve."[48]

Organizations must not expect customers to necessarily know what they want. "Customers' expectations are only what you and your competition led them to think," Deming said. "Customers have not asked for some of the most important developments. No customer asked for a telephone, a fax, or a pocket radio."[49]

Business customers also do not understand their needs alone. Deming said the customer "needs the help of the supplier. The supplier has specialized knowledge that the customer cannot have."[50]

Even that may not be enough. "We can't make it on satisfied customers," he said. "They will switch. We need loyal customers who will wait in line and bring friends. Profit is six to ten times greater with a loyal customer."[51]

"Doesn't anyone give a hoot about profit anymore?" Deming often thundered. "The aim is the lowest total cost. Shrink variation. Improving incoming quality month-by-month, at ever lower and lower prices, with better profit to the customer and the supplier."[52]

Organizations must adjust constantly, Deming declared. "Change is upon us. It is not optional."[53] Companies who focus on increasing their share of the market may fail to see other opportunities, because increasing market share means taking it from competitors. If they focus on expanding the market through new products and services, everybody wins. "He that only hopes to become competitive is already licked,"[54] Deming commented. Management guided by theory, not short-term results, is the wisest.

Government interference in the economy is not the answer to America's global competitive challenge. "Better quality is the answer to industrial survival in the western world,"[55] said Deming, noting that Japanese industrialists revived the nation's economy by nurturing a vigorous pursuit of knowledge and the industrial application of knowledge. The Japanese have much to teach Western enterprises, such as the "eagerness of top management to learn and to treat people as treasures, not as assets."[56]

Deming's work provokes people to think, whether it's in a classroom or on a drive across town. At New York University, where he taught for many years, Deming often liked to ask his students which other courses they were taking that would help them have a positive impact on the U.S. balance of trade. "Looking at their faces, you can see them getting mad"[57] as they realize their other classes really do not contribute to reducing the balance of trade, he said.

"Good intentions are not enough," he continued. "They must be accompanied by profound knowledge. Quality for international trade must be good enough to command a market."[58]

Individuals also must be guided by principles, Deming said. Although he made no public statements about his personal religion, Anna Maravelas, a psychologist at Process Management International, asked Deming if his System of Profound Knowledge contained a spiritual element.

"What do you mean by spiritual?" replied Deming. "A belief? A guiding principle? One's entitled to (those), should have (them). Call it spiritual, if you wish. Once somebody has principles, then he creates for himself a theory for the world. You can call that spiritual if you wish. That leads him—his guiding star."[59]

One of Deming's guiding stars has been his lifelong commitment to learning and teaching. Acceptance of his teachings has been slow in the United States, but those who have adopted his philosophy and methods—from small companies to whole nations—have found themselves able to lower costs, produce more, and gain greatest profits even in markets believed to have been lost forever.

During his seminars, Deming was fond of saying that people do the best they can but are limited by the system in which they work. He concluded each four-day seminar saying, "I leave you with five words: I have done my best."[60]

3
Joseph M. Juran

Joseph M. Juran is often considered a cofounder of the 20th century quality movement. Like W. Edwards Deming, Juran worked his way from an impoverished lifestyle to become a foremost authority on managing for quality. He also was highly influential in the Japanese post-World War II quality movement and continued into the 1990s as a leader of quality efforts throughout the world.

Throughout his childhood, Juran was not a stranger to the lack of quality life could bring. Born in a small village that today is a part of Romania, Juran's family emigrated to Minnesota in 1912 when he was eight years old. Eight people lived in a small cabin in the poorest section of Minneapolis. Technology was nonexistent "but in other respects, [Juran] had indeed entered a new world. There was minimal suppression of human freedoms; opportunities for education abounded; work was available, although workers were exploited; the hope of escape from a life of poverty was based on realities – numerous earlier immigrants had already made that escape,"[1] Juran writes in a short autobiography written for the Juran Institute, his Wilton, Connecticut-based training and consulting firm.

At this time, Juran had just one goal – to move out of poverty. He worked as a newsboy, bootblack, delivery boy, shipping clerk, printer's devil, laborer, teamster, janitor, shoe salesman, grocery clerk, bookkeeper, and editor of a chess column. In 1924, however, he achieved the first step towards turning his dream into reality; he graduated from the University of Minnesota with a degree in electrical engineering and took a job with the Bell System's Hawthorne Plant.

"How did I happen to choose a career in quality?" Juran wrote in his autobiographical essay. "The choice was not mine. It was chosen for me. Hawthorne was a huge works—it employed close to 40,000 people. Each year it recruited graduates from college. After a brief indoctrination, those graduates were assigned to various branches of the factory. I was assigned to what was called the inspection branch. I had little knowledge of what the inspection branch did, and it never entered my mind to challenge the assignment."[2]

"As it turned out, Hawthorne was a marvelous place for starting a career in managing for quality," he continues. "In those years the Bell System very likely faced the most difficult problems in the world with respect to quality. They had to transmit feeble energies over long distances, and do so with minimal distortion of the inherent frequencies."[3]

In the beginning, Juran's job was to field internal quality complaints. However, it was yet another coincidence that truly began Juran's interest in managing for quality. When Bell Telephone Laboratories began an initiative to apply statistical methodology to control the quality of manufactured products, Juran was one of two engineers chosen to help build a new inspection statistical department. New innovations for sampling and controlling quality were constantly developed and implemented, and by 1941 Juran had held positions as both quality manager and corporate industrial engineer at Hawthorne.

In 1941, Juran left the Bell System to work for the lend-lease office of the federal government. This was a time of turmoil not just for the country but for Juran as well. He emerged from this job in 1945 with a realization that he was too individualistic to work for a large company. Consequently, he began a career in what he calls "freelancing in the field of management."[4]

"I undertook to do everything within that field: research, philosophize, write, lecture, consult, practice. I had already become familiar with several areas of management—general management, industrial engineering, and quality control, and I undertook activities in all three of these," he writes. "However, over the years, as quality grew and grew in importance, it began to crowd out everything else to a point that it dominated all of my activities."[5]

As Juran became more and more immersed in quality, his reputation began to grow, solidifying in 1951 with the publication of *Quality Control Handbook*, his third book and the flagship of his quality efforts. He subsequently was invited to Japan by the Union of Japanese Scientists and Engineers (JUSE) and arrived in 1954.

During this time, Juran continued to develop his theory that quality control should be conducted as an integral part of management control. Although the worker plays a key role in quality improvement, Juran maintains that only about 20% of all problems are caused by the workers and even those must be partially solved through management support.

For the next 28 years, Juran enjoyed the life he had envisioned during those hard days as a youngster in Minnesota. He remained a freelance consultant, writing and traveling around the world to consult and lecture on quality. However, in 1979, spurred by the desire to create a series of videocassettes—*Juran on Quality Improvement*—he created the one thing he had resisted throughout his career: an organization. The Juran Institute was born and would remain under his control for the next eight years. In 1987, he passed on the leadership of the institute. He did not retire but once again pursued only what he had wanted to do: to dispense with administrative duties and devote his time to lecturing and writing on the current state of the quality movement as well as to write his autobiography.

Like Deming, Juran has been honored in many countries. These honors include the highest decoration presented to a non-Japanese citizen, the Second Order of the Sacred Treasure, which was awarded by the Emperor of Japan in 1981 for the development of Quality Control in Japan and the facilitation of U.S. and Japanese friendship.

JURAN'S THEORIES

Similarities with Deming's career abound; both men were employed by the Hawthorne Works, both had highly diverse careers, both were instrumental in the formation of Japan's quality movement as well as the U.S. quality movement, and there are many often-subtle differences between Deming's and Juran's theories for running a quality organization. They agree that management and employees play key roles in quality improvement, but Juran focuses on planning , organizational issues, management's responsibility for quality, and the need to set goals and targets for improvement.

Juran's quality philosophy contains many interrelated messages. However, key to his philosophy is the belief that quality does not happen by accident. It must be planned and that planning must begin with top management. He believes that the majority of quality problems are the fault of poor management rather than poor workmanship.

In his 1992 book, *Juran on Quality By Design*, Juran defines the quality mission for management on two levels:

- The quality mission of the company is "fitness for use" as perceived by customers. Fitness for use is determined by a product's design, the degree to which the product conforms to the specifications of that design, the product's availability, reliability and maintainability, and the customer service available. He emphasizes the need for specialist knowledge and tools for successful conduct for the quality function. He also emphasizes the need for continuous awareness of the customer in all functions.
- The missions of individual departments in the company are to work according to specifications designed to achieve fitness for use.

The quality mission applies not only to the organization as a whole but also to its suborganizations. If a product or service consistently meets the customers' specifications, the quality mission has been achieved by the providers of that product or service.

The second major component of Juran's philosophy is a sense that quality is freedom from deficiencies. He defines quality literally with the following equation:

Quality = Frequency of Deficiencies/Opportunity for Deficiencies

This two-part philosophy is a direct result of Juran's observations regarding post-World War II consumerism. This era saw the rise of product quality to a position of prominence among consumers as a result of several trends: growing concern about damage to the environment, action by the courts to impose strict liability, fear of major disasters and near disasters, pressure from consumer organizations for better quality and more responsible redress, and growing public awareness of the role of quality in international competition. Postwar industrialization created many benefits for society, but it also made industrialized society dependent on the continuing performance and behavior of a huge array of technological goods and services. Juran calls this the phenomenon of "life behind the quality dikes,"[6] a form of securing benefits but living dangerously. Protective dikes in the form of good quality shield society against service interruptions and to guard against disasters.

Juran also warns that there are no shortcuts to quality. "The recipe for action should consist of 90% substance and 10% exhortation, not the reverse," he writes in *Juran on Planning for Quality*. His formula for results includes:

- Establish specific goals to be reached.
- Establish plans for reaching the goals.
- Assign clear responsibility for meeting the goals.
- Base the rewards on results achieved.

JURAN'S ORGANIZATIONAL VIEW

Before Juran's advice for organizations on quality improvement can be discussed, it is crucial to look at his view of the workings of the company itself. He begins by looking at the processes within the company: "Companies and their autonomous divisions conduct their principal affairs through major, repetitive-use systems that are inherently multifunctional in nature," he writes.[7] These are called macroprocesses. Examples include bringing out new products, processing customers' orders, collecting income, recruiting employees, producing goods, purchasing materials, and planning for manufacture. The ideal macroprocess is effective, adaptable, efficient, measurable, controllable, and formalized, and any macroprocess provides added value as a return on the work done. Because they are multifunctional, no single employee can take ownership of a macroprocess nor can one employee have control over a macroprocess. For this reason, they are "owned" by teams and most often the focus of upper management's quality goals.

"The anatomy of a macroprocess varies but most of them consist of a procession"[8] of microprocesses, Juran continues. Each microprocess is typically carried out within a single functional organization unit often presided over by a first-line supervisor. These are closely focused operations. Microprocesses are so numerous that the upper levels of companies cannot become involved with them individually. In addition, replanning of the microprocesses seldom solves the major problems of the macroprocess.

Employees within the organization function both individually and in teams that can be described in terms of The Triple Role Concept (TRIPROL).[9] Every unit of the organization carries out a process and produces a product. Each unit is called a processor team. Each processor team carries out three quality-related roles:

- Customer. The processor team acquires various kinds of input that are used in carrying out the process. The processor team is a customer of the suppliers who provide the input.
- Processor. The processor team carries out various managerial and technological activities in order to produce its products.
- Supplier. The processor team supplies its products to its customers.

MANAGEMENT'S ROLE

Planning for quality has always existed in industrialized society, Juran notes, but it was done on what he terms a "Little q level."[10] The scope was narrow and confined to selected operating entities such as factories. The "supercause" of the deficiencies of the past is this "Little q" outlook, or the lack of a systematic, structured approach to planning for quality. "During the 1980s, many upper managers adapted strategies that involved setting vague goals and then delegated to the rest of the organization the responsibility for meeting those vague goals. The most usual results were a loss of several years, a residue of divisiveness and a loss of credibility," Juran writes in *Juran On Planning For Quality*.

To emphasize his point on the importance of top-level planning, Juran is known for his analogy of the alligator hatchery. It begins with the scenario of a manager up to the waist in alligators. Each live alligator is a potential quality improvement project. Each completed improvement project is a dead alligator. A benign hatchery produces new, useful quality plans. A malignant hatchery, however, produces new alligators because the planning process has not changed. Quality improvement can take care of the existing alligators one by one. However, to stop the production of new alligators requires shutting down that malignant hatchery. Nothing short of leadership by the upper managers can shut down the alligator hatchery.

During the 1980s, partly due to Juran's and other quality leaders' influence, the U.S. and other countries saw a significant trend toward the adoption of the "Big Q"[11] concept—quality planning as an integrated, top-level function that encompasses all business activities—and an associated trend toward the adoption of the concept of strategic quality planning.

Juran has evolved a concept called Strategic Quality Management (SQM)[12] that incorporates all of the roles management must play in an organization for quality planning as well as quality results to occur. "SQM is a structured process for establishing long-range quality goals, at the highest levels of organization, and defining the means to be used to reach those goals," Juran says. "The structure for SQM is similar to that long used to establish and meet financial goals."[13]

SQM requires the following changes be made in the organization:

- the establishment of broad quality goals as part of the company's business plan.
- The adoption of cultural changes (e.g., "Big Q" in place of "Little q") that disturb longstanding beliefs and habits.

- The rearrangement of priorities, with resulting upgrading of certain skills and downgrading of others.
- Creating a new infrastructure including a quality council and a quality controller and fitting it in place.
- Extensive training for the entire organization.
- Upper management participation in managing for quality to an unprecedented degree.

The first step in mobilizing for projects collectively is to establish a quality council made up of top management.[14] It is the apex of the broader system of managing quality throughout a company and includes operational quality management and the work force. This broader system is often called Total Quality Management or companywide quality management.

This quality council is critical because it is not enough to establish policies, create awareness, and then leave all else to subordinates, Juran argues. Typically, it has taken several years to establish quality improvement as a continuing, integral part of a company's business plan. The major common elements in responsibility of these councils are:

- Formulating the quality improvement policy (e.g., priority of quality, need of annual quality improvement, and mandatory participation).
- Estimating the major dimensions and establishing quality goals (e.g., quality compared with competitors, cost of poor quality, and length of the new product's launch cycle).
- Establishing the project-selection process.
- Establishing the team-selection process.
- Providing such resources as training, time for working on projects, diagnostic support, and facilitator support.
- Assuring that project solutions are implemented.
- Establishing needed measures (e.g., progress on quality improvement, performance versus competitors, and managers' performance).
- Providing for progress reviews and coordination.
- Devising programs that recognize employees for efforts toward the overall corporate quality goals.

- Revising the reward system so that it is clear that quality improvement has high priority and so that department performance is not a detriment to overall performance.
- Facing up to employee apprehensions.

Juran has identified predictable obstacles in this process:

- People are not aware that they are creating quality problems.
- People are unable to give top priority to quality because other goals actually have higher priority and hence get in the way.
- Achievement of quality locally gets in the way of overall quality.
- Prior unsuccessful drives result in a cynical reaction to any new initiative, including an effort to give top priority to quality.

THE JURAN TRILOGY

Quality planning actually is part of Juran's *quality trilogy*: quality planning, quality control, and quality improvement.[15] These activities are both separate and independent; they also involve all levels of the organization.

Quality Planning

"This is the activity of developing the products and processes required to meet customers' needs," he says. It involves a series of universal activities called Juran's Quality Planning Road Map.[16] This map consists of steps examined in the following sections.

Establishing Quality Goals

Visions have little relation to reality until they are converted into quantitative goals that are to be met within a specific time span. Goals are a crucial first step because it is impossible to plan in the abstract; only after a target has been identified can the organization plan to meet that goal. Quality goals include tactical goals that directly relate to product features, process features, and process control features. These should encompass all aspects of the organization at all levels, and all tactical goals should include a number and a timetable. Strategic quality goals are established at the highest company levels and include the corporate vision or mission statement. They also often address product performance, competitive performance, quality improvement, the cost of poor quality, and the performance of major processes.

Identifying Customers

This includes identifying all external as well as internal customers, recognizing that noncustomers, suppliers, and even those only peripherally related to the product's use (e.g., the neighbors of someone who uses an overly-loud lawnmower) also are customers.

To identify customers, Juran advises breaking them into two groups: the "vital few" and the "trivial many."[17] He recommends using the Pareto principle to determine which customers make up the oepration's key customers, that is the vital few who contribute the majority of business. However, Juran also cautions that, though the trivial-many group are of limited importance to the organization individually, "collectively they should be regarded as a member of the vital few."[18] He notes, most marketers, therefore, prefer to call them the *useful many*. This group is made up of small-volume consumers, workers, and the noncustomer public.

Determining Customer Needs

Each customer brings a variety of needs to the table. Among these are stated needs, real needs, perceived needs, cultural needs, and needs traceable to unintended use. The customers' needs may be unstated, and they may seem unreal. Yet, they must be discovered and acted on. Customer needs are a moving target and must be continuously evaluated. In addition, the most serious mistake many organizations make is a failure to recognize the difference between a customer's stated need (e.g., a color TV) and the real need (i.e., entertainment); when real needs are looked at in this scenario, a good book, a health spa, a movie theater, a sailboat, and many other activities all become prime competition for the color TV.

Developing Product Features

Juran depicts the process of achieving fitness for use as a perpetual spiral of progress to be accomplished by areas of the company. Each of the functions in the spiral makes use of a body of specialized knowledge and quality-related knowledge, but all are interdependent, resulting in the need for strong, competent, company-wide quality management.

Developing Process Features

A process as Juran defines it, is "a systematic series of actions directed to the achievement of a goal. Processes include the human components as well as the physical facilities. All processes exhibit variability. The extent of this variability is a critical input to process design."[19] In some process redesign cases, the gain from changing the anatomy of the process has been much greater than the gain from new technology. "The process design should provide means to reduce and control human error," he says. "A process design should meet the following criteria: goal oriented, systematic, capable, and legitimate."[20]

Establishing Process Controls and Transferring to Operations

All control is centered on the specific thing to be controlled, called control subjects, a mixture of product features, process features, and side-effect features. In *Juran On Planning For Quality*, he wrote that each control subject is the focal point of a feedback loop that works as follows:

- The sensor evaluates actual performance.
- The sensor reports this performance to an umpire.

- The umpire also receives information on what the goal or standard is.
- The umpire compares actual performance to the goal. If the difference warrants action, the umpire energizes an actuator.
- The actuator make the changes needed to bring performance into line with goals.

An additional component of the quality planning map is to provide measurement at every step so that numbers can supplant the use of vague terminology. Examples of the types of measurement used in each step include:

- Establishing quality goals. Analysis of prior performance, competitive analysis and benchmarking
- Identifying Customers. Pareto analysis of customers and sampling of useful-many customers
- Determining customer needs. Market research on customer needs, analysis of customer behavior, and analysis of customer dissatisfaction
- Developing product features. Failure analysis, reliability, analysis and optimization of product goals
- Developing process features. Process capability analysis, failure analysis, and optimization of process designs

QUALITY IMPROVEMENT

Quality improvement is not fire fighting, or removing a sporadic spike from the trilogy diagram, Juran maintains. That merely restores performance to the prior chronic level, which was also the prior standard. More than that, quality improvement raises quality performance to unprecedented or breakthrough levels. Juran says the methodology consists of a series of universal steps:

- Establishing the infrastructure needed to secure annual quality improvement
- Identifying the specific needs for improvement (i.e., the improvement project)

- For each project, establishing a project team with clear responsibility for bringing the project to a successful conclusion
- Providing the resources, motivation, and training needed by the teams to:
  - Diagnose the causes
  - Stimulate establishment of remedies
  - Establish controls to hold the gains

Each of the departments within the organization works individually and interdependently to solve two types of quality problems:

- Sporadic problems. Those that cause production to fall below acceptable standards (analogous to Deming's special causes)
- Chronic problems that are inherent in the workplace and call for management intervention to eliminate (similar to Deming's concept of common causes).

Teams that pursue quality solutions take two journeys: the diagnostic and remedial journey. During the diagnostic journey, employees look at the outward symptoms of a quality problem and determine the cause. Employees understand the symptoms, theorize as to causes, and test theories. During the remedial journey, teams look at the known cause and end with an effective remedy in place. During this time, the team develops a remedy, tests the remedy under operating conditions, and establishes controls to hold the gains.

To accomplish these two journeys, Juran describes six activities:

- Convincing others that a breakthrough is needed. To accomplish this, one must collect factual information, use this information to show the potential benefits available to the organization, and recognize that personal attitudes in the organization are of crucial importance. The most powerful way to collect factual information is in terms of dollars with respect to quality costs, loss of sales or competition, or legislation. Using this information, one can readily show the potential benefits in terms of return on investment (ROI). Even with the facts presented, people often object to change because they are accustomed to the way things are. One must work to motivate the employees of an entire organization to see the good of such a change for themselves and for the company.

- Identifying the vital few projects. This is done by conducting a Pareto analysis to divide the vital few from the trivial many.
- Organizing to secure new knowledge. This calls for two distinct sets of activities to be carried out at the same time:
  - Oversight, direction, and advice accomplished by a steering arm to set the specific goals for the project, suggest possible causes, authorize experiments, and advise on how to overcome resistance to changes.
  - Diagnosis of causes of problems without regard to remedies which calls for a diagnostic arm that provides the resources required for the project, brings its diagnostic skills to bear on the project and conducts objective analyses.
- Diagnosis of the situation. This calls for a study of the controllability—to what extent is the situation manager-controllable rather than operator-controllable? Most errors or defects are manager-controllable, and are subject to a breakthrough project. A controllability study establishes who is appropriate to conduct the project. Juran has pointed out that a chronic ailment continues to exist precisely because nobody knows why. The diagnostic arm can be used to solve these ailments.
- Overcoming resistance to change. To gain agreement, one must first recognize that two types of change are being implemented when remedying a chronic ailment: technological and cultural. One must discover what the social change entails in order for the technological change to meet success.
- Implementing the change by gaining any required approvals

from the senior management team and by effectively installing the solution.

QUALITY CONTROL

The control sequence is in place in a company to handle sporadic problems that arise, Juran has said. It refers to problems where solutions restore performance to its standard level but do not change the standard itself. This control sequence is defensive or reactive in nature and calls for many people to perform a lot of little things well. This sequence also is the final step of the breakthrough sequence because its success is dependent on the highest standards necessary. It consists of the stages examined in the following sections.

Evaluating Actual Quality Performance

Before sporadic problems can be solved, they must be determined. The first step is to choose worthy control subjects. This initiates the control sequence, of which there are two approaches. The negative approach is the boss-initiated drive or the infatuation with some current technique. This negative approach often results in overkill, defensive politics, frustration, some success, but ultimately failure. The positive approach addresses the actual choice as a problem in its own right. This results in a reasoned choice and consequently a higher likelihood for a successful control sequence. An advantage of the positive approach is that anything not chosen as a control subject could be eliminated.

Once the subject is chosen it is crucial to define the unit of measure. This is essential to effective communications. Without a unit of measure, one must live with the confusion, irritation, and animosity. If a subject cannot be measured, it cannot be scheduled. If it cannot be scheduled, it cannot be controlled.

Next, it is important to establish the standard level of performance. This is typically done by historical data. Although this is practical, it has the drawback of perpetuating mediocrity, making it crucial, as discussed previously, that the breakthrough sequence has occurred first so that the standard level is the best achievable. The standards for many functions within a company or plant should be set quantitatively, qualitatively, and verifiably, with the focus on the performance rather than the person.

With standards determined, the next step in evaluating performance involves creating the sensing mechanism that enables actual performance to be measured. Anything that can sense is a sensor. Trends in some data series are used as sensors. Shewhart control charts are sensors. A variety of mechanical sensors are available for the production cycle. A sensor may also be a human being who is in tune to what is happening. This human sensor may be able to provide ideas about trouble on the production line or worker morale.

Sensing can occur before, during, and after the fact. Sensing before the fact is the most desirable. Sensing during the fact denotes direct controls by deeds rather than by data; such control by deeds provides no advantage to a company. Sensing after the fact is suited only for longer range decisions based on patterns and not on instances.

Once sensing devices are in place, the next step is to mobilize for measurement. This is essential to good decision making and calls for:

- Measuring stations to collect data.
- Analysis stations to convert this data into information for interpretation, decision making and action.
- A network to transmit all information from the analysis stations to usage stations at all levels of the company.

Measuring Performance

Comparing actual performance to quality goals is done by:

- Verifying the validity of the differences.
- Evaluating the economic and statistical significance of the differences.
- Discovering the factual causes of the differences.

- Evaluating the alternative ways to restore performance to the standard level.

Acting on the Difference

Because most control action is at the worker level of the company, the people at that level must be given the right to decide the best actions to follow. Although this means delegating the control as far down the organization as possible, only when a person exhibits self-control can be delegation process take place.

Self-control applies to everyone in the company. It is a prerequisite to motivation and it is risky for managers to hold workers "responsible for quality unless the workers are in a state of self-control. Allocation of responsibility for producing nonconforming products at the worker level should be in accordance with the state of worker controllability. Ideally, responsibility for control should be assigned to individuals. "Such assignment is inherently clear. It also confers status, a form of ownership, which responds to some basic human needs. Ideally also, responsibility should be coextensive with authority."[21]

To give maximum delegation to the work force requires being specific about which decisions and actions are to be delegated. The work force must understand the purposes behind the goals. It requires providing each worker with a clear answer to the question, "What should I do that is different from what I have been doing?"

To create such a state of self-control, Juran writes, the process designers must provide the operating forces with:

- The means of knowing what the quality goals are. This criterion is met by providing the work force with specifications and procedures.
- The means of knowing what the actual performance is. This criterion is met by providing the work force with a system of measurement.
- The means of changing the performance in the event of nonconformance. This criterion is met by providing the work force with a process that is inherently capable of meet-

> ing the quality goals and is provided with features that enable the work force to readjust the process as needed to bring it into conformance.

A key concept within self-control is the control of operator-controllable defects. The operator controllable elements of quality improvement account for approximately 20% of defects, Juran notes. Operator errors are either inadvertent, technique-related, or willful and can be reduced in one or more of the following ways: foolproofing, keeping people attentive, training, changing technology, improving communications, establishing accountability, removing the error-prone person, and motivation.[22]

By matching the types of error against the way to reduce them, it often can be discovered how to remedy errors. For example, in some cases of willful error, the error may seem to be operator initiated, but its root lies in inadequate communications with the manager. It is important that decisions made by the managers are communicated to the workers. It is also important to communicate the rationale of decisions so that errant interpretations are not left to flourish. What may seem like a decision to push a product out the door may indeed have been a situation resolved between management and the customer. This information must be relayed to the workers so an incorrect opinion about management's support of a quality product is not allowed to take root.

The concept of the artisan exemplifies this example of self-control, Juran maintains. An artisan is someone who undergoes an apprenticeship and becomes qualified to practice a skilled trade. In many cases, the artisan has direct access to customers, external and internal. The artisan's skills are based on knowledge of a process. Artisans also conduct operations; they execute their own planning by running the process and producing the products. In short, this concept enables workers to participate widely in quality related activities and to accept a broader delegation of responsibility.

As a side note to the theory of self-control, Juran has cautioned that one should distinguish between theories that help build continuing programs and those for developing appropriate approaches to motivating people. Motivational programs often have two parts: a motivation package and prevention package, with the results often short-lived and unable to be documented. The most obvious reason for motivational programs being less than effective is that they are aimed at operator-controllable errors though only a small proportion of errors are operator controllable. So any benefit of such a motivational program is short-lived. Once the small percentage of operator-controllable errors is lessened and a large percentage of errors continue to occur as a part of the process, frustration sets in and the motivational program is effectively abandoned.

Juran's use of the Pareto diagram to separate the vital few from the trivial (i.e., useful) many has made that statistical tool one of the mainstays of many organizations' quality efforts. By emphasizing the need for breakthroughs to achieve quality, Juran has placed the onus on managers to work hard and look for new ways to motivate those beneath them. Like Deming, Juran came to fame late in life, at least in his own country; the Japanese had known and appreciated his work for decades. His ideas now form the backbone of quality efforts in hundreds of organizations in both the East and the West.

4
Homer Sarasohn

Homer Sarasohn's story begins in 1945 with a telegram on his desk at the Massachusetts Institute of Technology's (MIT) Radiation Laboratory, where the young product development engineer had a reputation for quickly converting preliminary product designs to manufacturable prototypes. The telegram, from a colonel in the U.S. War Department, said:

> General MacArthur's Headquarters has requested your services earliest possible date. Upon receipt reply your availability. Instructions for processing will follow.[1]

MIT's engineering crew was full of practical jokers, and Sarasohn assumed they were at it again. "Two weeks later, I got a call from this very irate colonel in Washington, upset that I hadn't even had the decency to respond to his message," he recalled later.[2]

Sarasohn went to Washington to hear more about the request and agreed to a nine-month assignment in Japan. He went that fall, joined the Civil Communications Section (CCS) of MacArthur's headquarters, and stayed five years.

His task was to figure out how to supply the Japanese populace with radios to receive communications from Occupation Headquarters so that it could nip in the bud insurgent hostility from doubts, rumors, and speculation. The problem was that Japan had been essentially destroyed as a functioning nation and a functioning economy. (This was 1945, and the men we acclaim as gurus in the worldwide quality movement had not yet arrived to impart their knowledge and advice to a resurgent Japanese industrial sector.)

Sarasohn recounted the situation he found on arrival: "The nation and its economy was at that time at a standstill. It was virtually impossible to do any manufacturing of any kind. For all practical purposes, factories, production equipment, tools, supplies, raw materials—none of it existed. The shops that were still standing had very little to sell and the people had very little to make any purchases with. Such personal items as they had been able to save or salvage were used as currency to buy whatever they could."[3]

It was a climate ripe for guerrilla warfare. According to U.S. Army intelligence, approximately three million Japanese soldiers had been held in reserve to defend the home islands against an invasion; civilians had reportedly been given wooden clubs and spears with which to make a last stand against the enemy on the beaches. Arriving Americans were concerned, typically going armed among a people many Americans had come to see as barbarous through the long, bitter years of war. In the first months and the years to come, however, not one incident of public disorder occurred.

According to Sarasohn, there was more at work in the prevailing calm than a benevolent occupation force imposing its will. The people of Japan, he reasons, were compliant and obeyed the occupation directives because their own authorities, who they had been taught to believe were infallible, had been discredited. Victory was not inevitable; it was not to be. The home islands were not impregnable; the Americans were everywhere. The Japanese were a people conditioned to following their leaders. Now, history had brought them a vacuum in leadership. If the American occupation could provide direction and begin to nurture new leaders, as much as possible without reparations or recriminations, the wounds of war might be allowed to heal in peace rather than become the festering sores that so often lead to still more hostilities.

To the Civil Communications Section of the occupation force fell the important task of involving the Japanese in the reconstruction of their nation and convincing a vanquished but still proud people that the United States did not intend to humiliate or terrorize them. Three initial objectives were set for Sarasohn to accomplish:

- Meet the occupation forces' own requirements for domestic radio and telephone services, but do so through Japanese sources.
- Supply the Japanese populace with radio receivers so they could receive broadcasts from the Civil Information and Education Section, Supreme Command Allied Powers (SCAP) bureau charged with communicating messages and directives of the occupation forces to the people. Although U.S. Army transmitters could be used to broadcast, the Japanese lacked receivers.
- In the process of accomplishing the first two objectives, build a progressive communications industry that would contribute to the revival of Japan's economy.

Sarasohn took the second task as his starting point because he knew that the ripple effects from that would work to accomplish the first and third. Getting reliable radio receivers into the hands of the Japanese people was a challenge of major proportions. As he recalled: "We had no production facilities to start with. We had very little material resources. The machinery that might have been available either had been destroyed or damaged by the bombing, or had been deployed by the Japanese into the countryside to escape the bombing. These machines or parts had to be located, returned, refurbished, and installed. We had to locate people to be brought in as workers. We had to start getting factories built. We had to start, literally, from the ground up to produce vacuum tubes, resistors, transformers, chassis—and all this had to be done from resources within Japan. We had no possibility of getting supplies from anywhere else." In fact, the occupation policy did not permit, except for extreme circumstances, the importation of materials from the United States.

Ironically, in the light of global business in the 50 years since, one of the most troublesome issues to resolve, beyond the pressing plant and material concerns, was the lack of management expertise. Japan's prewar and wartime leaders in government, industry, and the military had been removed from their positions of influence when the occupation began. They were barred from any positions of authority. The situation was similar to dismissing every senior and upper level executive at AT&T, destroying its production and distribution facilities, and then trying to reconstitute telecommunications services in the U.S. Just as new factories were needed, new leaders also had to be identified, trained, and thrust into positions of management responsibility. The need for Japanese managers was recognized as critical by the small staff that made up Sarasohn's section—just seven, including interpreters. The Americans there couldn't possibly do the job that had to be done just by themselves.

Some of the individuals picked for managerial positions were chosen almost at random. Until that time, they had been intermediaries in their organizations, passively passing instructions from superiors to subordinates. They had not been involved in business planning, strategy formulation, personnel and resource management or quality control. Suddenly, they had to be. Not only were they inexperienced, nothing in their past manufacturing traditions had prepared them for anything resembling what is known as quality today. "The Japanese style of management, which today is so highly regarded, at that time was a prime example of confusion and inefficiency,"[5] Sarasohn said. "There was no real understanding at the top level of either government or industry of the methodologies of mass production and its specific requirements for organization, for supervision and for measurement. It was absolutely impossible, based on their manufacturing methods, to get consistent production and reliable products."[6]

Industry in prewar Japan had hardly been a quality-driven enterprise. The problems, as Sarasohn encountered them, were fundamental and systemic. For starters, though Japan had prepared for and carried on a major war, it was far from a fully industrialized nation. What machinery it had was antiquated. Many prewar manufacturing operations were prone to adapt universal-type machines to the production of single-purpose products, a costly practice because it was inefficient and all but impossible to maintain quality tolerances. In the prewar era and after, "Made in Japan" often meant junk.

Yet, out of the post-war reconstruction would come a pantheon of new names that would set worldwide standards for quality: Sony, Matsushita, Sharp, Fujitsu, Toshiba, and NEC. These businesses cut their eye-teeth on the making of radios and other communications products and the rebuilding of their nation's infrastructure. In the process, they would learn important lessons about management's role in a quality-driven enterprise.

The conditions in which people had to work when the post-war reconstruction period began were daunting. Factories were hot and humid in the summer, cold and damp in the winter. Many were little more than sheds where equipment could be sheltered from the elements; construction materials for new buildings, like every other vital commodity, were all but impossible to come by. Inside, work surfaces were thick with dirt and dust, frequently contaminating products. Vacuum tubes were manufactured in buildings with dirt floors. Waste was high, and output by any measure of productivity was low.

Amid such defeating conditions, the newly minted production managers had little reason to expect high yields or high quality, and they acted accordingly. Although Sarasohn found line workers trying their hardest to improve their own lives and help reestablish Japan, managers trained for passivity had not yet accepted the challenge of their own new positions.

In late 1946, Sarasohn brought the situation to a head by calling the Japanese plant managers to his office at the Civil Communications Section headquarters. He listed the poor results being accomplished to date and asked them for their ideas on how to improve. For beginners, he wondered, what did they think was the major obstacle to getting better product yield?

Never having been asked previously for their opinions on anything, the managers got up, moved down to the end of the table and started talking among themselves.

"I asked the interpreter what they were talking about," Sarasohn recalled. "He said they were talking among themselves about what answer they could come up with that would be most pleasant for me to hear."[7]

For Sarasohn, the moment was a personal turning point, bringing him to two contrasting conclusions. First, it illustrated how much he needed to learn about the Japanese character and culture and how critical the language barrier was. He resolved to cross it by learning Japanese to remove the dependence on interpreters. It was of major importance to be able to communicate with the managers both in their own language and in their own cultural frame of reference.

At the same time, he decided this was the time for direct and forceful action. Secure because of General MacArthur's authority, he acted with American brashness to do what needed to be done—no more standing on ceremony, no more tolerance for circumlocution. To get the on-site managers to face up to the need for such basics as workplace cleanliness and scheduled machine maintenance, he defined quotas and insisted that they be met. When it became obvious that meeting those quotas would involve the generation of new standards and measurements, Sarasohn and his Civil Communications Section colleagues picked managers at each site to take on the standard-setting task. Their demands were simple: quality or else.

To enforce the demands, Sarasohn created an outside agency, the National Electrical Testing Laboratory in Tokyo, to assure that standards would indeed be met and not simply logged on a quality assurance sign-off. Every product by the new communications industry, from radios to telephones and components, was subject first to type approval and then subsequently to random testing, using products from a company's inventory or off the store shelf. Any product that failed was completely pulled from the marketplace until it passed.

From that first meeting and subsequent sessions on performance measurement came the broad outlines of participative management. Top managers received their training in fundamental business concepts from Sarasohn, then were charged with going back to their businesses and teaching their subordinates how they could do what was supposed to be done. The subordinates, in turn, communicated the new standards and values to their workers on the shop floors, in the process setting the stage for the development of quality control circles to close the loop on the information flow.

To get everyone involved in the quest to improve productivity, Sarasohn believed three basic values had to come to the fore:

- Commitment. The spirit of the organization has to spring from a total commitment by everyone in the enterprise to defined performance goals.
- Ownership. For everyone to be motivated to contribute to the group's success, everyone has to have a sense of personal ownership of the work and the organization.
- Feedback. Communications, up, down, and across the lines of the organization is the lifeblood that carries the information needed to do the job right the first time and places each individual's contribution in the broader context of the organization.

Information, Sarasohn reasoned, keeps the sense of commitment and ownership alive.

As the revived businesses began to function more productively, yields rose and quality problems dropped. However, there was still a noticeable shortfall in the capabilities of the new managers. Responsible as they were willing to be, it was clear they had a lot to learn about modern methods of management. In 1948, Sarasohn proposed to teach them, in the process incurring the ire of many, including some from other sections of SCAP headquarters. These objectors were determined to keep Japan a weak and subjugated nation. He was told not to share knowledge with the enemy. Undaunted, he presented his case directly to General MacArthur, who listened to both sides and told Sarasohn to go ahead. The Civil Communication Section Seminar was born.

Working with Charles Protzman, a new Civil Communications Section arrival from Western Electric, Sarasohn holed up in an Osaka hotel where they spent a month building an eight-week curriculum and writing a textbook for the seminar. Protzman, a pragmatist, took on manufacturing, finance, accounting, and distribution. Sarasohn, an idealist, handled quality control, management organization, research and development, and product innovation.

The seminar that resulted was anything but a course in the American style of management. Drawing on their own experiences, whatever books they had brought to Japan or could requisition through General MacArthur's headquarters, British sources on industrialization, and a sense of what should be rather than what usually is, Sarasohn and Protzman cobbled together a mini masters of business administration program, which they dubbed "The Fundamentals of Industrial Management." Then they hand picked groups of 30 to 50 senior managers from the best of their fledgling businesses and select ministries of the government to attend. No refusals, substitutions, and absences were allowed.

Initially, Sarasohn was adamant that no one from the outside would be allowed to stump for their own peculiar ideas: "I wanted to keep the carpetbaggers out. I had that very much in mind. When we talked about raw materials, or production processes, or factory organization concepts, I did not want to import a rigid philosophy . . . to say, 'I'm an American, this is what we do in America, you do what we say.' My approach in our lectures was to take a very fundamentalist point of view: how you go about process innovation, how you go about design, how you go about manufacturing, and winding up with the ultimate measure of your success – customer satisfaction."[8]

Nothing made a more immediate or profound impression than the idea of statistical quality control (SQC), introduced by Walter Shewhart in the U.S. in 1924. Officials of the Union of Japanese Scientists and Engineers decided that that was why America won the war. They termed it the "secret weapon" the United States used to gear up its industries for the war effort. Their infatuation with the concept worried him at first; he feared they would see SQC as merely a mathematical tool for use in manufacturing, as a magic wand, rather than a multifaceted management approach to continuous improvement and quality control. Despite repeated requests, he refused to bring in the author of the concept, Walter Shewhart, until it was time to build a second level of the Civil Communications Section Seminar, this one targeted directly to plant managers.

By then it was 1950, and events were rapidly changing the face of the U.S. occupation effort. Japanese companies were back on their feet and the communications industry as well as others were now self-sustaining, relieving many of the earlier needs to rebuild and nurture. The onset of hostilities in Korea changed the operating priorities in General MacArthur's headquarters. Originally contracted to spend just nine months surveying the post-war situation, Sarasohn was by then a five-year veteran of Japan's revival. He was ready to return to the U.S. It was time to hand off parts of the management training program he had so carefully created.

Due to ill health, Shewhart was unable to make the trip to Japan. Sarasohn and the Japanese turned to W. Edwards Deming, then a professor at Columbia University who had been a protege of Shewhart and had earlier visited Japan to help with the census. Deming arrived in the summer of 1950 to teach SQC; Sarasohn returned to the United States in the fall of that year. He spent the next seven years with Booz Allen & Hamilton, a management consulting firm, then 20 years with IBM before retiring to become a private consultant and lecturer.

Ironically, on returning to the U.S. in 1950, Sarasohn would find himself unable to duplicate the Japanese results with the American businesses he worked for as a consultant. In Japan, he would later recall, workers on the shop floor, their line-level managers, administrators and executives throughout the organization, understood firsthand the need for harmony and cooperation toward a common goal. The war and its aftermath demonstrated that they were all in a small boat and if it sank, all would drown together, regardless of title or position in the pecking order.

American businesses seemed beset on one hand with arrogant, unimaginative, and outright greedy management more interested in making as much money as possible as quickly as possible and, on the other hand, workers, especially unionized workers, accustomed to playing an adversarial role in search of their own piece of the pie. Nowhere did he find the sense of community interest and willingness to work for a common goal that made it possible to do so much so well and so quickly in the devastated conditions of postwar Japan.

Although the history of quality does not record Homer Sarasohn's name in the bright lights reserved for Deming, Juran, Crosby, and others, his contributions are noteworthy:

- He helped fast track the revival and growth of the postwar Japanese electronics industry.
- He sowed the seeds of participative management through

his insistence on extensive top-down communications from the new generation of Japanese business managers to their subordinates and line-level workers.
- He helped prepare the Japanese for learning statistical quality control and the many other lessons that Deming would later teach them.

Although he was not a quality theorist, Homer Sarasohn was a right man in the right place. He was a tough-minded facilitator who helped engineer many of the basic processes and nurture many of the new breed of Japanese business leaders that together would set the pace for a worldwide quality movement.

5
Allan Mogensen

Although not a household name in the total quality movement, Allan Mogensen laid some of the groundwork for many later quality theories. "Work smarter, not harder,"[1] Mogensen said, and proceeded to show what he meant by pioneering the area of work simplification. He developed techniques and methods for ensuring that any job—from clerical work to large production processes—is completed as efficiently as possible.

Mogensen's work simplification theories were developed before the Second World War, when they were put into use by many large U.S. companies. In many cases, the theories Mogensen developed for work simplification mirror key total-quality concepts.

For example, he came up with the following precepts that were outlined by Ben Graham, Jr., one of his associates:

- Treat workers with respect.
- Expect and insist upon proud craftsmanlike performance.
- Seek and use workers' experience in the continuing maintenance and redesigning of systems.
- Resist any temptation to build systems that are more complex and intricate than the combined skills of the people who will operate them.
- Stop trying to design foolproof systems and blaming clerical error for systemic faults. Foolproof systems require exorbitant amounts of checking and double checking. Design systems around the capabilities and goals of people who are rewarded for improvement and elimination of problems.

People are never foolproof but they can be taught and encouraged to be self correcting.

- Don't turn over the design of systems to people who don't really know what it is like to do the work.
- Get participation in system improvement from many people including managers, systems professionals, and operating personnel, who together can bring to systems the direction of management, the technology of professionals, and the sound common sense of firsthand experience.
- Fancy office equipment is a bromide and promises only temporary relief. Fix the system first, then bring in the new equipment.[2]

HOW IT STARTED

Mogensen was born in 1901 in Paxtang, Pennsylvania. His father was a civil engineer, and Mogensen has frequently claimed that he inherited his father's penchant for perfectionism. He entered Cornell's Sibley College in the fall of 1919 and began to study mechanical engineering. In those summers, he gained experience as a laborer at such jobs as making the exhaust castings for the Duesenberg automobile.

After graduation, Mogensen taught in the University of Rochester's industrial engineering department while continuing to work at odd part-time jobs. For example, he operated a rental film library and was one of the first people to take movies of weddings and funerals. In 1925, after hearing about some experiments in rating workers' performance at the Gleason Works Company, Mogensen got an evening job at the company and was first introduced to time studies.

In the summer of 1927, he was hired part time by Eastman-Kodak to plan the layout of equipment, machines, and working spaces. "I was also tasked with simplifying the manufacturing process wherever I could,"[3] he writes in his autobiography, *Mogy*. "I was urged to take pictures of people doing their jobs. By watching the film it was easy to denote flaws or movements which weren't essential to the task at hand, flaws or movements missed by the human eye when observed in real time."[4]

"I certainly didn't believe then that I would get involved in time and motion studies in intricate detail,"[5] he adds. "On the other hand, I sensed that a fertile field existed in the world of manufacturing wherein a motion picture camera could produce enlightening information on how people work with their hands."[6]

In addition to starting him on the road to work simplification, the job also taught him to incorporate the worker's views of performance into any work simplification program. "I think it was here, at Eastman Kodak, working on these time and motion films, that I recognized a new dimension in the working man,"[7] he writes in his autobiography. "I sensed that the person actually doing a job probably knows more about that job than anyone else and is therefore the one person best suited to improve it. My intuition told me this was vital and shouldn't be forgotten."[8]

In 1928, Mogensen left his teaching position to become associate editor of *Factory and Industrial Management* magazine. He interviewed company officials and tried to convince them to try his ideas. "The only agreement was that if I had convinced a company that techniques I proposed were in their view, potentially successful, the company would compose an article attesting to the presentation's merits and how it could help a particular company improve its operations."[9] His client roster soon included such companies as Cadillac Motors, Hood Rubber, and American Hard Rubber.

During this time, Mogensen also began to realize the importance of work simplification in the white collar world. "I firmly believe we are saving pennies on the plant floor while frittering away big bucks in the office,"[10] he writes. "One of my most rewarding experiences in this business has been to see the advances achieved in paperwork simplification."[11]

In 1933, Mogensen decided to spend more time consulting. He worked part-time with the magazine and officially started spreading his theories about work simplification to companies. It was during this time that his theories solidified. "Our overriding goal was the elimination of unnecessary motions and substitution of smooth, rhythmic motion patterns to reduce fatiguing work tensions,"[12] he writes. "We sought systems whereby operators could work slower, yet produce more. The premise I have set forth from the beginning of my career is that work simplification is the organizing of common sense to find better ways of doing work."[13]

THE THEORIES

To perform a motion and time study, Mogensen found that several things were necessary. As outlined in his autobiography,[14] they are:

- Measurement must be insisted upon from the very beginning. "In order to achieve measurement, tools are needed and the most important of these is the process chart, a detailed record indicating the sequence of any process, a device for visualizing a process as a means of improving it."[15]
- Records of measurement must be in such form that they can be used by those who did not make them.
- Through such measurements skill and experience may be transferred.
- Actual results of the measurements are incorporated into actual and universal practice as soon as they are properly synchronized into practical methods.

He also saw work simplification as a five-step process:

- Selecting a job to improve
- Getting the facts and making a chart
- Challenging every detail
- Developing a better method
- Installing the improvement[16]

In addition to this outline, Mogensen developed an intricate set of 20 guidelines each for industry and office that can be used to actually simplify a work process through "motion economy."[17] For industry, he suggests, "Begin each element of a job simultaneously with both hands," and includes such advice as "provide foot operated ejectors, to remove finished products"[18] and "design workplace height for sitting-standing positions, with posture seat, adjustable backrest, and footrest."[19]

The parallels between Mogensen's concepts and those of the early-day total quality masters are not surprising. They followed each other's work closely. For example, when working at the Bridgeport Ammunition Plant, Mogensen attempted to introduce Walter Shewhart's ideas regarding statistical quality control.

Although Shewhart was the father of the control chart, Mogensen might be considered the father of the flow chart. His methods for demonstrating work flow and analyzing processes still stand as pioneering work in the field. Not nearly as visible as most of the others mentioned in these pages, Mogensen provided methods for examining work processes that are still in use.

6
Armand Feigenbaum

The Japanese, in their drive to learn everything they could about improving their industries, called the best and the brightest consultants to their shores during the 1950s. One of them was Armand Feigenbaum.

Born in New York City in 1920, Feigenbaum was trained as a systems engineer and earned masters and doctorate degrees in engineering from the Massachusetts Institute of Technology. He spent the early years of his career at General Electric in a number of different positions ranging from training and managing production areas to quality control.

In Japan, Feigenbaum placed an emphasis on extending the quality tools and philosophies to every corner of the organization, calling his concepts "Total Quality Control." Japanese quality consultants and writers still cite Feigenbaum as the originator of the total quality concept, which he defines as "an effective system for integrating quality-development, quality-maintenance, and quality-improvement efforts to enable marketing, engineering, production, and service to achieve full customer satisfaction."[1]

In 1969, Feigenbaum founded General Systems Co., an international engineering firm specializing in systems for quality control and new product development. Feigenbaum's long career in the quality field has included a seat on the Board of Overseers of the Malcolm Baldrige National Quality Award Program.

At the forefront of his total quality control theory is product design. "The two entry points to getting better quality are to find out what the customer wants and then develop a design process to answer those wants," he said in an interview for *Design News* magazine.[2] "That's quite different from the old way of simply trying to use existing manufacturing facilities and design concepts more efficiently."[3]

This theory derives from his recognition that in the past, it became commonplace in American industries to provide for defective products and problems. Feigenbaum refers to these costs of quality—personnel and equipment used to rework unsatisfactory parts or field returns and reinspect or retest rejected parts—as the "hidden plant,"[4] and further contends that this form of organized wasted effort accounts for 15%–40% of production capacity.

"We encourage very systematic design methods that detect errors much earlier, such as thorough failure mode and effects analysis," he said in the *Design News* article.[5] "The goal is to produce robust designs that are immune to minor process variations."[6]

A QUALITY CONTROL SYSTEM

Reflecting his diverse background with General Electric, Feigenbaum's concept of total quality control defines eight stages of an industrial cycle:

- Marketing
- Purchasing
- Manufacturing engineering
- Manufacturing supervision and shop operations
- Mechanical inspection and functional test
- Shipping and installation
- Service

He has also delineated four classifications of quality control jobs:

- New design control. Quality control efforts on a new product during the phases of marketing, design, manufacturing, prototype testing, and quality standards.
- Incoming-material control. Procedures for acceptance of materials, parts, and components purchased from other companies or other operating units of the same company.
- Product control. Control of products and processes at the source of production

- Special process studies. Research and tests to determine probable causes of defective and nonconforming products and to establish permanent corrective action geared toward product and process improvement with reduced costs

He writes in *Total Quality Control,*[7] the tasks of each of these classifications is to:

- *Set standards.* Quality control cannot be performed without guidelines and information provided by the company. This includes information about the accuracy and capabilities of machines and processes as well as factual data about a product's quality that can be used for marketing activities.
- *Appraise conformance.* The mass inspection at the end of a production run must be replaced by checks of samples of the product. This means recognizing and emphasizing the need for orientation to customer satisfaction. Feigenbaum describes quality as that which is best for satisfying an organization along with a clear, customer-oriented quality management process that people understand and are a part of. Consequently, he recommends continuously measuring and monitoring actual customer quality satisfaction with the products in use.
- *Take corrective action.* Feigenbaum stresses that in-line management of quality, or worker-controlled quality management, is essential for success, and that quality is what the customer says it is, not what an engineer or marketing representative says it is. Knowledge, skills, and attitudes of an organization's people are as important to quality as the machinery and systems with which people work.[8]
- *Plan for improvement.* Management can incorporate quality most effectively into a company when it recognizes that quality is a process that extends throughout all functions of the organization, Feigenbaum says. The management of quality is effective only to the degree that it provides genuine quality improvement participation opportunities for each person in the company.

Feigenbaum insists that the management of quality must be quality-driven and customer-oriented rather than focused only toward factory efficiency. This occurs through management's encouragement and the introduction of new quality technology into the company. Management must recognize that quality must be managed as directly and effectively as sales, production, and engineering to produce high-quality products.

INTERRELATED ACTIVITIES

Feigenbaum maintains that total quality control must be interwoven through all areas of a company. "A modern TQC system must be developed and maintained so key activities are established for both their own effectiveness and for their interrelated impact on total quality effectiveness," he writes in *Total Quality Control.*[9] "The hallmark of modern total quality improvement systems is the concept of integration—a meshing of people-machine-information structures to economically and effectively control technical complexity."[10]

He states that four characteristics of a TQC system are particularly important for achieving this integration of people, machines and information.[11]

- A point of view, or attitude, for thinking about the way quality really works in a modern company and how quality decisions can be made. This viewpoint presents quality activities as continuous work processes, starting with the customer's requirements and ending with the customer's satisfaction. Processes must be developed to improve the way each person, machine, and organizational component works—both individually and together—to achieve this quality.
- The system as the foundation for thorough documentation. This documentation identifies the key quality activities and people-machine-information relationships that make a particular activity viable and understandable throughout the company. It is a complete task analysis and detailing of a

process that results from each person being able to visualize each work assignment and decision-making responsibility, then communicating it to others.
- The quality system as the foundation for making quality activities of the company manageable and broader in scope. It permits the management and employees of the company to grasp and understand their "customer requirements to customer satisfaction"[12] quality-related activities. It also allows the company the flexibility to provide alternatives under given quality situations. A closely linked relationship between all components of a company must be established before this foundation can allow that kind of flexibility.
- The system as the basis for the systematic engineering of improvements of the major quality activities of the company. The total quality system provides the framework and discipline, so changes in a key area of work anywhere in the customer-to-customer activities of the company can be understood and absorbed into the ongoing production system.

Feigenbaum has listed two general management steps to establish quality as a business strategy in a company:

- The concept of total customer satisfaction, together with reasonable costs of quality, must be established. They should serve as performance measurements of the marketing, engineering, production, industrial relations, and service functions of a company.
- To assure this customer satisfaction, quality and cost results must be established as primary business goals of the quality program of the company and of the quality control function itself.

Feigenbaum is well remembered in Japan. The foremost Japanese quality experts cite him for introducing the concept of total quality into their organizations. His hidden plant concept provides a brilliant graphic representation of waste and rework in all businesses and is a lasting symbol of his contributions.

7 Philip B. Crosby

Deming and Juran labored for years virtually unnoticed before solidifying their reputations in the quality pantheon. Philip B. Crosby came to prominence relatively suddenly with the 1979 publication of his first book, *Quality Is Free*. A concise, briskly written case for quality, it quickly found a receptive audience among American business executives just becoming aware of the size of the threat posed by growing international competition and just beginning to sense the depth of the hole they'd dug for themselves in the 30 years of easy pickings after World War II.

If his public prominence came somewhat quicker than Deming's and Juran's (however, Crosby was 53 years old when the book first hit the stores), his own work on quality at that point spanned more than 25 years, beginning with Bendix Corp. in Ohio and then inspecting radar equipment at Martin Marietta for $75 a week. By 1961, he was supervising quality for the company's Pershing missile program, where Zero Defects (ZD) was about to be born. To this day, that uncompromising approach to quality remains closely associated with Crosby's enduring work in the field.

Yet, even though his quality roots are in pioneering the manufacturing application of Zero Defects, the stage for Crosby's later consulting and writing work was actually set during a legendary elevator ride in the late 1960s. His companion on the journey was his then-boss, Harold Geneen, chairman of the board of ITT, for which Crosby had become director of quality. As the floors passed, Crosby argued a case for improved quality regardless of the business at hand; ITT's Sheraton Hotels division was his current focal point. To make sure his boss was listening, he started with dollars before sense: The cost of not doing things right, he told Geneen flatly, was at least 20% of corporate sales. Before the doors opened, Geneen agreed to back an attempt at a cultural revolution. With top-down participation assured, Crosby got his chance to implement his ideas.

He didn't waste it. An American Express survey had rated Sheraton the worst hotel chain in the country when it came to the quality of what it offered the traveling public. Five years later, the same survey showed Sheraton ranking first. During the next 10 years, Crosby's ITT turf expanded as he became vice president and director of corporate quality worldwide. His horizons expanded as well. As word of the transformation at Sheraton and ITT got out, and Zero Defects found its own hard core of business adherents, he was invited to carry the word to other organizations.

Ultimately, he left ITT in 1979 to form his own management consulting company, Philip Crosby Associates, in Winter Park, Florida. Other books besides *Quality Is Free* include *Cutting the Cost of Quality* (1975), *Quality Without Tears* (1984), *Let's Talk Quality* (1989), *Leading: The Art of Becoming An Executive* (1990) and, most recently, *Completeness: Quality For The 21st Century* (1992).

Popularizing the disciplined ZD approach to quality and broadening the overall focus of quality efforts to integrate them into the corporate culture are his two primary contributions to the field. The essential philosophy builds on the tenets laid out in *Quality Is Free*, which Crosby dedicated to Geneen, crediting his former boss for observing: "Quality is not only right, it is free. And it is not only free, it is the most profitable product line we have."[1]

ZERO DEFECTS

In 1961, the U.S. Army was looking to the introduction of the Pershing missile as a major new addition to its firepower. (For historical perspective, this time frame falls between the Bay of Pigs invasion in 1961 and the Cuban Missile Crisis of 1962.) Quality was a very real concern: Each missile had thousands of parts, virtually all of which had to be assembled defect-free for the system to work. Although test firings of the Pershing had been uncommonly successful—the first six worked flawlessly, and only four of the first 33 experienced partial failures—the cost of inspecting-in quality on such a scale was significant, involving constant testing and rework of components all the way up to the time the missile was shipped from Martin Marietta's plant in Orlando, just west of Cape Canaveral.

In early 1962, the Army accelerated the delivery date for the new missile system by a month. To meet the deadline, the Martin Marietta team pledged to deliver "Pershing Artillery Set Number 7" with zero discrepancies in both hardware and documentation. There simply wasn't going to be time to rework parts found to be out of spec; each job had to be done right the first time. To many people's amazement, they were. Martin Marietta delivered on the accelerated schedule defect-free.

Afterward, Crosby and his colleagues were asked how they could account for this stellar performance. As head of the quality personnel involved, he could find only one answer. A certain "acceptable quality level" had always been assumed as part of the missile program. This one time, zero defects had become the expectation and had been achieved. Basic cause and effect was at work. Ever since, Crosby has had to continually hammer home the point that Zero Defects is *not* a motivational slogan. It's a management performance standard.[2]

In Crosby's analysis, two factors cause defects or mistakes: lack of knowledge and lack of attention. He maintains the former can be measured by tests and improved through training and education. He describes the latter in *Quality Without Tears*: "Lack of attention is an attitude problem. The person who commits himself or herself to watch each detail and carefully avoid error takes the giant step toward setting a goal of Zero Defects in all things."[3]

It's at this point that Crosby sets himself apart from those whose approach to quality proceeds from a statistical base. Indeed, his approach emphasizes management and organization theories rather than implementation of statistical tools. His theories derive from a pair of related, multi-element principles:

- Four absolutes of quality improvement
- A 14-step program for quality improvement

THE FOUR ABSOLUTES

Crosby's four absolutes are designed to answer two basic questions:

- What is quality?
- What standards and systems are needed for the achievement of quality?

He holds that understanding and following these four absolutes takes the "hassle" out of management and improves quality.

Absolute 1: Quality has to be defined as conformance to requirements, *not* as goodness

In simplest terms, quality means meeting the requirements set forth for a product's production or a service's delivery. It's Crosby's belief that it is management's job to set the requirements and that, once set, they become ways to communicate with employees so everybody knows what is expected.

In keeping with his emphasis on creating a predisposition toward quality at the frontline, Crosby preaches DIRFT (sometimes whimsically pronounced as *dirt foot*) which stands for "Do It Right the First Time." Of course, the philosophy of DIRFT can take hold only after the requirements for quality are thoroughly understood and accepted. That's when requirements become an effective communications medium. In Crosby's view, employees should complete the job exactly as required or follow a formal procedure for changing the requirement.

Absolute #2: The system for causing quality is prevention, not appraisal

Here, Crosby echoes the process orientation of other quality proponents but still with a distinct cultural orientation. The first step toward defect and error prevention is to understand the *process* by which the product is produced, which is a knowledge issue for quality-focused workers. When a defect or error occurs, the discovery and elimination of the cause then becomes a top priority. There's no point in continuing to make and fix the same mistakes; fixing the process eliminates the variation.

Crosby has emphasized that conformance to requirements is not the same thing as *fitness for use*. If a finished piece of work has an attribute error totally unrelated to its form, fit, or function, it is still fit for use. Consequently, the attribute error must either be made a requirement (in other words, all subsequent pieces must have the same attribute error), or an engineering change order must be completed to correct the attribute error. Workers are expected to complete their work per requirements until the requirements are changed.

Absolute #3: The performance standard must be Zero Defects, not "that's close enough"

As Crosby learned firsthand at Martin Marietta, such common and undeniably comfortable business practices as shipped product quality level (SPQL) or acceptable quality level (AQL) proved very powerful in lulling people into believing that Zero Defects was an unattainable goal.

However, as was proven with the Pershing missile—and countless other processes since, including services as well as manufactured products—it is indeed possible to do it right the first time. That being the case, the only performance standard for "dirt foot" that makes any sense is Zero Defects. Central to Crosby's case for quality has been his insistence that ZD needs to become a personal performance standard of everyone in the company from top management down to the workers on the line.

Absolute #4: The measurement of quality is the price of nonconformance, not indexes

By Crosby's math, the cost of quality (COQ) can be figured in dollars by determining the difference between the price of nonconformance (PONC) and the price of conformance (POC). The former is the expense of doing things the wrong way—from 20% to 35% of revenues, he has argued. The latter is the expense of continuing to do things right—typically from 3% to 4%. On this evidence alone, quality makes sense.

According to Crosby, however, it is important to realize that COQ is not a standard to be met. Rather, it is a flow. Managers should spend time identifying where it is occurring and address what makes it occur. By solving for the factors that underlie the cost of quality, the Zero Defects standard takes on real-world significance.

CULTURAL IMPERATIVES

Statistics aside, Crosby has strongly emphasized the process of changing the corporate culture and attitudes to build toward a commitment to quality from everyone at every level of the organization. In that context, and in marked contrast to Deming, Juran, and the Japanese approach, Crosby does not highlight statistical quality control techniques. His 14-step process is oriented toward providing guidelines for developing a quality improvement attitude throughout the organization.

To set a framework for his 14-step regimen, Crosby believes companies committed to improving their product quality need to address three general areas for improvement:

1. *Determination*

As his own experience at ITT confirms, quality improvement starts from the top or it doesn't start. Once the members of the top management team decide that they cannot accept the status quo any longer, they must also recognize that only they can launch the change process in the organization and ensure that it will continue.

2. *Education*

In Crosby's analysis, this takes three forms:

- Orientation to the concepts and procedures of quality
- Direct skill improvement
- Continual quality data communications

In order to conduct quality education, he advises, people need to develop a common language for communication, which means everyone should be well-versed in the four absolutes of quality. Employees also must know and accept their individual roles and have the skills and knowledge to accomplish their assigned tasks within the preset requirements of quality. Finally, specialized knowledge relating to all aspects of quality must be available for use by the workers.

3. *Implementation*

With the will and the skills in place, the crucial task of quality comes down to guiding the flow of improvement throughout the company. Crosby has devised guidelines for the implementation through 14 steps designed to help a company move toward and beyond a mythical but motivating Zero Defects Day, when defects will no longer be accepted or occur.

BUT FIRST, A GRID

Basic to Crosby's cultural approach is his understanding that not every company is ready, willing, or able to jump right in and "do" quality. In response, Crosby developed his Quality Management Maturity Grid to enable a company to assess where each of its operating units is in the context of quality (see Figure 7.1). Management, he notes, must have matured considerably before the first step toward quality improvement can even occur. As he explains in *Quality Is Free*: "Quality management has always been looked at as a subjective operation, hard to define and measure. That is because it has been relegated to the role of a results-oriented procedure rather than a planning operation. . . . the folklore of business management states that if you have good in your heart, you will produce quality."[4]

QUALITY MANAGEMENT MATURITY GRID

Rater ____________ Unit ____________

Measurement Categories	Stage I: Uncertainty	Stage II: Awakening	Stage III: Enlightenment	Stage IV: Wisdom	Stage V: Certainty
Management understanding and attitude	No comprehension of quality as a management tool. Tend to blame quality department for "quality problems."	Recognizing that quality management may be of value but not willing to provide money or time to make it all happen.	While going through quality improvement program learn more about quality management; becoming supportive and helpful.	Participating. Understand absolutes of quality management. Recognize their personal role in continuing emphasis.	Consider quality management an essential part of company system.
Quality organization status	Quality is hidden in manufacturing or engineering departments. Inspection probably not part of organization. Emphasis on appraisal and sorting.	A stronger quality leader is appointed but main emphasis is still on appraisal and moving the product. Still part of manufacturing or other.	Quality department reports to top management, all appraisal is incorporated and manager has role in management of company.	Quality manager is an officer of company: effective status reporting and preventive action. Involved with consumer affairs and special assignments.	Quality manager on board of directors. Prevention is main concern. Quality is a thought leader.
Problem handling	Problems are fought as they occur; no resolution; inadequate definition; lots of yelling and accusations.	Teams are set up to attack major problems. Long-range solutions are not solicited.	Corrective action communication established. Problems are faced openly and resolved in an orderly way.	Problems are identified early in their development. All functions are open to suggestion and improvement.	Except in the most unusual cases, problems are prevented.
Cost of quality as % of sales	Reported: unknown Actual: 20%	Reported: 3% Actual: 18%	Reported: 8% Actual:12%	Reported: 6.5% Actual: 8%	Reported: 2.5% Actual: 2.5%
Quality improvement actions	No organized activities. No understanding of such activities.	Trying obvious "motivational" short-range efforts.	Implementation of the 14-step program with thorough understanding and establishment of each step.	Continuing the 14-step program and starting Make Certain.	Quality improvement is a normal and continued activity.
Summation of company quality posture	"We don't know why we have problems with quality."	"Is it absolutely necessary to always have problems with quality?"	"Through management commitment and quality improvement we are identifying and resolving our problems."	"Defect prevention is a routine part of our operation."	"We know why we do not have problems with quality."

FIGURE 7.1. Crosby's Quality Management Maturity Grid. (Reprinted from *Quality Is Free* by Philip B. Crosby by McGraw-Hill, Inc., New York, 1979.)

He adds, "However, quality management has just become too important to leave to chance. In this day of crushing taxation, mysterious methods of accounting, rollicking inflation, and unsettled politics, it may be that quality is the last chance we have to make profits controllable. But if quality is to be 'first among equals,' then management must have a way of measuring and controlling."[5]

Used appropriately, the Quality Management Maturity Grid is a diagnostic tool through which "even the manager who isn't professionally trained in the quality business can determine where the operation in question stands from a quality standpoint. All that is required is knowing what is going on. If the manager doesn't know that," Crosby wryly notes, "then we are both in the wrong book."[6]

CROSBY'S 14 STEPS – PRELIMINARY ACTIONS

In *Quality Is Free*, Crosby introduced his transformation process through a narrative case study that traces the 14 steps as taken by the HPA Corporation, "an old-line manufacturer and distributor of small appliances."[7] Each step is capsuled in the following, along with the expected accomplishments at each phase. (The "Purpose" description is in each case quoted directly from the book; the "Actions" precis are the author's summations of what Crosby is envisioning.)

Step 1: Management Commitment

Purpose

To make it clear where management stands on quality.

Actions

Prepare a quality policy that states that each individual is expected to perform exactly as specified in the requirements of the specific process or cause the requirement to be officially changed to what the customer and company really need. From the very beginning, it becomes clear that management is and must be personally committed to the program, raises the level of visibility for quality itself, and ensures everyone's cooperation as long as there is some progress.

Step 2: Quality Improvement Team

Purpose

To run the quality improvement program.

Actions

Orient team members to the content and purpose of the program, and fully explain their role in it. The objective is to bring together all the tools necessary to do the job on one team.

Step 3: Quality Measurement

Purpose

To provide a display of current and potential nonconformance problems in a manner that permits objective evaluation and corrective action.

Actions

Determine the status of quality throughout the company to show where improvement is possible, where corrective action is necessary, and to document actual improvement later on. Placing these results of measurement in highly visible charts helps establish the foundation of the entire quality improvement program.

Step 4: Cost of Quality Evaluation

Purpose

To define the ingredients of the cost of quality and explain its use as a management tool.

Actions

Provide the comptroller's office with detailed information on what constitutes the cost of quality: not just the obvious, such as scrap, rework, warranty and service provided beyond regular maintenance; but inspection, test and quality control labor, auditing, the cost of acceptance equipment, changes in engineering and purchase orders, software correction, consumer affairs activities, and "other costs of doing things wrong." This creates a measurement of quality management performance in the company's system.

Step 5: Quality Awareness

Purpose

To provide a method of raising the personal concern felt by all personnel in the company toward the conformance of the product or service and the quality reputation of the company.

Actions

Share with employees the measurements of what nonquality is costing the company. According to Crosby, this may be the most important step of all. Ideally, this awareness cycle sets the basis for the corrective action and error-cause-removal steps that follow.

Step 6: Corrective Action

Purpose

To provide a systematic method of resolving forever the problems that are identified through previous action steps.

Actions

Point out the opportunities for correction in the supervision meetings at each level of management. The quality improvement team established as Step 2 should take actions to establish these meetings in every department to help identify problems and correct them, assuring that the new procedures become habits.

CROSBY'S 14 STEPS – PROCESS ACTIONS

Up to this stage of Crosby's 14-point program, the approach has been to understand and accept the underpinnings of dollar-related measurements and the nature of taking corrective action. The remaining eight steps get to the heart of the matter: establishing Zero Defects as the performance standard, setting goals, removing causes of errors while engaging the people dimension of the entire process.

Step 7: Zero Defects Planning

Purpose

To examine the various activities that must be conducted in preparation for formally launching the Zero Defects program.

Actions

Communicate to all employees the literal meaning of Zero Defects and emphasize that everyone should do things right the first time. Set up the planning that ensures the goals of the program are firmly supported by the company's leaders.

Step 8: Supervisor Training

Purpose

To define the type of training that supervisors need in order to carry out their part of the quality improvement program.

Actions

Ensure that all managers understand each step well enough to explain it to their workers. This education helps get all supervisors tuned into the program so they realize its value for themselves and for the company.

Step 9: Zero Defects Day

Purpose

To create an event that lets all employees realize through a personal experience that there has been a change.

Actions

On Zero Defects Day, all supervisors explain the program to their people and do something different, so every employee in the company recognizes the new attitude the company is trying to put in place. The purpose of this special day is to make the ZD commitment a memory that is long-lasting for the workers. In many implementations, it lends itself to a companywide special event.

Step 10: Goal Setting

Purpose

To turn pledges and commitments into action by encouraging individuals to establish improvement goals for themselves and their groups.

Actions

Supervisors request employees to establish the goals they wish to strive for, usually within short-term frameworks of 30, 60, and 90 days. All must be specific and capable of being measured. Such goal-setting activities help people think in terms of accomplishing specific tasks as a team.

Step 11: Error-Cause Removal

Purpose

To give the individual employee a method of communicating to management the situations that make it difficult for the employee to meet the pledge to improve.

Actions

Individuals describe problems that prevent them from performing error-free work. All such problems described by workers must be acknowledged quickly by management to make it clear that line-level problems have been heard and will be addressed.

Step 12: Recognition

Purpose

To appreciate those who participate.

Actions

Crosby has maintained that an award program should be established to recognize those workers who meet their goals or perform outstanding acts. The awards must not be financial, however. Individual recognition is the important element. "The contest and the measurement are the key,"[8] he writes, "the prize is not significant."

Step 13: Quality Councils

Purpose

To bring together the professional quality people for planned communication on a regular basis.

Actions

Regular meetings of the company's quality professionals and team chairpersons are held to determine new actions as they become necessary and to improve the quality program being installed. This helps develop the best source of information on the programs and ideas for action.

Step 14: Do it Over Again

Purpose

To emphasize that the quality improvement program never ends.

Actions

Set up a new team of representatives and begin again, because the program is never over.

Each 14-step cycle in Crosby's process typically takes from 12 to 18 months. By repeating the cycle the program progressively becomes a part of the company's culture and quality becomes ingrained in everyday business activities. More so than the implementation of statistical quality tools, active top management participation is crucial to Crosby's process, because he believes that workers' performance reflects the attitudes of management. (His consulting company, Crosby Associates, however, has become a full-service quality company, melding his philosophy with statistical process control and other managerial tools and in total quality management for small businesses.) Therefore, quality Crosby-style demands that all managers adopt zero defects as their personal standard of conformance. Only after managers have accepted this attitude, can a quality improvement program be aimed at the company's workers with any chance of long-term success.

TOP-DOWN COMMITMENT

To succeed, Crosby insists that top management must be serious about committing the entire organization to quality improvement. In his analysis, organizations determined to improve their quality have the following characteristics in common:

- Quality improvement is seen as an ongoing, everlasting process.
- Quality education and philosophy begins at the top of the organization.
- Quality control departments believe in ZD.
- Quality training materials and instruction must be excellent.
- Management is patient and never decreases effort or enthusiasm for quality improvement.

In the end, Crosby remains an organizational realist. Nothing happens through goodness alone, he says. Quality must become a pervasive influence throughout the corporate culture by systematic effort at every level. Or, in his words: "Quality is free. But it is not a gift."[9]

8
Myron Tribus

Myron Tribus brings a unique outlook to total quality theories in two distinct areas: the practical problems of everyday total quality programs and the application of total quality theories to nonmanufacturing settings. A disciple of W. Edwards Deming, Tribus has drawn heavily from Deming's works but has taken them beyond general theory to provide specific methods for implementing the concepts in individual settings.

Tribus received a B.S. degree in chemistry from the University of California, Berkeley in 1942 and a Ph.D. degree in engineering from the University of California, Los Angeles (UCLA) in 1949. He was a design engineer for the jet engine department of General Electric and senior vice president for research and engineering for Xerox Corp., where he was in charge of research, development, and engineering of the entire line of Xerox copiers, duplicators, and telecopiers. He was assistant secretary for Science and Technology in the U.S. Department of Commerce during the Nixon administration. Tribus also helped found Exergy, a company devoted to the commercialization of a new power cycle for electric power generation and still serves as a partner. He was also one of the founders of the American Quality and Productivity Institute.

In addition to this work, Tribus established a distinguished career in the academic world. He served for 16 years on the faculty of the College of Engineering at UCLA and two years on the faculty of the University of Michigan. For eight years he was dean of the Thayer School of Engineering at Dartmouth College. He served as director of the Center for Advanced Engineering Study at the Massachusetts Institute of Technology for nearly 12 years.

Tribus published more than 100 papers on topics ranging from such academic topics as heat transfer, fluid mechanics, and probability theory to such applied topics as sea water demineralization and the design of engineering curricula. In more recent years, Tribus became known for his papers on Deming-style management philosophy.

THE THREE-SYSTEM CONCEPT

The combination of work as an educator and engineer led Tribus to develop a unique perspective on bringing total quality concepts to the world. Tribus developed a concept that shows what factors must be considered when introducing quality management into any enterprise, whether it be industry, service, government or education (see Figure 8.1).

The innermost circle represents the "know-how" of a company, the actual tools and techniques required to run the business. It includes all the machinery, the technical tools of quality science, and the quantitative aspects of quality.

The next circle represents the social system within which the tools and techniques must operate. It defines the power structure of the organization by including the reward structure, the symbols of power, the relationships between people and among groups, privileges, and politics. Whenever new technology arrives, the social system inevitably changes (e.g., the introduction of two-person bucksaws in lumbercamps that forced the workers to shed autonomy and work in teams).[1]

Likewise, the social systems can inhibit the introduction of new technology, he notes. "It is not possible to consider only the set of tools and techniques without considering the social system in which the processes are imbedded," Tribus writes in his paper, "Quality Management in Education."[2] "If the tool for improvement calls for cooperation and the social system promotes competition, then the tool cannot be used," he adds in his paper, "When the Enterprise Opts for Quality, What is the CEO Supposed to Do?"[3]

The outer circle represents the managerial system. It is the way practices, procedures, and protocols are established and main-

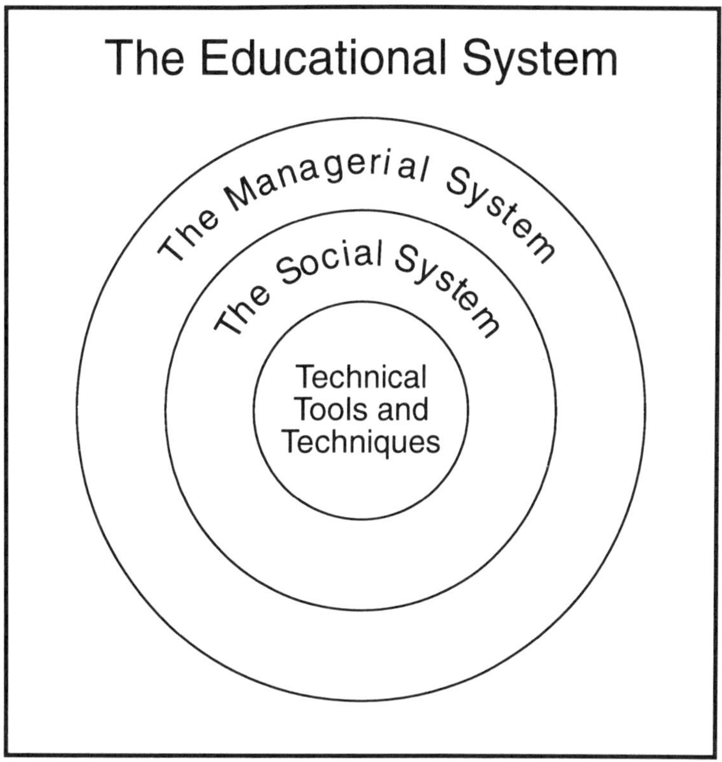

FIGURE 8.1. Tribus' Three-System Concept.

tained. Thus, it has great influence on the social and technical systems. "If the managerial system emphasizes individual behavior, giving rewards to 'outstanding' contributors, then the social system will not be a cooperative one," he writes.[4] "If the managerial system shoots the messenger, then it will be very difficult to get at the truth."[5]

The outer box represents all of the preconceived ideas that are brought to the workplace as a result of education, both formal and informal. It is the source of management paradigms, self images, problem solving techniques, knowledge, know-how, wisdom and character. Although management is boxed in by its own and by workers' paradigms and education, the box can be enlarged and changed with specific training and education.

Tribus remarks, "The people work *in* a system. The job of the manager is to work *on* the system—to improve it, continuously, *with their help*."[6] The CEO is responsible for the continuous improvement of all four systems. "It is the responsibility of management to change the social, technical and managerial systems so that the circles become larger—this is the definition of empowerment," he writes.[7] "Once we understand this linkage among these systems, it becomes clear why top management has to be deeply involved in the quality movement. While it is possible for the lower levels of management to introduce the tools and techniques of quality management, they cannot succeed unless the social system is also changed to accommodate these tools and techniques."[8]

With this as the nexus of his theory Tribus goes on to give advice to managers. He writes that the organization must have a well-defined process to:

- Recognize a system
- Define it so others can recognize it, too
- Analyze its behavior
- Work with subordinates in improving the system
- Measure the quality of the system
- Develop improvements in the quality of the system
- Measure the gains in quality, if any, and linked these to customer delight
- Take steps to guarantee holding the gains.[9]

Managing for continual improvement must be a companywide imperative, Tribus says; everyone must have a role. Figure 8.2, displayed by Tribus during a June 29, 1986 talk to the Minnesota Federation of Professional Engineers, suggests how employees in various positions should allocate time for working on continuous improvement.

When everyone engages in improvement activities, the entire organization becomes more receptive to new ideas and designs which flow from research. The chart is useful in telling everyone in the organization how to prioritize their time.

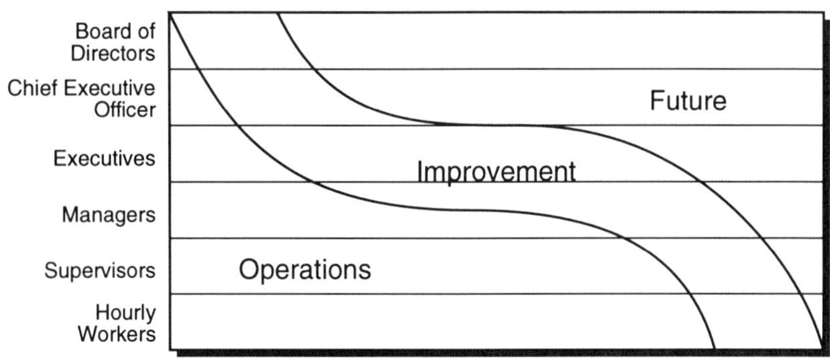

FIGURE 8.2. Employee Time Allocation for Continuous Improvement.

TRANSLATION TO EDUCATION

Tribus' theory takes on many different nuances depending on the organization. However, because of more than 30 years as an educator and the fact that his theory involves education boxing in the other three systems, he has made a great deal of progress in bringing his ideas to the world of education. When translating Deming's total quality theories to education, Tribus writes in his paper, "Quality Management in Education," the basic principles are unchanged, but the specifics of the application involve new elements. To begin, it is well to keep in mind some of the important differences between education and industry:

- The school is not a factory.
- The students are not the product.
- Their education is the product.
- The customers for the product are several (i.e., the students themselves, their parents, their future employers, and society at large).
- Students need to be comanagers of their own education.
- There are no opportunities for recalls.

He also makes the following observations:

- In education, the teachers work in a system. The job of the administration is to work on the system to improve it continuously with their help.
- The students study and learn in a system. The job of the teacher is to work on the system to improve it continuously with their help.
- Quality in education is what makes learning a pleasure and a joy. Some measures of student performance may be increased by threats, competitions for grades or prizes, but such an attachment to learning is unhealthy. It takes a quality experience to create an independent learner.
- Quality has to do with the way the teaching and learning process is carried forward. It is possible to have a high quality education in a one-room school house with few amenities. Of course, the students may not be adequately prepared for work in a high-tech industry, but the foundation for life-long learning can be laid.
- In the classroom, the students are the customer of the teacher, i.e., the people who most directly receive the teaching service. This does not mean that the students are in charge of the process. They do not decide upon the features of the educational system, though they ought to be consulted. They do, however, have a voice in defining quality.

TRIBUS AS ADVOCATE

Many of Deming's disciples disseminate Deming's theories in hope that organizations will see the value, but Tribus prefers a frontal attack, explaining not just what Deming believes but how it differs from other management tools and why it is critical to business success. His papers give succinct, easy-to-understand explanations of how to use Deming's theories in the real world.

For example, he writes in his paper, "Deming's Way," "the basic idea that Deming had is this: If management is to be responsible for improving something as complicated as a modern assembly of machines and people (whether in the factory, the hospital, the office, or anywhere else), managers must have a way of learning (1) which parts of the problems are due to the workers and (2) which parts are due to the system."[10] Tribus says Deming understood that this can happen only if two circumstances are fulfilled:

- The workers and the management can speak the same language.
- The management uses the workers as essential "instruments in understanding what is happening at the place where the work gets done."[11]

"Too many people believe that Deming merely teaches simple statistical quality control," he adds in the same paper. [12] "Deming's way is not taught in any school of management in America. Indeed, many things taught to managers in our schools and seminars about how to manage enterprises are actually *contrary* to Deming's way."[13]

Tribus' well-written, easy-to-understand papers provide a primer for those wanting to understand basic quality and, at the same time, insights for those already well versed in it. He offers them for reproduction gratis.* Though a disciple of Deming, Tribus himself will be remembered for his own well conceived ideas, particularly the Four-System Concept, and for his ability to communicate all aspects of quality. His nationwide connections, in government, industry and education, give him a range of influence second to none. His ability to communicate and disseminate both his own ideas and Deming's resemble the impact of Kaoru Ishikawa, the Japanese guru discussed in the next section.

*Write: NSPE, 1420 King Street, Alexandria, VA 22314.

II

THE JAPANESE

World War II will prove to be one of the great watersheds in history, a sharp dividing line between the modern world and an older, more hierarchical social paradigm. North Americans emerged from the war with their society and industrial structure not just unharmed, but stronger than it was when the war began. America's ability to mobilize such a large nation and turn its considerable energies into the development of war material astounded other nations.

Not the least among them was Japan. Although its industries and its perception of the world were shattered, Japanese pride and determination were intact. They wanted to know how to become an industrial power. The Japanese lapped up all that Deming, Juran, Feigenbaum and others could teach them. Then they took off on their own, and many of their industries now have a 40-year headstart on western competitors just sorting out what quality means. The Japanese quality masters tend to overlap each other in expertise, probably because of their longstanding tradition of collaboration. Japanese quality efforts tend not to be steeped in philosophy but in disciplined practical applications of techniques and concepts. These applications include such tools as Kaoru Ishikawa's cause-and-effect diagram, Yoji Akao's quality function deployment matrices, and Genichi Taguchi's loss function method.

9
Kaoru Ishikawa

Kaoru Ishikawa practically grew up in the Japanese quality movement. His father, Ichiro, was a key member of the group that invited Deming to Japan in 1950. Born in 1915, the younger Ishikawa was a newly trained scientist when the movement was just starting, and today his experience serves as a reminder of how much evolution has occurred in Japan's business environment. As a result, his theories provide a solid framework for the "typical" Japanese approach to quality.

Ishikawa received a degree in chemistry from the University of Tokyo in 1939. He was commissioned as an engineer lieutenant in the Japanese Navy and, following World War II, was employed at Nissan Liquid Fuel Company. It was this point in history, when Ishikawa and many other young scientists were trying to help rebuild their country's obliterated production facilities, that saw the divergence between the U.S. and Japanese quality control efforts. "After the end of World War II, modern quality control blew like a breath of fresh air through Japan's ravaged industries," writes Ishikawa in his 1989 book, *Introduction to Quality Control.*[1] "It was a major force in helping rationalize the country's manufacturing, and it revolutionized the management policies and organizational structures of Japanese companies."[2]

JAPANESE TOTAL QUALITY

Built on the foundation laid by Deming, Juran, Sarasohn, and Feigenbaum, the theories and practices promoted by Ishikawa and the other Japanese Total Quality experts today are very different from those originally adopted in the mid-1950s. Nevertheless, the basic concepts have remained constant. Most importantly, the definition of quality in the Japanese theories continues to revolve around the customer.

"Talk of making good-quality products is often misunderstood as making products of the best possible quality. However, when we talk about quality in quality control, we are talking about designing, manufacturing, and selling products of a quality that will actually satisfy the consumer in use," Ishikawa writes in his landmark book, *Introduction to Quality Control.* "In other words, 'good quality' means the best quality that a company can produce with its present production technology and process capability, and that will satisfy the consumers' needs, in terms of factors such as cost and intended use. Which would you buy, a newspaper printed on top-quality paper costing $10, or the same newspaper printed on ordinary newsprint prices at 50 cents?"[3]

With the customer's needs determined, writes Ishikawa, the next step is to consider the four aspects of quality, and plan, design, and control them comprehensively. The four aspects are:

Q (Quality): quality characteristics in their narrow sense. Performance, purity, strength, dimensions, tolerances, appearance, reliability, lifetime, defects, rework, non-adjustment ratio, and packing method.

C (Cost): characteristics related to cost and price as well as cost control and profit control. Yield, unit cost, losses, productivity, raw materials costs, production costs, defects, overfill, cost price, selling price, and profit.

D (Delivery): characteristics related to quantities and lead times (i.e., quantity control). Production volume, sales volume, changeover losses, inventory, consumption, lead times, and changes in production plans.

S (Service): problems arising after products have been shipped and product characteristics requiring follow-up. Safety and environmental character-

> istics, product liability and liability prevention, compensation period, warranty period, before-sales and after-sales service, parts interchangeability, spare parts, ease of repair, instruction manuals, inspection and maintenance methods, packing method.[4]

Quality control is impossible without numerical data. In Japan, the goal of Total Quality Control has remained the same over the years—defect-free processes and not just quality end-products. Ishikawa states that it is possible to build quality into every step which makes every process 100% defect-free. This is achieved through process control. A process is actually a collection of cause-and-effect factors and must be controlled to obtain better products. His approach anticipates a problem and prevents it before it actually occurs.

In the Japanese theories, however, it's not enough to justify or explain defects or flaws when they are discovered. Rather, one must determine the causes that create the flaws and remove the causes. "The aim of quality control is to assure quality by controlling it," Ishikawa sums up. This "means implementing quality assurance using the TQC approach by building quality (including reliability) into a product during its development stage (which starts from the planning of the new product), then carrying out properly executed process control and, if necessary, performing inspection. When implementing quality control, we need to manage the five Ms: men, materials, machines, methods, and measurements."[5]

Workers should view the next step in each process as their "customer," Ishikawa says. Therefore, they are always working to please the next process or their customer. It is a frame of mind that can be used to break through barriers in other business climates as well. Quality control functions work best where there is a sense of mutual trust and respect, and where the organization's managers accept the fundamental belief that workers are by nature good and that trust can always be cultivated. This is a break with the older form of supervision, where workers were admonished to perform but not think. The older form is dehumanizing for both workers and those supervising, and it has contributed to labor unrest.

This concept of working together has the added advantage of opening up channels of communication throughout the company. With such all-encompassing communication, failures can be discovered before they turn into disasters. The increased communication also makes it possible to maintain closer contact with the marketplace and keep ahead of the changing pace of customer preferences.

Finally, Ishikawa notes that total quality control must be continued as long as the company exists. Once begun, the movement must be continuously promoted and renewed. "Quality control should not be practiced simply because it is fashionable,"[6] he says. "Its purpose is to rationalize industry, establish technology, and enable companies to develop the ability to secure good profits and beat international competition through quality rather than through unfair trading practices such as dumping. Quality control must be continued throughout the life of a company."[7]

DIFFERENTIATING FACTORS

In December 1965, a symposium on quality control detailed six characteristics that distinguished Japanese theories about quality from Western theories. Although U.S. efforts have progressed in many of these areas, the extent to which they are identified strongly with Japanese efforts continues to set them apart. These characteristics go a long way toward illustrating the essential differences between quality as practiced in postwar Japan and as belatedly recognized in U.S. businesses in recent years.

Participation by All Members of the Organization in Quality Control

From the very beginning of their total quality movement, the Japanese insisted on participation by all workers, from the chief executive officer down to the line. According to Ishikawa, total quality control is the participation of all employees, including the president, in an effort to create better products or services at a lower cost. This effort, in turn, leads to increased sales and improved profit and makes the company into a better, more cohesive organization. "Real TQC is a complete revolution in the old-style approach to management," Ishikawa writes. "It means that top and middle management, engineers, administrators, and all other employees, as well as affiliated companies, must work together as a team to understand the philosophy of statistical quality control, acquire a feeling for TQC, put it into practice, and build up an effective management organization."[8]

Ishikawa also addressed the issue of maintaining positive relationships with workers. He cautioned against getting angry with subordinates when they make mistakes—problems may be the fault of the process rather than the individual. By getting angry, it becomes more difficult to determine the truth behind the situation. Subordinates become more inclined to provide management with false data and reports if they think it helps them avoid conflict. Likewise, several factors may prevent a manager from encouraging total quality control and quality improvement, Ishikawa says. These occur when managers:

- Are passive, avoiding responsibility.
- Believe there is no problem, remaining satisfied with the status quo and lacking the understanding of significant company issues.
- Think their own company is already the best (i.e., egotists).
- Think the easiest and best ways of doing things are those which are familiar to them and rely only on their own limited experiences.
- Think only of themselves, their own company, or division.
- Don't consider other people's decisions.
- Compete for distinction and always think of themselves.
- Promote despair, jealousy, and envy throughout a company.
- Are unaware of what is happening beyond their immediate surroundings and know little or nothing about other divisions, other industries, or the outside world in general.
- Continue to live in the past, don't improve, or lack common sense.

To overcome these situations, quality control is needed. Each of these factors is closely linked to the people working in the company. The spirit of cooperation, pioneer spirit, and the desire to make new breakthroughs must be fostered. Managers also need confidence in their own abilities to persevere and use tactics and strategies for overcoming difficulties.

One result of this approach is that the Japanese have long encouraged their consumers to complain when they encounter defects. In this way, they help the manufacturers create better products. The basic reason for fostering this involvement is that consumers normally do not complain—they simply switch products or brands. If they are encouraged to communicate with the manufacturer, they can work together to produce a better product, and everyone benefits from this process. The producing companies must, therefore, be proactive and solicit their customers' complaints.

Education and Training in Quality Control

Ishikawa has always maintained that quality control begins and ends with education. To promote quality control with participation by all, quality control education must be given to all employees from the president to assembly line workers.

The Japanese believe that when people are educated, they become more reliable and authority can be delegated to them. Japanese organizations work toward having one supervisor for several hundred people, but Americans are taught in management classes that only three to seven people should report to one supervisor. The Japanese believe that by educating their people, a supervisor can lead hundreds of workers just as an orchestra conductor does, bringing out the best music from the entire group.

With that philosophy as the guiding force, Japanese industry traditionally takes a leadership role in the continual presentation of opportunities for their employees. This is partly due to the lifetime employment practices used in Japan; industry knows that any education given to its employees is an investment in the future. Employers are willing to spend time and money on workers' educations when they are sure they'll be staying on the job.

The basic quality control theory designed by the Union of Japanese Scientists and Engineers serves as a model for all Japanese requirements for quality control education. These courses last for at least six months, with five days of classroom instruction per month standard. That translates to 30 days of instruction time per year, per participant. Participants study for one week then put to use what they learned during the three weeks they are back on their jobs. When they return for the next session, they come with their own data and applications. This course is a continuous repetition of study and practice, not unlike American military training (e.g., two hours of lecture followed by two hours of laboratory work). In Japan, education does not end with formal training. It is the responsibility of the supervisor to teach subordinates continually through actual work experience.

Ishikawa asserted that quality control is a vanguard revolution in management. Therefore, thought processes must be changed as well as activities before theories truly become ingrained in everyday business practices. To accomplish this, training must be repeated over and over again. The Japanese achieve this by introducing statistical methods in their primary schools. It continues through their formal school levels, and continuing education courses on statistical methods are televised each morning so workers can take lessons before they begin their day's activities.

Quality Circle Activities

It is sometimes said that standards can lead to arrogance within the industry, both by the company and the consumers. According to Ishikawa, if standards and regulations aren't revised within six months, there's proof no one is using them.

As a result of this view, the Japanese continue improvement by looking forward and working together in quality circles in a preventive mode. Once again, this is in marked contrast to the United States, where quality circles were imported and simplistically used as a way to delegate a problem to the line workers with no management participation. "QC circles are small groups of people from the same workplace who carry out quality-control activities voluntarily,"[9] Ishikawa writes. These small groups carry out self-development and mutual development as part of companywide quality control activities and use QC tools to control and improve their workplaces continuously, with everybody taking part.

"The basic philosophy of QC circle activities carried out as part of companywide quality control activities is:

1. To contribute to the improvement and development of the corporate culture.
2. To create cheerful workplaces that make life worthwhile and where humanity is respected."[10]

Guided by Ishikawa, the Japanese Union of Scientists and Engineers developed and published ten defining characteristics of quality control circle activities, five of them structural and five functional. The structural characteristics are:

- Circles are small enough to allow face-to-face communications between members.
- Members work in the same place and meet frequently.
- Circles perform quality control activities; that is, matters pertaining to product quality, process quality, safety, communication and morale.
- Circles are voluntary.
- Quality Control Circles should be part of company-wide quality control activities.

The functional characteristics are:

- Informing and educating the circle's members.
- Using quality control methods and techniques; that is, making decisions based on facts, not feelings.
- Relating the activities to improving and managing the workplace.
- Continuing as long as the work continues, regardless of personnel changes.
- Involving everyone in the workplace, so that no one feels left out.

A text published by the JUSE titled *QC saakuru Koryo* also specifies three principles for quality control circles, including:

- Quality control circles contribute to the improvement and development of the enterprise.
- Quality control circles respect humanity and build a happy, bright workshop that is a meaningful place to work.
- Quality control circles fully and eventually draw out infinite possibilities.[11]

Quality Control Audits

Because the Japanese believe in continual improvement, one can understand that they also believe standards and regulations are always inadequate. Consequently, Ishikawa maintained that top management must be visibly involved in applying quality techniques themselves and demonstrating to their co-workers that they not only have understanding but believe in the results and expect results from others. Management must regularly visit the workplace, and the manager should have a definite purpose in mind and check what is seen, comparing it against previous knowledge.

The presidential audit, one of the cornerstones of a Japanese total quality control program, is one way management ensures the program is on track. In addition, the Japanese encourage consistent quality throughout a company by each year awarding the Deming Application Prize to companies and individuals who have demonstrated the most skill in applying total quality concepts and techniques done the most to improve quality.

Utilization of Statistical Methods

Ishikawa notes that statistical data is the most important concept in quality control. Without a tightly constructed statistical process, no analysis or control is possible. In following through on the total quality control cycle and taking corrective action, it is important to take measures to prevent any future recurrence. Adjustments and preventions of recurring problems are two separate issues, and managers should seek to prevent problems. In removing the cause for the problem, one must go back to the very source and take steps to prevent the problem from recurring.

Statistical methods are useful at all levels of the organization, but must be kept in perspective as an organization improves. "Statistics and statistical methods are continuing to make great advances, but it is not necessary to know all about them to promote quality control and business management," writes Ishikawa. "On the contrary, it can in fact be harmful to teach too much about them, and statistical methods courses should be divided into introductory, intermediate, and advanced grades to suite the level of students, with due regard to the actual conditions in the workplaces where the methods will be used."[12]

Ishikawa is credited with inventing the cause-and-effect diagram (see Figure 9.1), one of the seven process management tools discussed in Chapter 17. Ishikawa first used it publicly to summarize the opinions of engineers at a plant, but his staff at the University of Tokyo already used it in research activities.[13]

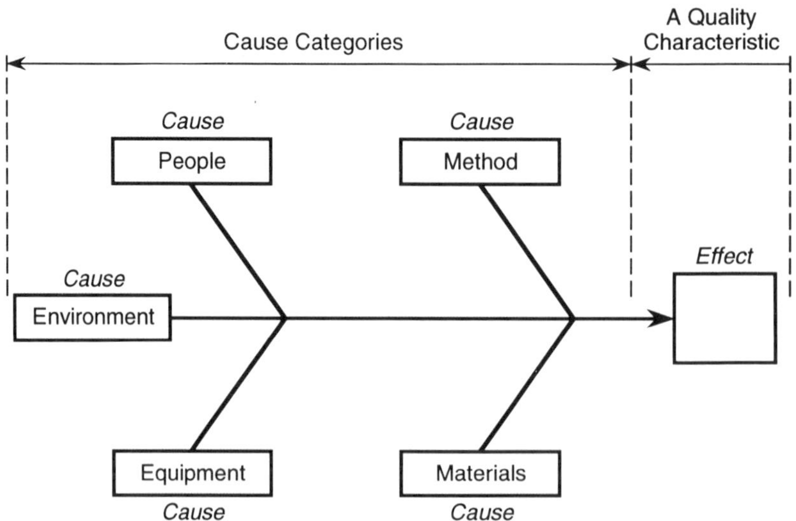

FIGURE 9.1. Ishikawa's Cause and Effect Diagram.

Nationwide Quality Control Promotion Activities

Ishikawa in the years leading up to his death held that people were beginning to understand the true value of quality control. The many years of education on the subject in Japan have contributed to this understanding as well as further attention as other nations have adopted similar activities.

However, he also believed that continual promotion activities are necessary at the individual business level. "In promoting total quality control, a long-term program must be set up as a matter of management policy. It is also important to make the program an integral part of the company's long-term business plan," he has written. "If quality programs are not unified with other business plans, total quality control and management will be regarded as separate entities and people will easily fall under the delusion that total quality control is something apart from their normal daily work."[14]

He suggests the following items should be included in a long-term total quality control program:[15]

- Policy management
- Plans for new-product development and the discontinuance of obsolete products
- Quality improvement programs
- Quality assurance programs
- QC education and training programs, organization and personnel plans
- Standardization promotion plans (i.e., materials and regulations)
- Subcontracting, purchasing, and raw materials plans
- Sales, distribution, service, and consumer plans
- QC circle activity promotion plans

Ishikawa was a professor of engineering in Japan and a consultant to businesses across the world for more than 40 years. He is considered one of the handful of Japanese who helped bring total quality control to his country and was awarded the Order of the Sacred Treasure, Second Class, and the Blue Ribbon Medal by the Japanese government. He received the Deming Prize in 1952 for his work in bringing quality concepts to Japanese industry and also has been awarded the Shewhart Medal from the American Society for Quality Control for outstanding contributions to the development of QC theory, principles and methods, and QC circle and standardization activities for improved industrial quality and productivity both in Japan and abroad. A prolific writer, Ishikawa is the most prominent of the Japanese quality experts, not so much for original ideas or concepts as for his firm grasp of the requirements of total quality and his ability to disseminate that understanding to others.

10
Shigeru Mizuno

Just after World War II, Shigeru Mizuno, an electrochemical engineer, joined the Union of Japanese Scientists and Engineers (JUSE) as part of a group assigned to study wartime production methods, particularly those of the United States. There was little material available on quality control, though the group spent hours translating a text on control charts which, Mizuno later wrote, "may have confused as many people as it helped."[1]

The group persisted, however, offering a basic course on quality control, and in the early 1950s, the group put together a quality control course that was broadcast over Japanese radio. Out of the script came a book that gained enormous popularity in Japanese industry. An understanding of quality was launched—and so was Mizuno's career.

In 1954, he was appointed head of the Tokyo Institute of Technology's Resource Utilization Research laboratory where he redirected the organization's attention toward scientific measurement, control, and other concepts learned at JUSE. Mizuno particularly emphasized the statistical methods required for quality control. He retired from the institute in 1970, took a professorship in management engineering at the Science University of Tokyo, and became involved in launching the Japanese Society for Quality Control that year. Later in his career, Mizuno sought contact with the growing international quality community, took numerous speaking engagements abroad, and hosted conferences on statistics, quality control and production engineering.

Mizuno's theories, developed while advising more than 300 companies on quality control, are compiled in his 1988 book, *Company-Wide Total Quality Control*. The book, highly popular in Japan and available in an English translation, uses a modular design, setting forth self-contained chapters and sections on such topics as management's role, planning, functions of quality assurance, product liability, education, production and purchasing, and quality control in the office.

PRODUCT QUALITY

Quality, Mizuno notes, once was the responsibility of the buyer, who had to check whether the product was safe and would do what it was supposed to do. The manufacturer's emphasis was mainly on quantity. Today, however, products are more complex, and the seller must assure the buyer that the quality is good. The product should be easy for the customer to use and maintain safely.

By using total quality control, Mizuno contends, organizations can develop safe, high-quality products, help workers acquire the technical know-how required to improve products and systems, strengthen the company for greater adaptability to change, and emphasize its social and public responsibilities.

Product quality is defined as those qualities which characterize the product's fitness for use; that is, the characteristics the product must possess if it is to be used in the intended manner.[2] In cases where it is difficult to measure the desired quality characteristics, substitute characteristics may be applied so long as they reflect customer requirements. Other elements of product quality include a reasonable price, economy of use, durability, safety, ease of use, simplicity of manufacture, and easy disposal. Although a product lacking any of these elements is inferior or defective, their presence does not guarantee quality. Still other elements must be present in a winning product, including a good design, superiority over the competition, physical appeal and distinctiveness and originality.

All parts of a company play a role in product quality, Mizuno emphasizes. Purchasing must buy the best supplies. Marketing must research consumer needs, conveying these to the company's product designers and explaining the product's proper use to the customer.

ACHIEVING CONTROL

Mizuno advocates use of the PDSA cycle, which he learned from Deming, to achieve control. First, there must be a reasonable plan. Second, the plan is carried out. Third, there is a review of the results. Fourth, changes and improvements are made.

Detecting defective products and fixing them is not true quality control, he says. Quality control is composed of revising designs, work standards and work procedures to eliminate defective products. "Quality control is prevention,"[3] Mizuno says.

None of this is unusual, he adds, "in fact, it should be all too obvious. In this sense, it might be said that quality control is the art of doing the obvious and doing it right."[4]

Consumers have become more demanding regarding product safety and use. Product guarantees are expected to extend throughout the product's useful life. Simultaneously, the pressures to reduce both manufacturing costs and the cost to the consumer have risen, Mizuno notes. Quality control also must be applied to unintended by-products of the manufacturing process, especially when the waste is in the form of harmful industrial pollution.

Each nation has a different perception of total quality control, Mizuno believed. In Japan, it is practiced throughout the company, with total involvement by everyone. Sensing a need to make the distinction between Japanese total quality control and that of other nations, the Japanese coined the phrase "company-wide quality control,"[5] influenced by a paper presented by Mizuno on "Company-Wide Quality Control Activities in Japan."

Quality control cannot be limited to technical functions. Everyone must participate—administration, sales, line managers, and employees at every level. Quality control begins with clarifying problems and seeking their causes; it is based on factual evidence, using solid tools to reach solid decisions.

MANAGEMENT

Mizuno notes that in Japanese, management and control are the same word. Managers play a crucial role in total quality, but often are the very ones who obstruct it. There is a large distinction between understanding the theoretical importance of total quality control and actually implementing it. As busy people, corporate managers too often settle for understanding quality control through a few books or introductory lectures, failing to learn the details of implementation. Cloistered in the executive suite and pressed with a huge workload, managers may lose touch with floor workers and day-to-day operations. They may lose the sense of urgency, awareness of quality control requirements, and determination essential to success.

Managers' attitudes reverberate through the organization, however, and those with no interest in total quality control should be weeded out.[6] Managers may send employees off to seminars and educate everyone in the company in total quality control, but if they fail to educate themselves and participate actively in quality control, the organization will be like a chicken with its head cut off. Consequently, managers should do two things to promote total quality control: participate in product quality assurance activities and participate in practical management of total quality control by establishing clear policies, making sure that everyone is familiar with them and working to achieve the goals expressed in them.

According to Mizuno, defects in products or services can be placed in two categories: chronic defects and occasional defects. Chronic defects often are difficult to identify, whereas occasional defects, are localized (like a toothache), and hence easier to detect and cure. Chronic defects are traceable to many causes, but it is management's responsibility to seek them out and correct them.

Management should promote quality control through policies, which Mizuno subdivides into administrative, work, and management for the long-term and short-term (i.e., business year). These policies should include one company quality that places priority on the product's advantages to the consumer. Such a policy should include guidelines for the direction and nature of the organization's activities, as well as goals to be attained and methods to be used.

Quality control always involves activities within and among divisions, referred to as vertical activities and horizontal activities.

To implement total quality control, Mizuno cautions that a company must do more than have each division pursue its own activities. To achieve total quality, the divisions must cooperate closely with each other.

MIDDLE MANAGEMENT

According to Mizuno, middle management also promotes quality control by elaborating on policies outlined by management, following their own programs, evaluating results and developing new plans, analyzing and evaluating product quality, collecting information and data on product quality, encouraging quality circle activities, and standardizing their innovations and performing cross-functional activities.[7]

Middle management also must plan for quality control and its introduction. Often quality control has been delayed or rendered ineffective because of a poor introduction. The pitfalls of quality introduction rarely are publicized, so few organizations have the benefit of others' problems. Planning should be done in two stages:

- Dissemination and education
- Implementation and organization

It must be noted, however, that there is no definitive point where introduction ends and implementation begins. Introducing total quality control involves education, dissemination, and organization.[8]

EDUCATION

Education of employees is a major way to disseminate the quality control concept. Workers need to know how to maintain quality using a control chart, how to create standards, how to improve quality and how to develop new product quality. Educating top managers, who usually have strongly held opinions based on their experience, is sometimes the most difficult part, Mizuno observes. The best way is to educate them through short lectures, reports and recommendations emphasizing the economic impact of activities, reading material, and study groups inside and outside the company.

Quality control, as presented by Mizuno, has little to do with statistics,[9] though statistics, which provide specific, solid data, must be carefully considered in any organizational training program. They should not be overemphasized, however, and employees should only be taught what they need to know, such as how to use a control chart to detect abnormal conditions.

People need to know how statistics are used, but effective quality does not result from having a small group spend time on esoteric facts and figures not understood by other employees. "The last thing you want to do in instituting quality control is to create an elite corps of statisticians," Mizuno writes.[10] People who have dedicated themselves to learning statistics sometimes develop a superior attitude, which can kill the cooperative work atmosphere among their fellow employees.[11]

Middle managers should learn that quality control involves probing for problems, diagnosing the causes, and eventually correcting the causes of mistakes. Research and development staff members must learn how standardization can help them become more creative and not hinder their creativity.

The level of education is different for each company and its requirements. Separate courses should be conducted for various job types simultaneously. Actual work situations provide material for study.

DISSEMINATION

Management should create an information network to communicate data and other quality control information to everyone concerned. Clear procedures, defining what to write and where to send it, are a part of Mizuno's plan for dissemination.

Cross-communications, memos, and other written materials sent between departments, make up another mode of dissemination. There should be horizontal as well as vertical contact between employees and departments, Mizuno says. Committees comprise another communications forum, as do meetings in departments or other operating units.

A total quality control promotion center may draft proposals to promote quality and quality policies. It also keeps tabs on current issues and problems in the company's policy and functional management systems, lists critical problems and checks on action to solve them. It might also plan educational activities and workshops and other quality control activities.

QUALITY CONTROL ACTIVITIES

Corporate management involves maintenance, reform, and development, Mizuno says.[12] Total quality control covers a broad range of activities, but "the heart of all quality control activities, quality maintenance, is implemented through analyses, process analyses and the establishment of work standards,"[13] he adds.

Deciding on standard quality requires consideration of customer requirements and manufacturing requirements. Work standards must take into consideration the process required to manufacture the desired product. There also must be control standards, explained in writing.

There are two approaches to quality control: the project approach and the system approach. The project approach concentrates on specific problems, seeking out priority problems, and correcting them. The system approach is more usual, though a project approach may prove more effective. The project approach is unlikely to uncover everything, and the system approach should be tried as well. "Quality control should be an all-encompassing grid, projects being the vertical lines and systems the horizontal lines," Mizuno writes.[14]

Quality control activities include:

- Quality planning and designing
- Purchasing and storing materials
- Institutionalizing quality control procedures

- Analyzing and controlling manufacturing processes
- Studying and measuring to determine nonconformance
- Equipment and installation management
- Personnel management, including education, training and placement
- Managing supplies and subcontractors
- Technology development
- Diagnosis and supervision[15]

There are always problems in implementing total quality control. Mizuno has outlined the following as the major ones:

- Uninterested top management
- Middle management's failure to recognize its role in total quality control
- Unclear total quality control targets
- Lack of product quality policies
- Failure to clarify the scope of activities
- Lack of a clear-cut program
- Too much stress on theory and too little effort to learn methodology
- Ritualized QC activities with little meaningful content
- Assuming that total quality control is limited to QC circle activities
- Lack of interest
- Problems in total quality control headquarters
- Incomplete understanding of what you want to achieve
- Lack of well-defined and uniform total quality control terminology.[16]

Everyone must participate in quality control, Mizuno insists. Assigning quality control activities to quality circles does not do, because others may then tend to feel absolved of doing anything in their own areas to improve quality. As noted earlier, quality control consists of revising designs, work standards, and work procedures to prevent the production of defective products. Employees must develop the skills to maintain, improve, and develop quality in their own areas.

Mizuno, perhaps more than any other quality expert, defined how quality should be disseminated and promoted throughout an organization. He also demonstrated that quality is a part of every corner of the organization, and that no one is exempt from the effort. His breakdown of each area of the organization makes clear that simple, easy-to-understand steps may define every process. Quality control is, to repeat some of Mizuno's most noted words, "the art of doing the obvious and doing it right."[17]

11
Yoji Akao

The Japanese industrial wagon was rolling smoothly in the mid-1960s, a remarkable recovery less than two decades after the country's devastation. Still, the nation's quality control wizards, steeply versed in the teachings of Deming, Juran, and Feigenbaum, were not satisfied. Although Japan's exports were growing, they reckoned, the quality of designs had to improve for Japan to move to the front of industrial nations. Many tried using fishbone charts to identify customer demands and to establish design quality.

Yoji Akao, a professor of industrial engineering at Tamagawa University in Tokyo, was among those foreseeing the need to probe deeper into customer interests. He developed a series of concepts to spread the critical aspects of quality throughout design and manufacturing. His ideas, refined, and formalized over the next several years, became known as quality function deployment (QFD).

Quality function deployment was first used in the Kobe Shipyard, where consultants, including Shigeru Mizuno, developed a matrix of customer demands and quality characteristics. The concepts spread quickly, soon permeating major Japanese industries.

Almost 20 years later, Akao, still virtually unknown in the United States, wrote a short article in *Quality Progress*, the official journal of the American Society for Quality Control, introducing quality function deployment to American businesses. The concept, based on use of a series of matrices to understand customers' wishes and to deploy them into product development, soon gained popularity in the U.S.

Born in 1928, Akao founded in 1974 a quality function deployment research committee for the Japanese Society for Quality

Control, which helped support quality function deployment's development as a technique for improving the transition from design to manufacturing. His posts and honors include: membership on the Deming Prize Committee (1964); recipient of the Deming Prize (1978); vice president of the Japanese Society for Quality Control; vice director of the editorial committee for the Union of Japanese Scientists and Engineers' *Journal of Statistical Quality Control*.

Akao's landmark book, *Quality Function Deployment: Integrating Customer Requirements into Product Design*, originally came out as a series of magazine articles. Published in 1988, it became the definitive work on quality function deployment.

Consumers, Akao writes, express their perceptions of product quality through "negative quality" comments—that is, complaints—or through unspoken "positive quality" ideas in the form of consumer demands.[1] Companies should analyze complaints about an existing product and then move upstream into the production process to search for factors contributing to the problems. With new products, the approach must begin from the upstream end, looking downstream toward the qualities that consumers demand. This method is called the *design approach*.

Quality function deployment is such an approach. It helps focus employees on the needs of the customer by using matrices and charts to help companies hear and express the customer's voice, develop a definition of quality, and then deploy that definition to the development and production of all services and parts of the product. It is not a design tool or a problem-solving tool; its purpose is to focus managers and employees on the product characteristics that will interest the customer.

THE DEMANDED QUALITY DEPLOYMENT CHART

"Planning is determining what to make; designing is deciding how to make it," says Akao.[2] Quality function deployment begins at the planning stage, which depends on gaining an accurate comprehension of what qualities customers want and translating these customer wishes, or demands, into such technical specifications as precise measurements. Questionnaires help to determine these wishes and their degree of importance. Then the qualities can be arranged in a demanded quality deployment chart, using symbols to show the degree of importance of each characteristic. In the United States, these often are referred to as a customer needs analysis table, which provides an ongoing record of customer needs with importance, performance and sales point data (see Figure 11.1).

THE QUALITY CHART

The demanded quality deployment chart, or customer needs analysis table, becomes the basis for a quality chart (see Figure 11.2).

Computer Desk Customer Needs Analysis Table Rev Date 3/8/93

Customer Process	Primary Needs	Secondary Needs	Importance	Performance		Competitors' Performance				Sales Points	Total Weight	Relative Weight
				Performance Now	Perception Target	O'Sullivan Computer Wk Stn.	O'Sullivan Swiss Army Desk II	Fixtur Oak Desk	Improvement Ratio			
Install	Easy to use	Simple assembly process	0.05	3	4	3	3	4	1.33	⊙	0.09	8%
		Assembles quickly	0.01	3	4	3	3	3	1.33		0.02	1%
Use		Can fit it to my work area	0.02	3	4	3	5	3	1.33	○	0.03	3%
		Good selection of accessories	0.03	3	4	3	3	3	1.33		0.04	3%
		Place printer close to my computer	0.07	3	3	4	4	3	1.00	○	0.09	8%
		Space to display papers, etc.	0.12	3	3	3	4	3	1.00		0.12	11%
		Feel comfortable viewing the monitor	0.14	3	3	4	5	3	1.00		0.14	12%
		Plenty of room for my legs	0.09	4	3	3	3	3	0.75		0.07	6%
	Good storage space	Plenty of storage for my supplies	0.02	4	5	3	4	3	1.25		0.02	2%
		Quickly access stored supplies	0.10	3	3	3	4	3	1.00		0.10	9%
		Easy to organize my supplies	0.11	3	3	3	4	3	1.00		0.11	10%
		Plenty of space for my computer equipment	0.04	3	3	3	4	2	1.00		0.04	4%
		Can control access to files	0.03	3	3	1	1	1	1.00		0.03	2%
Aesthetics	Looks good	Looks rich	0.02	3	5	3	3	5	1.67	⊙	0.05	4%
		Keeps equipment out of sight	0.01	3	3	3	5	2	1.00		0.01	1%
		Stays looking good	0.08	3	4	2	2	3	1.33	○	0.13	11%
	Feels good	Feels sturdy	0.04	4	4	3	3	4	1.00		0.04	4%
		Level surface	0.01	3	3	3	3	3	1.00		0.01	1%
		Even surface	0.01	4	4	3	3	3	1.00	○	0.02	2%

FIGURE 11.1. Customer Needs Analysis Table.

Computer Desk - Quality Characteristics by Functions		Rev Date 7/23/93																									
Quality Characteristics / Functions		Installation			Ease of use						Storage						Aesthetics									Function Weight	
					Flexibility				Comfort		Supply storage		Physical dimensions				Look				Feel						
		# of assembly steps	Time to assemble	Assembly tools required	# of configurations	# of standard document sizes	Maximum shelf height (all shelves)	Accessories rating	Monitor height range	Leg room width	Storage volume	# of storage configurations	Weight	Height	Depth	Width	Fit of parts	Color match of components	Resistance to surface mars	Routine maintenance time	Weight tolerance	Stability loaded	Surface warp	Surface sag	Leveling adjustment range		
Quality Characteristics Weight		4%	4%	1%	1%	4%	0%	13%	7%	3%	5%	8%	2%	3%	10%	10%	8%	1%	7%	4%	2%	2%	1%	1%	0%		
Hold computer equipment	Hold monitor				◕			◔	●																	1.1	6%
	Hold CPU				◑			◔																		0.45	2%
	Hold keyboard																									0	0%
	Hold peripherals				◕			◑																		0.74	4%
Hold computer supplies	Hold printer paper				◑			◑			◑	◑			◔											1.66	8%
	Hold diskettes, etc.							◑			◔	◑														1.21	6%
Hold books							●	◑			◑	◑		◕	◑											1.99	10%
Hold files						●		◑			◕	◑		◑												1.88	9%
Control access to storage								◑																		0.66	3%
Hide stored items								◑				◑														1.06	5%
Provide workspace	Hold documents							◑							◕	◕										2.06	10%
	Provide flat area														◕	◕							◕	◕	◕	1.6	8%
Fit the user								●	◑	◕		●		◑	◑	◑									◔	3.59	18%
Communicate image								◑					◔			◔		◕	◑	◔		◕	◔	◔		1.78	9%

FIGURE 11.2. Quality Chart

Akao defines a quality chart as "a two-dimensional matrix consisting of a demanded quality chart combined with a quality characteristics deployment chart."[3] The matrix is coded with symbols to indicate the strength of relationships between demanded qualities and quality characteristics. Its purpose is to convert customer's quality demands, usually expressed in abstract language lacking the details necessary for design activities, into quality characteristics in terms that may be understood by the engineers who design the product.

The quality chart provides a visual presentation of a product's or a company's quality characteristics. Quality charts that do not reflect these characteristics do not help much, Akao says, warning beginners not to pay too much attention to charts produced by other companies. Instead, they should seek to understand and copy the meaning of those charts. Some copying may be unavoidable, Akao says, but "copy the spirit, not the form."[4]

A quality chart improves communications between manufacturers and their suppliers. It also can be used to attain higher efficiency in new product development and to enhance sales.

PRODUCT DEVELOPMENT

Quality function deployment techniques can be a very effective methodology for developing new products. The charts and concepts used in quality function deployment can help convert de-

Key to Figure 11.2:

Symbol		Correlation Factor
Blank	No correlation	0
○	Weak correlation	1
◔	Some correlation	3
◐	Moderate correlation	5
◕	Strong correlation	7
●	Very strong correlation	9

manded quality into understandable characteristics. Then they may be used again to determine which structures work best to implement the characteristics (see Figure 11.3). By deploying such structures, employees may identify potential bottlenecks before beginning development work.

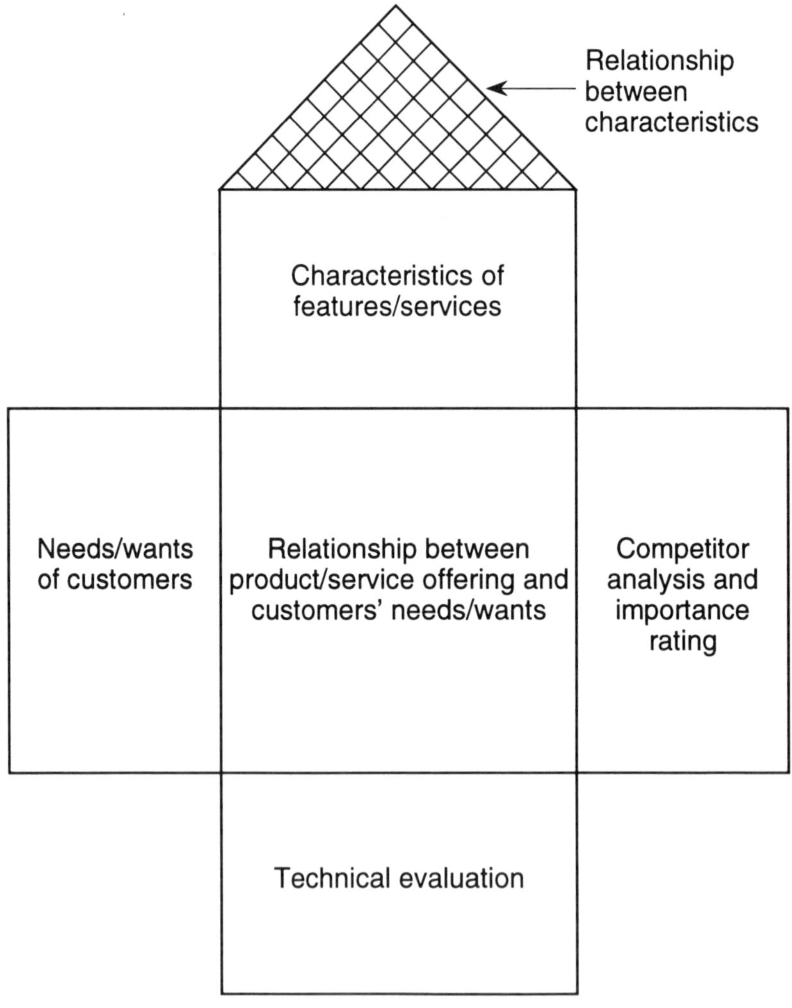

FIGURE 11.3. Quality Function Deployment.

The charts and matrices also help people involved in the development, who may be from different functions or departments, to view the total picture, develop logical development routines, and communicate with each other.

In some industries, using quality function deployment has enabled research and development to move closer to the market, generating new and improved requirements for product preparation, production, and service. It also facilitates an improved response to the growing social needs that influence almost every market. This may be particularly relevant for process industries, whose improvement efforts include upgrading raw materials. For instance, making tires, a consumer product, relies partially on formulas for developing synthetic rubber. Tires should provide a good ride and not slip on wet pavement; these are their demanded qualities. They are also the demanded qualities of the raw material. The charts and matrices of quality function deployment enable the tire manufacturer to demonstrate and communicate these requirements as well as determine key purchasing criteria for raw materials.[5]

VERSATILITY

Likewise, quality function deployment is effective in all sorts of businesses, including service industries, where quality elements are typically intangible, immediate, and often include feelings and subjective impressions. It helps establish targets for improvement or development during planning and designing while clarifying what services or products to offer.

Akao's concepts now pervade thousands of businesses, in Japan, the United States and elsewhere, though many managers who use quality function deployment may have never heard his name. Although he is an industrial engineer, Akao's work also is noteworthy for its contribution to communications in the workplace, where the matrices and other concepts quickly convey the importance of quality features and the means for achieving them. A recent revision and translation into English of another of Akao's seminal works on QFD (with Shigeru Mizuno)[6] promises to further his contributions.

12 Genichi Taguchi

Since Genichi Taguchi first brought his concepts to Xerox Corp. and Ford Motor Company in the early 1980s, his Taguchi Methods have helped to transform several large U.S. companies' product-design and manufacturing methods.

Born in 1924, Taguchi attended Kiryu Technical College and received a doctorate of science from Kyushu University. Trained as a textile engineer, he was hired by General MacArthur during the postwar reconstruction of Japan to help repair the country's phone system. He soon became frustrated with the time and money spent on tests and retests and began searching for ways to use statistics to design experiments that could reach the same conclusions in much less time. This quest for ever-increasing precision was to remain a theme in his work for the next 50 years.

Following the postwar reconstruction work, Taguchi entered academic life, teaching and continuing to perform research on statistical methods for reducing manufacturing costs and product development time. In 1962, he spent a year at Princeton University as a visiting professor, his first introduction into U.S. business. However, the experience apparently left no great mark on either his U.S. students or on his theories. He returned to Japan to teach at Aoyama Gaguin University in Tokyo.

In 1980, however, Taguchi adopted a different tactic to learn more about the U.S. and bring his ideas here. He took a one-year sabbatical to offer free consulting services to Bell Laboratories, the famous think tank. When he returned to Japan, he decided to become a consultant.

At the same time, Xerox executives had heard of Taguchi from their Japanese counterparts at Fuji Xerox and hired him as a consultant in the U.S. Soon after, Ford also hired him as a consultant.

Although his work has matured from the first postwar frustrations, it continues to center on the concept that companies only gain a worldwide marketing advantage if they cost-effectively produce quality products. According to Taguchi, the drive for quality should begin as a drive to control costs in product design then continue as a prime goal through all production stages, sometimes going so far as to assert that controlling cost is more important than striving for high quality.[1]

In many cases, he has built on other quality theorists' work, advocating "horizontal" communication that begins with the customer, for example. However, where other quality theories expound on the value of first setting up employee teams, Taguchi's work says the teamwork follows naturally from a focus on quality. If all employees are working to meet specific targets, "conditions change dramatically, teams prosper, and valuable data proliferate to support better product and process design," he writes in a paper entitled "Robust Quality" published in the *Harvard Business Review*.[2] "It is only through the efforts of every employee, from the CEO on down, that quality will become second nature. The most elusive edge in the new global competition is the galvanizing pride of excellence."[3]

This consistency begins at the design stage, Taguchi asserts. "If U.S. managers learn only one new principle from the collection now known as Taguchi Methods, let it be this: Quality is a virtue of design," he writes. "The 'robustness' of products is more a function of good design than of online control, however stringent, of manufacturing processes. To improve quality, you need to look upstream in the design stage. At the customer level, it's too late."[4]

Instead of tightening tolerances, the Taguchi method advises manufacturers to concentrate on hitting the design target—almost to the extent of ignoring tolerance limits, writes Lance Ealey in *Quality* magazine.[5] On the other hand, "with Taguchi's methods, an engineer keeps unimportant tolerances as loose as possible because they have little effect on a customer's perception of product quality."[6]

To visualize this concept, Taguchi has frequently used the analogy of a television set trying to send a signal. "The signal is what the product (or component or subassembly) is trying to deliver. Noises are the interferences that degrade signal, some of them coming from outside, some from complementary systems with the product. Robustness then becomes a product with a high signal-to-noise ratio."[7]

To maximize signal-to-noise ratios, he writes, world-class companies use a three-step decision-making process:[8]

- They define the specific objective, selecting or developing the most appropriate signal and estimating the concomitant noise.
- They define feasible options for the critical design values, such as dimensions and electrical characteristics.
- They select the option that provides the greatest robustness or the greatest signal-to-noise ratio.

PRODUCT ROBUSTNESS

Taguchi's principles of quality surround a spectrum of ideas centering on the concept of product robustness. "For customers, the proof of a product's quality is in its performance when rapped, overloaded, dropped, and splashed,"[9] he writes. "Then, too many products display temperamental behavior and annoying or even dangerous performance degradations. We all prefer copiers whose copies are clear under low power; we all prefer cars designed to steer safely and predictably, even on roads that are wet or bumpy, in crosswinds, or with tires that are slightly under- or over-inflated. We say these products are robust. They gain steadfast customer loyalty."[10]

He has thus focused all areas of the company on one goal: producing products that are as near perfect as possible. "You gain nothing in shipping a product that barely satisfies corporate standards over one that just fails," he writes.[11]

Taguchi has referred to functional variations of products as *noise*, of which he identifies three types:

Outer noise.	Environmental conditions, such as temperature, differences in customer use, or other variables

Inner noise.	In the deterioration of product elements or materials
Variational noise.	Individual variability of products

There are two ways to minimize the loss caused by these noises: offline and online measures. Because they come in the design phase, offline measures are the more important of the two. Online measures, which take effect after the product is built, are good for variational noise, but have little or no effect for inner noise or outer noise, being too late in both instances.

Taguchi views the design of a product or a process as a three-phase program consisting of system design, parameter design, and tolerance design, according to Phillip J. Ross in his book, *Taguchi Techniques for Quality Engineering*:

- "System design is the phase when new concepts, ideas, methods, etc., are generated to provide new or improved products to customers."[12]
- Parameter design is crucial to improving the uniformity of a product. Products are subject to a wide degree of operating conditions after purchase, including temperature and humidity. For a product to be robust under such a wide array of conditions, certain parameters of a product or process design must be determined to make the performance less sensitive to variation.
- Tolerance design, which improves quality by tightening tolerances to reduce the performance variation, is used when the efforts of parameter design have not proved adequate in reducing variation.[13]

In Taguchi's parameter design method, "the meaning of quality improvement is changed from problem solving to reducing variability around target values, with the important point being how to measure quality improvement,"[14] writes Lawrence P. Sullivan in an article in *Quality Progress*. "Spec limits or tolerances that theoretically represent engineering needs are no longer acceptable."[15]

"This requires a change in marketing intelligence and engineering knowledge to develop target values that are at the best level for function, fit, or appearance,"[16] writes Sullivan. "When target values are established, the engineering function must optimize product designs early in the product development stage, especially where conflicting requirements exist. Trade-offs and compromises are eliminated where possible, or moved to the last stages of product development."[17]

The need for this tightening of product parameters is a function of today's complex products. Complex products cannot be robust when manufactured under a system of specifications, Taguchi notes, because of defect "stacking" (that is, the accumulation of products just within the specification limits). "Robustness," he says, "derives from consistency. Where deviation is consistent, adjustment to the target is possible; catastrophic stack-up is more likely from scattered deviation within specifications than from consistent deviation outside."[18] He uses the case of Ford vs. Mazda as an example:

> "Ford owns about 25% of Mazda and asked the Japanese company to build transmissions for a car it was selling in the United States. Both Ford and Mazda were supposed to build to identical specifications; Ford adopted Zero Defects as its standard. Yet after the cars had been on the road for a while, it became clear that Ford's transmissions were generating far higher warranty costs and many more customer complaints about noise.
>
> To its credit, Ford disassembled and carefully measured samples of transmissions made by both companies. At first, Ford engineers thought their gauges were malfunctioning. Ford parts were all in-spec, but Mazda gearboxes betrayed no variability at all from targets. Could that be why Mazda incurred lower production, scrap, rework, and warranty costs?
>
> That was precisely the reason. Imagine that in some Ford transmissions, many components near the outer limits of specified tolerances—defined by the definitions of Zero Defects—were randomly assembled together. Then, many trivial deviations from the target tended to stack up. An otherwise trivial variation in one part exacerbated a variation in another. Because of deviations, parts interacted with greater friction than they could withstand individually or with greater vibration than customers were prepared to endure.
>
> Mazda managers worked consistently to bring parts in on target. Intuitively, they took a much more imaginative approach to online quality control than Ford managers did; they certainly grasped factor conformance in a way that superseded the pass/fail, in-spec/out-of-

> spec style of thinking associated with Zero Defects. Mazda managers worked on the assumption that robustness begins from meeting exact targets consistently—not from always staying within tolerances."[19]

REDEFINING COSTS

By loosening tolerances and only concentrating on important product design features, Taguchi's methods produce higher-quality products for lower costs. "Indeed—though not nearly so obvious—an inherent lack of robustness in product design is the primary driver of superfluous manufacturing expenses,"[20] Taguchi writes. The cost of quality losses cannot be reckoned only by the costs of defective products; high quality is not equivalent to zero defects. "The more a manufacturer deviates from specific targets, the greater its losses. Overall loss is quality loss plus factor loss."[21]

From this thought, Taguchi developed the quality loss function, a quadratic formula designed to roughly approximate the geometric increase in losses from not meeting targets; "loss increases by the square of deviation from the target value, where the constant is determined by the cost of the countermeasure that the factory might use to get on target"[22] (see Figures 12.1 and 12.2).

In other words, he writes, "Let's say a car manufacturer chooses not to spend, say, $20 per transmission to get a gear exactly on target. Quality loss function suggests that the manufacturer would wind up spending (when customers got mad) $80 for two standard deviations from the target ($20 multiplied by the square of the two), $180 for three, $320 for four, and so forth."[23]

"The quality loss function creates an economic perspective that redefines the traditional cost control guidelines under which most U.S. companies operate,"[24] Sullivan wrote. "Every major company has a financial system with payback ratios for capital expenditures and product design improvements. The quality loss function quantifies annual cost savings as product characteristics improve toward target values even when they are within specification. This puts a whole new economic perspective on quality and encourages continual improvement as a method to reduce costs."[25]

For example, according to Taguchi's Methods, only after ex-

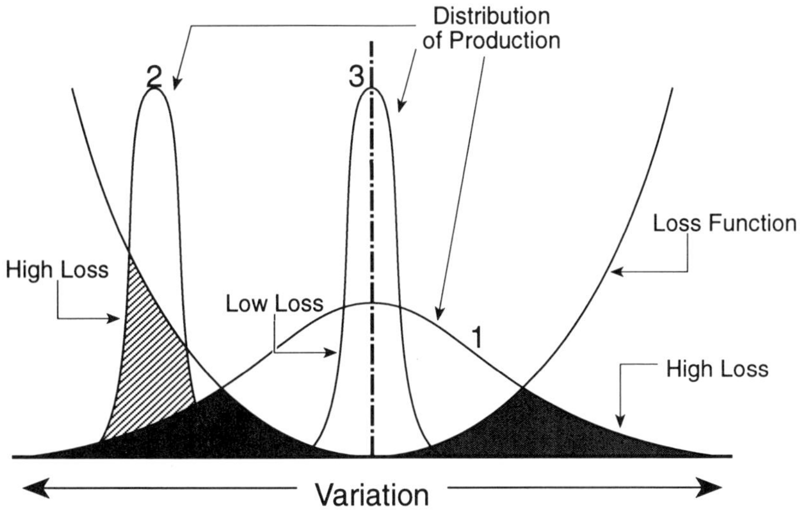

FIGURE 12.1. Taguchi's Quality Loss Function.

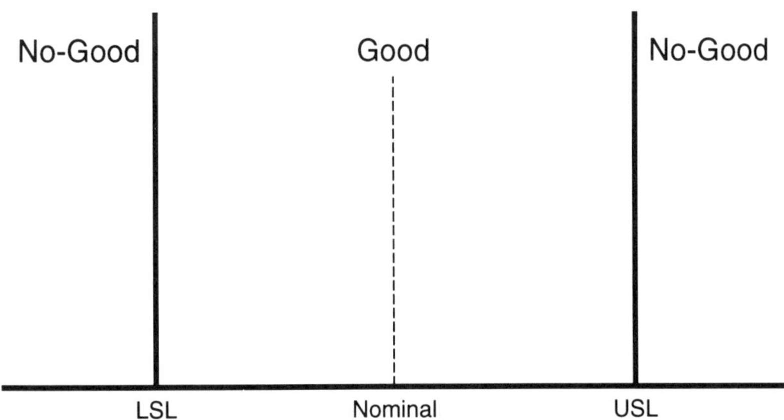

FIGURE 12.2. Normal Manufacturing Goal.

hausting the possibility of creating a robust product with inexpensive materials should an engineer use more expensive products.

Taguchi has stirred some debate with his use of orthogonal arrays to pinpoint areas where variation might be reduced. Orthogonal arrays originally were proposed by Sir Ronald Fisher, who developed them as a strategy for systematic experimentation. Taguchi's orthogonal arrays method allows few trials to produce exacting results, thus saving costly experimental trials during the product design stage. Management then simply examines the production cost of a product plus the quality loss function (from expected deviations) to decide which of competing factory processes to use and determine if the savings are worth the future losses.

Invariably, says Taguchi, management finds that "You gain nothing in shipping a product that barely satisfies corporate standards over one that just fails."[26] Getting on target, not staying in spec, is what produces low-cost quality.

Taguchi has been well-honored for his efforts. He has received a Deming Prize on three separate occasions for contributions in the field of quality engineering. He received the Willard F. Rockwell Medal in 1986 for "combining engineering and statistical methods to achieve rapid improvements in costs and quality by optimizing product design and manufacturing processes."[27] And he was awarded the Blue Ribbon Award from the Emperor of Japan in 1990 for his contribution to the industry. His loss function concept has provided a new understanding of how to aim for higher quality in products, and given him a worldwide reputation as a quality master.

13 Noriaki Kano

Quality is like a house, suggests Noriaki Kano; it must be built well and maintained or it will crumble.

That simple explanation highlights the clear and insightful explanations offered to organizations by Kano, one of Japan's most respected quality experts. Indeed, he may be best known for his House of Total Quality Control theory and graphic, which provide a model for understanding quality and what it demands of those who wish to achieve it.

An applied chemistry major at the University of Tokyo, Kano earned a masters of engineering degree in 1966 and a doctorate in 1970 under the supervision of Kaoru Ishikawa. His extensive international experience includes consulting and lecturing in dozens of nations, including every country in North America. Kano also has been active with the Japanese Union of Scientists and Engineers, the Japanese Standards Association, the Deming Prize Committee, the Japanese Society for Quality Control, the American Society for Quality Control, and several other committees and publications.

Kano's House of TQC demonstrates the organizational components of total quality control. (As noted in a previous chapter, the Japanese use the word *control*, because the Japanese have only one word to mean either management or control. In the West, Kano's illustration is often called the House of TQM.) "If we think of Total Quality Management as a complex, interconnected structure of ideas, practices and values, it may be compared to a house,"[1] Kano says (see Figure 13.1). The ground beneath the house represents the general education and mores of society.

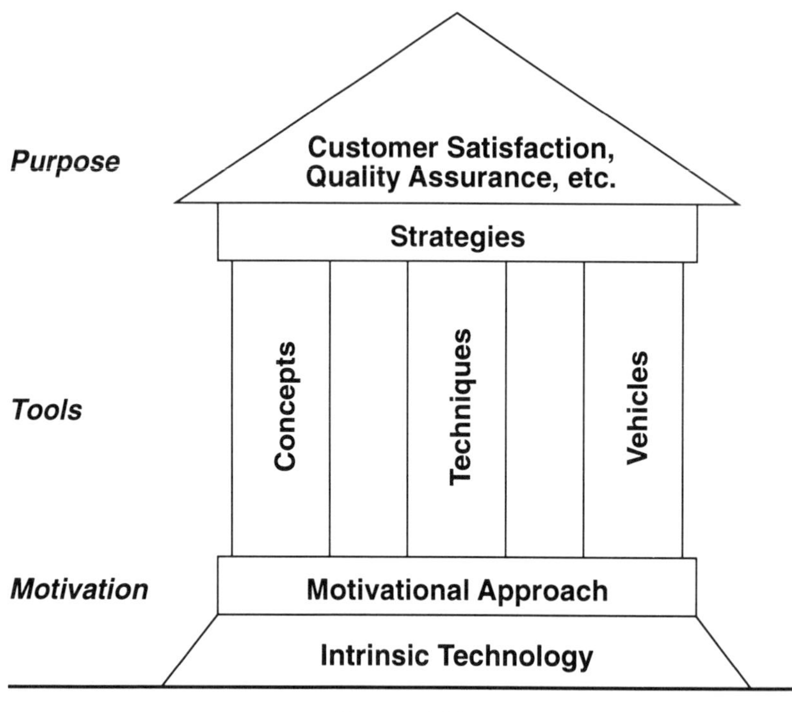

FIGURE 13.1. Kano's House of Total Quality (Reprinted by permission of Noriaki Kano from his paper, "The Right Way to Quality," delivered to the 1993 World Quality Congress).

Upon that rests the organizational foundation of intrinsic technology, then a ground floor of motivational approaches. Three pillars, concepts, techniques and vehicles, hold up the roof of the organization, that is, its purpose, which is assuring quality.

INTRINSIC TECHNOLOGY

Intrinsic technology is the business's driving technology. For instance, electrical engineering is intrinsic to the electric or electronics industry. It depends on having people educated in that specialty who serve as the foundation for the business.

MOTIVATIONAL APPROACH

Once the intrinsic technology is in place, there still must be a motivation for quality. Kano has called this the "sweating work,"[2] that is, promoting standardization, educating and training, collecting and analyzing data and other work to achieve quality. "The problem is this: How to create the conditions that will impel management and employees to take up such sweating work," Kano observes. Success depends on this sweat.

According to Kano, there are two approaches that make people sweat. One is labeled CLSQ for Crisis Consciousness and Leadership Make People Sweat for Quality; the second is VLSQ, which stands for Vision and Leadership Make People Sweat for Quality. The Crisis Consciousness approach occurs when an organization (or a nation, for that matter) feels the need to achieve a breakthrough in quality, a need to improve and stay competitive. Crisis Consciousness marks the outset of a growing business or quality effort or economic effort by a nation. The Vision and Leadership approach is the mark of a more mature quality effort. The Vision and Leadership approach may lead a company into a new enterprise or innovation of new products or services. Often an organization begins with the Crisis Consciousness approach and matures into the Vision and Leadership approach.[3]

The United States is an example. Quality efforts nationwide began in the late 1970s with the awareness that foreign competition was weakening major U.S. industries. Some of those industries, such as the automobile industry, responded by beginning quality efforts, which led to greater competitiveness during the 1990s.

Either path, Crisis Consciousness or Vision, should lead to what Kano terms *Quality Consciousness*, a secondary, more mature motivation for quality. In no case, however, can quality advance without leadership. The organization must be guided by people willing to lead its employees in spending the time and energy for quality, what Kano calls "a tough and sweaty job."[4]

STRATEGIES FOR QUALITY

Companies just beginning quality efforts frequently do so without first developing a strategy for quality, Kano says. Others develop strategies in the belief that if a strategy is good, its aim will eventually be realized. He adds, however, "if we do not take care of how to realize the strategy, it will not automatically succeed, no matter how good the idea. Thus, we need to install a system for both preparing a plan to execute strategy and a plan to precisely measure results and improvements"[5] from quality efforts.

COMMON ERRORS

Kano also warns managers to guard against certain common errors that often defeat quality efforts. He lists three:

- *Chasing too many rabbits at once.* Companies seeking to establish management by policy often set up too many strategies to implement. Even organizations cautioned to avoid this trap forget during the early stages, resulting in poor performance in some areas.
- *Inadequate data analysis regarding current status; a preference for pursuing dreams.* When top executives choose strategies, they tend to chase their dreams rather than analyze data relevant to the current situation. Dreams are essential, but it takes years of sweat to realize them. Managers first should identify, through data, the current status of product or service quality, tackling specific chronic problems first.
- *Insufficient Cross-Functional Coordination.* An example is a company that sets up a strategy to develop a new product with specific targets for sales and profit. At the end of the sales period, the company achieves its sales target, but falls short on its profit target. The product incurs unexpectedly high warranty costs because of poor reliability design and inadequate design review. Marketed with only new product development in mind, the designers never contact the service department, which might advise them on reliability, an example of poor strategy preparation.[6]

Organizations may share common concepts, techniques, and vehicles for promoting quality but still be very different in achieving success with them. They may even have the same level of intrinsic technology and exist in the same society, yet attain different results. The difference, Kano says, lies in the differing strengths of motivation for quality—their willingness to sweat—and variations in their strategies. Attention must focus on both, he insists, before concepts, techniques, and vehicles work to their maximum potential.

CONCEPTS

Once management has a strategy and the willingness to sweat, it must choose or develop the concepts to hold up part of its house. Concepts show how to proceed from the organization's particular view of its industry, society, or other situation. Concepts consist of a quality theory or philosophy and a theory of management. The philosophy might be something like, "quality is customer satisfaction" or "the next processes are our customers." A theory of management might be summed up by such statements as "building quality into processes," "managing by facts," or simply "plan, do, study, and act."

TECHNIQUES

Management must choose how it carries out its concepts; that is, it must choose the tools for doing so. These may be such quality control tools as histograms, control charts, run charts, or other data-gathering and analytical tools (see Chapter 17). The Japanese believe in using a series of data and analytical tools, expressing them in a chart called the *QC Story*. (An American version of this chart, called the *Quality Journal*, is explained in Chapter 18.)

VEHICLES

Vehicles are highly important, because they convey management's choices of concepts, techniques, and motivation to the general work force. There are numerous vehicles, and organizations may differ on which they use. In various papers, Kano has listed several vehicles:

- Promotional organization
- Management by policy
- QC Diagnosis
- Education and training
- Quality circles
- Team activity

Promotional Organization

Who should promote quality on a company-wide level? Kano asks. The answer is the key factor to successful implementation. It differs from company to company, but usually rests with someone such as the executive vice president or director. Companies that choose to promote someone in the personnel area to do it seem to encounter difficulty. The newly promoted director, vice president, or quality manager must be able to persuade the highest executives to take action. "When it comes to promoting quality in implementation units—such as a division, factory and branch office—successful results depend on whether or not their heads, general staff, and managers are actively leading the promotion,"[7] Kano writes. "On this point, I found no differences between American and Japanese companies."[8]

Management By Policy

Management by policy begins with the recognition that quality control must be based on business policy. Like other vehicles and concepts and techniques, policy benefits from rotating the PDSA cycle. To do this, managers might use the following steps:

- Make individual/departmental facility plans based on the president's policy on how to make the business plan.
- Discuss and adjust the overall plan in the business plan committee.

- Preparing an actual performance report
- Analyzing differences between performance and the plan
- Checking progress
- Providing feedback on the result of checking actual performance of the previous year to next year's plan

Quality Control Diagnosis

The Quality Control Diagnosis, also known as *QC diagnosis* or *QC audit*, may be the job of internal employees or hired consultants. A presidential diagnosis would be an example of the former, and an audit by a prize committee, such as the Deming Prize one, or possibly an ISO 9000 audit, are examples of the latter. Most importantly, says Kano, "it is a system for checking a company's own quality control system and to clarify its strengths and weaknesses, and to promote its strengths and to improve its weaknesses."[9] Kano prefers the word *diagnosis* instead of *audit* for the Japanese word *kansa*, which means checking. A diagnosis, he notes, is done for the sake of the patient and not to look over the patient's shoulder. Whatever the term used, managers should make sure that they or their designated auditors perform the review with a benevolent, helpful attitude.

Education and Training

American companies promote very intensive training programs for quality, but seem to have difficulty adapting the learning to the workplace. Kano believes this is due to the shortage of seasoned quality experts who can support and encourage managers to promote company-wide quality management.[10] Nevertheless, training, and education are major vehicles for promoting quality, and as the experience factor grows exponentially, the exchange of quality information between companies also grows.

Quality Circles

In 1989, Kano coauthored a book titled *Continuous Improvement: Quality Control Circles in Japanese Industry*. The book analyzes survey data gathered by his co-author, Paul Lillrank, during a six-year stay as a visiting research fellow studying under Kano at the Science University of Tokyo's Department of Management Science. (The first component of Japanese quality to be imported to the West in the early 1970s, quality circles were considered a flop for a time during the 1980s. This was due partly to the failure of management to relate them to the rest of Japanese quality efforts. For some managers, quality circles became a way to assign quality to someone else rather than taking it on themselves. Other managers appeared to believe that quality problems related to low worker morale and saw quality circles as a way to improve morale. Quality circles may be making a comeback, however, under a different label—empowerment teams. These, however, may not function precisely as Japanese quality circles.)

The goals of quality control circle activities are to benefit the company by improving its products and services and to build up people by motivating and training them and providing an environment for growth. The circles use the PDSA cycle (outlined in Chapter 5) and the seven management tools and the Quality Journal (outlined in Chapter 18).

Much of a quality control circle's success is dependent on its *kanji*, the frontline supervisor who advises and coaches the circle's daily activities. The *kanji* helps define projects to work on, advises on technical problems, and provides a role model. Japanese refer to the *kanji* as the linchpin connecting quality control circles and the company's policies and targets.

Quality control circles help make an organization stronger and more flexible, able to correct itself by spontaneous action within the ranks of its employees. Modern manufacturers and service organizations require this kind of flexibility to implement new strategies and processes. The success of Japanese quality control circles illustrates that organizations can create their own subcultures to further organizational goals and human needs.

Cross-Functional Teams

One American twist to the team approach would be cross-functional teams who work on a project and then move on to another.

Sometimes the employees on a project may switch jobs, with each person doing multiple jobs, with the collaboration of their union if necessary.

Management also may become cross-functional to facilitate a companywide approach to quality. Cross-functional management often consists of basic management elements such as quality, cost, quantity and delivery date. It also may balance the work loads of individual departments to ensure objectives are effectively met. Cross-functional management ensures that objectives are mutually linked and that employees know they are linked. Companywide objectives become deployed cross-functionally among operating units together with the methods for achieving them.

BEHAVIORAL SUBSYSTEMS

Using a computer metaphor, Kano has detailed a simple classification of behavioral subsystems, including hardware, software, and humanware:[11]

- *Hardware* describes the physical or measurable objects like technology, raw materials and facilities. There may also be nonmaterial but still such measurable factors as finance, quantitative aspects of markets, and the labor force.
- *Software* refers to rules, routines and institutional arrangements created for a specific purpose, much as computer software tells the computer what to do. Software operates on a "logic of efficiency," addressing how to assure cooperation between individuals and groups. It can be determined and explained through clearly written and well understood rules.
- *Humanware* follows a "logic of sentiment" governed by human feelings, social atmosphere, and traditional notions of how work should be done. It has rules as well, though they may not be explicit and some people may not be aware of them. Humanware behavior, as the term is used in Japan, is influenced by values internalized during a person's socialization at an early age or during the formative time of employment at an organization.

Management of organizations relies on a mix of hardware, software, and humanware methods. Organizations manage hardware through physical setups such as factory layouts, machine specifications and material flow. Software management uses order and rules enforced by administrators. Humanware management operates by establishing common objectives, giving employees the information to make informed decisions and by enthusiasm and a positive environment. (See Figure 13.2.)

Managing quality control circle activities requires managers to invest time and money in hardware resources, including education, compensation, facilities, and executive time; software resources, by providing a structure, organization, and promotion; and humanware resources, through personal effort and enthusiasm, also referred to as the quality control circle promotion style.

Managing hardware is mostly a matter of budgeting funds and executive time to encourage and administer the quality effort.

Managing humanware effectively creates a corporate culture—including a strong set of values—that encourages quality efforts. Managing humanware can also be improved by managing

	HARDWARE	SOFTWARE	HUMANWARE
ORGANIZATION:	Technical	Formal	Informal
LOGIC OF:	Cost	Efficiency	Sentiment
BEHAVIOR GOVERNED BY:	Law *	Rule	Value

* Refers to "law" in the sense of a law of nature.

FIGURE 13.2. Hardware, Software, and Humanware. (Reprinted by permission of the publisher, from Paul Lillrank and Noriaki Kano, *Continuous Improvement: Quality Control Circles in Japanese Industry*, Ann Arbor: Center for Japanese Studies, University of Michigan, 1989, 48.)

software and hardware so that barriers between workers can come down. For instance, changing certain jobs from individual to group tasks and providing greater flexibility and help may facilitate getting work done. Workers may then become more dependent on each other. Quality control circles help to give spontaneous behavior in organizations a direction, making the circles a systematic attempt to manage humanware.[12]

Kano's broad understanding of all aspects of quality, particularly organizational dynamics, have made him one of the most sought-after speakers and consultants worldwide. He represents one of the very aspects of quality he frequently comments on—a mature understanding of quality and what must occur to achieve and continue it. Like a kind uncle, Kano sounds a dire warning for managers who pay lip service to quality: There must be leaders who have a strategy in mind and the willingness to sweat and make others sweat for quality.

III

THE RINGS OF MANAGEMENT

The masters outlined in this book have provided the theories and techniques to pursue quality. The progression becomes clear with knowledge of which expert provided which theory. Each has built on ideas provided by others and in most cases, their ideas have grown (e.g., Deming's evolution of Profound Knowledge). There are others, of course. Studying Fisher, Shewhart developed the concepts that led to the control chart, the starting point—and still one of the chief tools—of modern quality. Akao, building on principles established by Deming, Feigenbaum, and Ishikawa regarding the pursuit of quality in every corner of the organization, developed quality function deployment. The list goes on. Every individual or organizational has put a special emphasis on quality that led to innovations and techniques that led to still others.

How, then, can your organization synthesize all these concepts into a strong, uniform effort that can take it into the next century and—even more—into an everlasting pursuit of perfection?

Deming's system of Profound Knowledge provides the theoretical base for continual improvement. Deming has not specified the tools to use but has provided the overall picture. The tools appear in a concept called here the *Rings of Management* (see Figure 14).

The largest ring *Environment Management*, circumscribes all

FIGURE 14. The Rings of Management.

the others, indicating the absolute necessity of creating the right organizational climate. If the organizational climate fails to support quality improvement processes, the other efforts will die. As the masters say, leadership must use the brainpower of everyone in the organization and create an atmosphere in which everyone feels invited and encouraged to use all their abilities to help reach the organization's vision.

The first inner ring, *Strategy Management*, provides a method for deploying the organization's strategies to every employee or department. The second ring, *Process Management*, refers to the tools and techniques used to improve and innovate processes, services and products. The third ring, *Personal Management*, refers to the actions of individual employees to improve their own work. The overlapping area that includes portions of all three rings is referred to as cross-functional management, which was mandated by Mizuno as a key to spreading quality throughout the organization.

14
Environment Management

Environment Management defines what managers do to transform their own thinking and adopt the new quality philosophy. Creating a quality work environment begins with senior executives establishing and communicating a vision of the company's long-term aim and, then, opening ways to realize that vision. What does the company stand for? What will it provide to society? These are some of the questions the senior managers must answer and communicate. The chapter on Strategy Management probes this further.

To transform the organization to what they envision, managers must fully understand the organization's process, culture, and subcultures. As managers communicate the vision—and the new quality philosophy—they quickly find that some employees are enthused, some are opposed, and most are somewhere in between. It is up to the managers to recognize employees who understand the vision and can lead others in the transformation. Deming addresses this under his first point, establishing "constancy of purpose toward improvement of product and service," (see Chapter 3).

As virtually all of the quality masters have said, management may not delegate quality to others. Instead, they must create and serve on cross-functional and cross-level teams with specific assignment to seek out deviations from Deming's fourteen principles and find ways to improve. The teams work closely with senior managers, members of the executive steering team, who champion the principles and plan the transformation.

Managers, aided by such teams, engage in a systematic exercise of identifying and eliminating the conditions that impede the

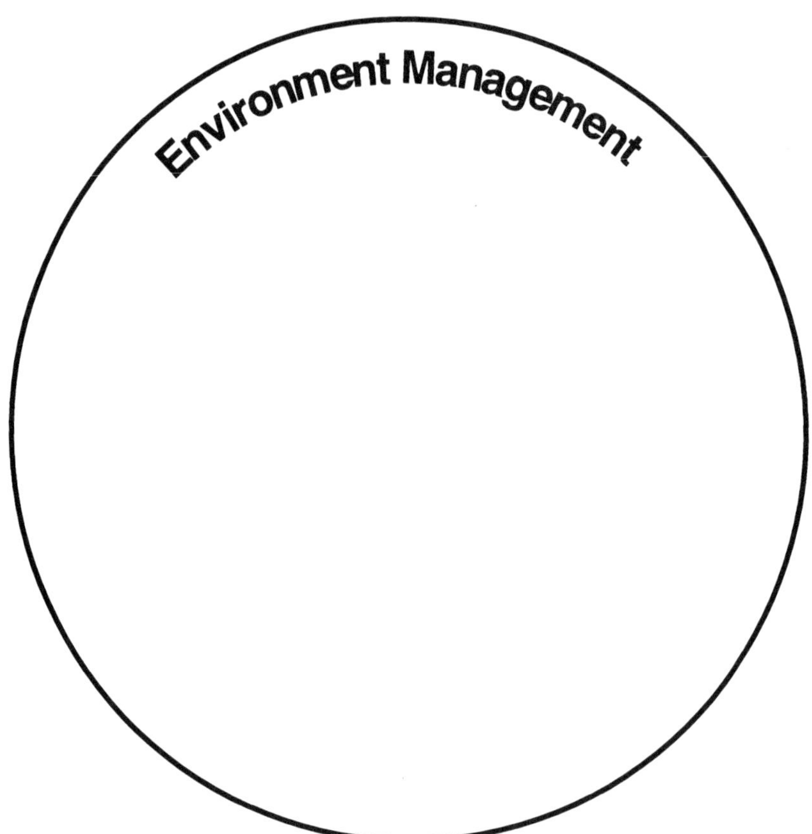

FIGURE 14.1. Environment Management.

path to continuing improvement. Their efforts represent a continuous rotation of the PDSA cycle as initiated by Shewhart and further developed by Deming. Establishing the concept of continual improvement in an important part of these initial steps.

In English there is no single word for continual improvement. The Japanese call it *kaizen*, and many American managers are now familiar with that term. In this book it is called *continual improvement* because that is something that everyone readily understands. Many companies set up continual improvement teams made up of people from every rung of the organizational ladder.

The team may identify barriers to the transformation and recommend ways to infuse the organization with the new management philosophy.

Senior management's commitment to change must be unequivocal and clarified for all employees. Experience shows that people further down in the organization are more receptive to new messages. Senior management, however, must initiate the messages and set an example by following the recommendations of the continuous improvement teams.

Every senior manager performs a critical role in the quality transformation. They cannot merely permit others to pursue quality but must serve as role models by practicing the philosophy and actively using the methods to achieve and maintain a quality culture.

LEADERSHIP

Leadership remains one of the most elusive qualities to define. Nations rise and fall based on leadership; vast corporations and society-changing innovations come from it. Yet defining it and training for it remain difficult.

The best way to define leadership may be to ask the followers. The American Management Association, AT&T, and business consultant Ron Wiley all did this, asking for adjectives to describe a good leader.[1] The results of those efforts are shown in Table 14.1. Wiley concluded that leadership already had been summed up in the Boy Scout manual.

In every survey, honesty stands as the first ingredient. The reasons seem rather obvious. How can people follow someone they cannot believe?

What does a leader do to exhibit these characteristics? On the surface, they seem simple. For instance, honesty means not lying. However, such an explanation tends to offer less than the term itself. These are personality and intellectual traits that make someone a leader. They support a new concept of leadership, based on what followers want in a leader, which is emerging from many quality experts. Deming probably has the most to say about it,

TABLE 14.1 CHARACTERISTICS OF LEADERS

	Ron Wiley[2]	American Management Association	AT&T
1.	Honest	Honest	Honest
2.	Knowledgeable	Competent	Competent
3.	Understanding	Forward Looking	Inspiring
4.	Good Listener	Inspiring	Courageous
5.	Fair	Intelligent	Forward Looking
6.	Considerate	Fair Minded	
7.	Positive	Broad Minded	
8.	Supportive	Straight Forward	
9.	Caring	Imaginative	
10.	Punctual	Dependable	

basing his theory on understanding people and work processes and instilling win-win behavior. Deming defines a leader as "somebody who accomplishes change."[3] He says a leader has three sources of power: the formal power of the leadership position, the force of a leader's personality and a leader's depth of knowledge. Formal power of position, Deming has said, should only be used to change the system—as in fostering a vision for quality. Otherwise, the leader uses personality and depth of knowledge to lead.[4]

The new network of ideas emerging from the demands of quality form the leadership technology of the 21st century. What does this require of a leader? "I think the management of the 21st century is going to be something quite different than we know today," says Kano. "I think that interpretation of theory and interaction of ideas such as we are now doing will become the foundation."[5]

If the foundation of leadership is the ability to interpret theory and understand ideas, then leadership obviously depends on education. That is not to say there are no leaders with, say, only a high school education. In every organization there are leaders who are not well educated and probably not in management, but education can develop their innate leadership abilities. Education itself improves when the educators alter their views of the teaching process and how to improve it. "If you want to improve the student's achievements, put your attention on the teaching/learning process and not on the achievements in examinations,"[6] says Myron Tribus.

Leadership can be trained, and it must be trained if we are meet the challenges of the next century. What do leaders do that makes them leaders?

Beginning with Shewhart's ideas that led to the PDSA wheel, Mogensen's flowcharts, and Deming's flow diagram of an organization viewed as a system, it is clear that leaders must view their organizations holistically. That is, they must think systematically, perceiving each part of the system as part of a continuous cycle. Using statistical tools, the masters showed how to challenge the process, another facet of leadership. These two activities—thinking systematically and challenging the process—imply yet other leadership traits: continuous learning, seeking new knowledge. The teachings of various masters, particularly Deming, call for a new perception of the manager's role, with a strong emphasis on modeling the behavior they wish to encourage in others. Once managers see that they are responsible for the system and that other employees are their customers and best assets, they have a responsibility to create an environment for intrinsic motivation.

So, by distilling the teachings of the quality masters, the leader can identify five broad areas to master and model: thinking and acting systemically, challenging the process, continuously seeking new knowledge, leading the way and creating an environment for intrinsic motivation.

THINKING AND ACTING SYSTEMICALLY

It is often said that Japanese think systemically, or holistically, more so than Westerners. If so, perhaps that explains why they absorbed quickly Feigenbaum's Total Quality Control concept and then expanded it into company-wide quality control. A company, after all, is a system, with each component dependent on the others. It operates in a greater system, society, and has a wide set of codependencies based on relationships with customers, stockholders, suppliers, government agencies, and the general public. Quality, says Mizuno, "requires the integration of such formerly independent functions as raw material purchasing, work procedure analyses"[7] and so on.

Education again plays a key role. One of the benefits of higher education is that it allows a person to see things broadly. Ideally, it is a place for training a leader, who must develop the capacity to envision how an organization will work together and what it will be like when it does.

The AT&T and American Management Association studies call this trait *forward looking*, but vision is a better word. Leaders must inform employees about what is going on in the organization and what shape their roles will take. This begins the process of inspiring a vision for their organization. Employees must be helped to attain a sense of ownership of the organization's long-term goals. Deming says management's role is to supply the aim of the organization. The aim, of course, takes into account how the organization operates as a system.

Leaders must see the whole system broadly. They must understand it enough to anticipate the impact of actions by one unit on the activities of another. For what is meant by a system other than a set of components, functions or activities that work together to achieve a certain end.

Leaders think in terms of the whole system, including the parts they may not be in control of, and work to optimize the whole system and not just their own areas. They think of the system and act for the system. A leader's intervention stems from knowing the difference between chance causes and assignable causes of problems, as Shewhart would call them, or, in Deming's terms, common causes and special causes. Education prepares leaders to know the difference, thus enhancing their ability to guide actions.

When leaders act, they must consider the impact on the whole system. Will it be positive or negative? Will it help the entire system? Juran wisely warns against allowing the achievement of quality in one area to suboptimize overall quality. A leader must act for the benefit of the whole. A car is a system. If one part of the engine is disconnected, other parts will not work well. Organizations, like car engines, have become highly complex, and it is essential that a leader become the high-tech troubleshooter of the modern organization.

An organization runs optimally when its leader practices win-win behavior. Deming refers to this as the theory of life. The theory of living is to practice win-win, to cooperate, to collaborate, to help each other. The clarity of the vision is essential to maintain a constancy of purpose. Leaders make decisions designed to stay with the vision and keep the components of the system in harmony with each other. Followers gravitate toward those with a clear sense of direction and the ability to act in line with that direction at all times.

CHALLENGING THE PROCESS

Along with understanding a system, leaders must understand the processes in the system. They must know what is going on right now, what the employees are doing and why they are doing it. Quality processes are achieved by learning about and applying statistical tools: Shewhart's control charts and scatter diagrams; Pareto's principle popularized by Juran; Mogensen's flowcharts; Ishikawa's cause-and-effect diagrams; and Akao's quality function deployment analyses. What do these tools and techniques do? They help promote understanding of—and reduce—the variation that exists in every process and give the means to develop higher quality products and services. A train does not arrive at the same time every day, no matter how efficient the engineer is. What does this variation signify? Is the system working better, worse, or about the same? A process gives different results every time, so the leader must know how to assemble and study the data to know what is happening. Shewhart first showed how to examine processes through control charts and other tools, which subsequent thinkers expanded on. Collectively their work allows issues to be probed with penetrating analyses and processes to be ceaselessly challenged.

Consultants have estimated the amount of waste and rework in manufacturing is about 35%. In such service functions as in administration, it is anywhere from 60 to 90%. Feigenbaum's hidden plant best illustrates this problem. By understanding variation and using statistical methods, leaders can identify—and find ways to eliminate—the waste and rework that exist in every process. That is why they must find the time and pay the costs for quality improvement. Then they can simplify the processes and eliminate complexity. After the process has been simplified, the organization can strive for continual improvement and innovation. By understanding processes, variation, and statistical methods, leaders can challenge the status quo—that is, the processes as they exist. Work processes always change, and the leader must be the catalyst for some of that change.

Most innovations come from ideas external to the organization or its management. By sharing problems and opportunities, the leader opens the door to the opinions of others who may provide solutions and innovations. Managers who discount the ideas of those who do not share the commonly accepted limits of the system deny themselves access to a wellspring of ideas. Sometimes leaders encounter rationalizations from employees as to why new ideas should be disregarded: "They don't understand how we work here" or "They haven't been working in our industry." The leaders' role is to explain that though these statements may be accurate, the idea of listening to others is to gain their fresh perspectives on what others do and how they do it.

These outside ideas provide leaders with opportunities to exercise another aspect of leadership—the chance to break old paradigms. This is where force of personality and depth of knowledge come in. When leaders hear that something has always been done a certain way, they should sense an opportunity. Many processes continue to exist because no one challenges their current or future usefulness. Sometimes the originator moves on, but the process has a life of its own and continues. For example, in one company, accounting employees were frustrated because some of the work was not getting done. Management refused to add more people. A Pareto analysis of their work revealed that 25% of their time was spent on a particular task. They developed a flowchart of the task but could not determine who used the output from the task. When advised of the dilemma, the vice president for finance instructed them to stop doing the task in question and see who screamed. They did so, and no one screamed.

A search for customers, the users of output, and discussions of how to improve or simplify the output, usually improve most processes. Initially, total quality management may present a problem, because it requires taking time from a busy schedule. Simple flow-charting of the work processes and discussions with customers, coupled with an open mind and a desire to improve, can simplify the processes and establish ways to remove waste and rework. When that happens, time for quality work becomes available.

CONTINUOUSLY SEEK TO ACQUIRE KNOWLEDGE

Quality, Ishikawa notes, begins and ends with education.[8] The fact is, the world is changing so fast that everyone must learn more and study harder than ever before. Leaders must be learners, always looking for new information and ways to meet the aim of the organization. Leaders, however, cannot possibly know all there is to know nowadays. They must rely on others and must encourage them to learn constantly and provide them with means and opportunities to do so. This has the effect of empowering people to take more responsibility and develop themselves as far as they can go. Ishikawa says education "generally increases people's span of control; that is, the number of people they can manage, and makes them more able to delegate authority."[9]

Leaders must understand the differences in how people learn. Do they learn by experience? By reading? By being told? Leaders must also understand the underlying theory of knowledge, how knowledge is obtained and how it is used. Deming says that experience alone teaches nothing; there must be a theory to accompany the experience.

Consistent with Deming's thoughts are those of Professor Richard Bawden of the University of Western Sydney in Australia. Two people might have the same experience, but learn different things from it because they are seeing the experience through their own windows (see Figure 14.2). These windows are formed through education and previous experience and can be likened to knowledge. Then, the two individuals ponder their view of the experience, forming theories about the experience. Bawden calls this step thinking; it results in theory to be supported or dis-

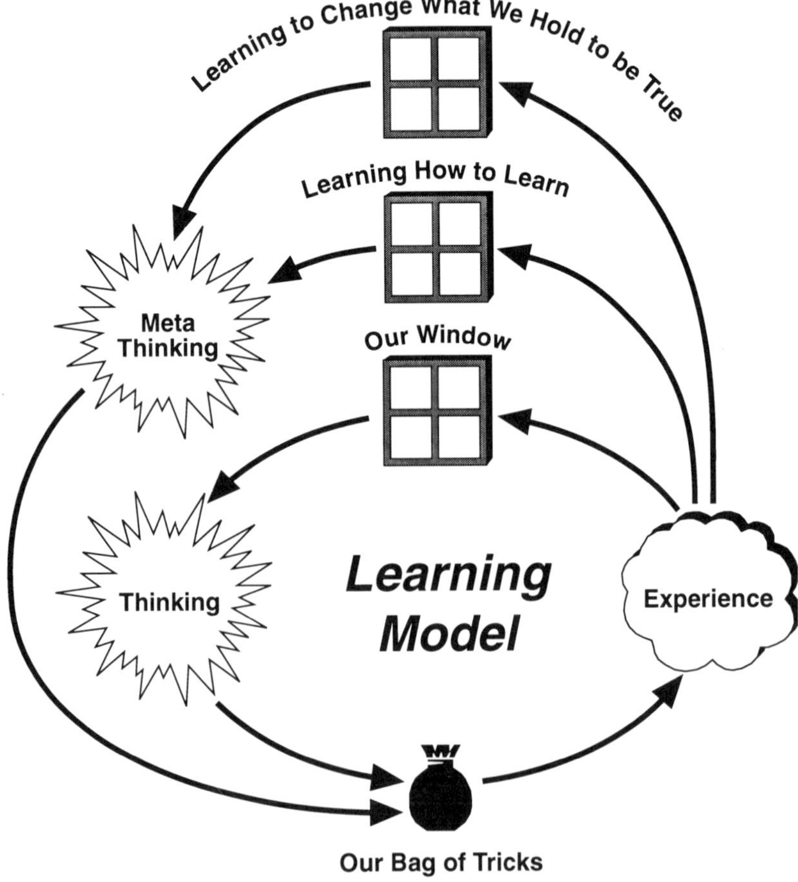

FIGURE 14.2. Learning to Create a Quality Culture.
(SOURCE: Dr. Richard Bowden, University of Western Sydney, Hawkesbury, Richmond NSW, Australia.)

proved. The following step is to take action to alter or improve the experience through knowhow acquired by training, or as Bawden states, using the individual's "bag of tricks."[10] This continuous cycle—increasing knowledge and know-how through experience and theory development—constitutes the learning cycle. Bawden then elevates his model to another level by improving the knowledge of how people learn and raising thinking to a metalevel. A still higher level is attained by breaking old paradigms through learning how to change what is held to be true.

Variation exists in the learning process as in all others because people learn in different ways. An older generation of workers in the U.S. is "paper trained"; that is, they tend to learn by reading. The latest generation tends to better utilize more of their senses by taking advantage of audio and video tapes. Many people learn better by doing.

Once documented and retained, lessons learned from experience and theory help others in the organization to know what their leaders are doing, making it easier to assist in these efforts. As Ishikawa says, "No good work can be expected if supervisors jealously guard their working secrets and fail to teach them to subordinates."[11]

LEADING THE WAY

Leaders lead; they model the way. For instance, Figure 14.3 shows three people with a team of horses. One is sitting in the driver's seat driving a team of horses with a whip in hand. Another is out in front of the horses leading them, and the third is sitting in

FIGURE 14.3. Leadership.

the wagon, hoping the horses are headed in the right direction. Traditionally managers have behaved autocratically, with a whip in hand. In 21st century leadership, that is not the way; instead, leaders must enable and empower. Certainly sitting in the back of the wagon, hoping to arrive on time in the right place, is not the way to lead. A leader must be up front, leading the horses down the trail, making sure they are going in the right direction. This way a leader enables and trains others to solve problems, empowers them to make decisions.

Many managers often state that their employees are their most valuable asset, but they tend to utilize only part of that asset—the body. They do not optimize their use of employee brainpower. Those who are closest to the work most often are the most insightful thoughts about it. "People are never foolproof but they can be taught and encouraged to be self-correcting," Mogensen says. "Don't turn over the design of systems to people who don't really know what it is like to do the work."[12] Managers often suboptimize their most valuable asset when they forget to use employees' brains.

If leaders say they want the whole person but act like they want only the body, they undermine their own most precious asset—credibility. A leader's credibility is developed by actions over time. This determines the type and magnitude of the followership.

Employees must feel that leaders truly understand their needs and wants and are dedicated to meeting them. There is no substitute for communicating with employees to understand their dreams. Communications has two parts: sending and receiving. Leaders share their thoughts and feelings on the performance and outlook of the future of the organization in clear, succinct terms. At least half their communications time, however, must involve listening to the thoughts and emotions of others. Leaders are obliged, therefore, to spend time refining their listening and speaking skills, particularly the listening skills, because those serve to educate and sensitize. They need to know what questions to ask, how to actively take an interest in the answers, and to be quiet so they can hear. No one learns by talking but by listening. Deming set the example for this. In almost every plant he visited,

Deming met with average employees to hear their views. Often he scolded management for not doing the same.

Leaders are risk-takers. Success, as Kano notes, depends on sweat. Leaders know that getting to the pot at the end of the rainbow is not on a well-trod path. They listen to the thoughts of others, employees, and customers, and then take action. Leaders encourage others to take risks and challenge themselves. To do this, leaders must have a keen sense of the limits of the organization and the individuals they may call on to take risks. New tasks that are easy have little motivational value, while those that are too hard stifle individual or the group spirit. Leaders know what their followers can do and how to stretch them to go just a little further.

Leaders encourage and empower their followers to make decisions and coach them on how to make good decisions and assume new responsibilities. By teaching others to use their own brainpower, the leader develops new resources for the organization. Leaders think and act positively. They visualize their dream, share it with others, and relate all the positive benefits of achieving it. They believe in it and convince others. They build up others, which tends to build the organization. Tearing down others destroys the organization.

AN ENVIRONMENT FOR INTRINSIC MOTIVATION

Why do people work? Do they work for incentives and money, carpet on the floor, name on the door? Or do they work because they want a sense of satisfaction doing something they feel is worthwhile and that they have pride in? Most people are motivated intrinsically by something they do themselves, not something external. Deming noted that everyone is born with a natural inclination to learn and to innovate. Leaders must provide an environment and systems to allow them to achieve it. Juran's breakthrough theory supports this as well and instructs managers to identify needs for improvement and establish the infrastructure to secure continual improvement.

People must be recognized for their accomplishments and share that recognition with others. A leader looks for ways to allow people a sense of pride and accomplishment in their work. People spend so much of life at work it's a shame if they don't have joy in what they do and make it fun for others.

Perhaps the most important ingredient in creating an environment for intrinsic motivation is to build mutual trust and respect in the organization. If leaders have mutual trust and respect, they can accomplish miracles. If they don't, they'll probably accomplish little. "Ethics is important in quality. You have to have trust,"[13] says Deming.

It has been said that money is not a motivator, but it can be a demotivator. So what turns people on?

The greatest motivator is the sense of pride and satisfaction that comes from doing something worthwhile, the inner feeling that comes with a self-satisfying sense of accomplishment. For example, I used to repair radios. When I received one that did not work, performed my trouble shooting, and took action to make it play as good as new, I experienced a good feeling inside. I was proud and happy. After graduating from college, I took a job in sales. I experienced the same feeling when I won a contract, particularly if it was the result of something special. It was the same proud and happy feeling of accomplishment I had when fixing radios. I was so turned on that I redoubled my effort to get more contracts so I could experience that satisfaction again and again. A leader's role is to create that environment in which the employee, having done a job well, experiences pride and satisfaction. It is tremendously more effective than the carrots and sticks of extrinsic motivation.

Meeting with employees to seek true understanding of what gives them the sense of satisfaction and pride, what obstacles they face and to learn their ideas for removing the obstacles and other improvements becomes the true job of a leader. Taking action to provide the opportunities for employees to succeed and grow provides more of sense of satisfaction for the leader and therefore pride and happiness than watching over them and administering carrots and sticks.

Leadership creates an environment where it is possible for

people to satisfy their own needs for a sense of achievement, pride, self-esteem, belonging, and living up to their principles and ideals. Ishikawa notes, "Finding a management posture that enables people to express their human qualities and motivates each individual in this way is one of the most important philosophies of total quality control."[14]

By viewing the organization as a system interacting with society, leaders can focus on their own roles in optimizing the system. They see how the subsystems work together, and where human beings fit in. The new leaders must be part psychologist, with a profound understanding of the inner forces that create a desire in people to want to work and a keen ability to listen to their ideas and wishes. By challenging the process, leaders create an environment in which continuing improvement can occur. By always challenging themselves to learn more and do more, leaders model the behavior of personal management and growth. Given the important characteristics of honesty, competence, understanding, vision and inspiration, leaders lead by modeling these characteristics. They may also lead by coaching and walking with workers through difficult tasks.

PERFORMANCE APPRAISAL AND COMPENSATION

There are two other important factors for leaders to consider in Environment Management—the annual performance appraisal and compensation. Both tend to be obstacles to creating an environment for intrinsic motivation.

PERFORMANCE APPRAISAL

The annual performance appraisal is like inspection at the end of the assembly line: It attempts to weed out what went wrong after it happened. It often makes little effort to improve the process as it occurs or to provide insight as to what caused the result. It usually provides few clues as to what the employee may do better in the future. Deming particularly disliked evaluations, saying they rob people of their right to pride of workmanship.

Many quality experts say controlling people appears to be an aim of the traditional performance appraisal, one of the most frequently cited sources of dissatisfaction with Western management. The appraisals attempt to measure the contributions of individuals in creating a product or service. The information used in the appraisal may be unreliable, because the individuals are caught in the systems and processes given to them by management. The inadequacies of the systems and processes are not taken into account.

Management seeks to reward behavior productivity but succeeds instead in forcing employees to focus on short-term individual goals. Appraisals may also lead to office politics, the destruction of teamwork and discouraging leadership development, because performance tends to cluster around standards set in the appraisals.[15] Employees may become less inclined to take risks.

Employees may seek appraisals so they can know how they are doing but usually come away with few clues. The performance appraisal presents a fundamental obstacle to changing an organization's culture from one of management to one of leadership.[16]

Most people want to do a good job but frequently are discouraged by the system they work in. Deming chastised organizations for such discouragements as "destructive effect of grading in school, . . . the so-called merit system, incentive pay, M.B.O.,"[17] or quotas. "People are born with forces to bring about intrinsic motivation, a yearning for learning, curiosity, inquisitive, eager to learn," he adds. "We crush that out with our system of handling people—from kindergarten and before, the university, and on the job."[18]

Human beings, like organizations and processes, can be optimized or suboptimized, that is, encouraged to live up to or forced not to live up to their potential. The manager's responsibility under the new quality philosophy is to see the organization as a system, made up of people, processes, materials, and facilities. The processes and materials may be mastered using the management tools, but people are different. A suboptimized human is not like a mechanical or procedural error but rather must be described with other words, such as individually depressed, discouraged, or not interested in performing up to ability.

To properly evaluate the individual, the supervisor must adopt a *systems* view, seeing the employee's performance within the context of the system. When that happens, it becomes clear that the individual is only partly accountable for the results of his work processes. It is imperative not to confuse people with systems.

Once the organization shifts from seeing itself as a producer of results to seeing itself as a series of processes, the appraisal based on results no longer applies. The concept of Personal Management (discussed in Chapter 18) takes over, encouraging, supporting, and empowering the employee to take charge of the work processes. Managers meet with employees individually at least each quarter to review progress and roadblocks in improving work processes. Such meetings become coaching sessions—not evaluations—where the manager seeks to help the employee dismantle roadblocks.

COMPENSATION

Compensation figures heavily into any discussion of fair or equal treatment in the work place. Many organizations are rife with animosities created when one employee hears through the grapevine that another employee just got a raise. The skyrocketing levels of some executive salaries in the United States often stir controversy. Western societies tend to believe that if an individual can persuade an organization to pay an astronomical compensation, the individual must be worth it. This blind acceptance fosters escalating salaries for executives, entertainers, and professional athletes.

The Japanese system for compensation is a good one to study because it attempts to be fair to everyone. The Japanese have a strong notion of what they call *wa*, which means *harmony* in English. Japanese executives typically are compensated on a fixed scale, taking into account level of training or education, seniority, number of dependents, and position in the company. Japanese compensation schemes attempt to achieve harmony in the pay scale. Needs are categorized according to employee age groups, taking into account marital status, and number of dependents. Blue collar workers also are paid on a salary basis, though similar gradations are also observed.

Pay levels for full-time employees are altered every year, taking into account market level, living costs, and the company's ability to pay. Allowances are also made for meals, dependents, commuting costs, and other such expenses. Seniority pay is provided, independent of job value and the work being performed. Job evaluation (i.e., the value of the position), merit pay, and bonuses are added to seniority pay. Bonuses in the Japanese system are typically given twice a year and average a total of about 4.7 months' pay and are dependent on the profitability of the organization.

Human beings are highly sensitive, requiring careful treatment by managers and peers. Treated with respect, people eagerly participate in improvements to the system, as called for by most of our experts. First, management must remove the obstacles to their participation—and to their enthusiasm.

15
Strategy Management

Strategy, like leadership, is an elusive concept. Merriam-Webster's dictionary defines it as "the science and art" of conducting a major campaign to achieve some objective. Strategy is the idea on how to achieve goals. It is based partly on prediction. That is, if certain activities are carried out effectively, the aim is achieved. Of all the quality theorists outlined in this book, Deming has made it clear that the leadership of the organization must determine its aim and establish a system for getting all employees involved in it. Management must determine where the organization is headed in the long term, and what ideal conditions, strategies, and values can get it there.

Great strategists no doubt use both science and art to develop and execute their plans. What about managers of organizations today? Can they be expected to mix science and art to develop and execute strategy? Some can, but most need to learn how to carry out a strategy.

Actually, most North American managers excel at planning strategies—whether for business, government or other endeavors. Their planning is probably the best in the world. When it comes time to carry out a planned strategy, however, they seem to lag behind some of their foreign competitors. Plans gather dust until it is time to write another one for next year.

Why is this so? U.S. companies lack a system of management for deploying strategies down through the organization. Kano notes that many organizations develop sound strategies only to fail to carry them out. Juran, noting the lack of organization to execute a strategy, developed a six-step program to put strategy to work.

FIGURE 15.1. Strategy Management.

Strategy Management goes further, offering a system for doing that, and for communicating the plans and organizational aim to the whole organization to get all employees focused in the same direction.

As noted in the chapter on Environment Management, a leader must see the organization as a system, with each part interacting with the others and with outside systems, including the larger system we call society. The organization must have an aim, expressed in a vision, a mission and values. The aim must be a vision of the future desired and endorsed by the organization's stakeholders. Who are the stakeholders? They include customers, employees, and stockholders, many of whom may have very different views of where the organization should be going. The purpose of Strategy Management is to help them acquire a common understanding for the company's long-term direction, so that all can be enlisted in a crusade to get there.

The crucial first step comes from the chief executive, who, perceiving a need to improve strategy execution, decides to act. An outside consultant may help to guide the steps that follow.

STRATEGY DEVELOPMENT

A workshop or retreat should be scheduled, with a preliminary or kick-off meeting scheduled about a month in advance of it. In this preliminary meeting of the planning team, usually the top executive and those who report directly to this executive, are presented a flowchart of the Strategy Management process. After the explanation of the process, the top executive presents the grid of planning components with the names of those on the planning team. Each of them is assigned a component, with responsibility for conducting the necessary research and developing a draft statement of the component to be presented at the workshop. Secondary responsibility may also be assigned if two- or three-person teams are desired. The balance of the day is spent with one-on-one meetings with the individuals with primary responsibility and a consultant discussing the assignments (see Figure 15.2).

For example, the individual assigned to customers' needs/wants has to research results from such sources as customer surveys, customer service reports, customer critiques, results from customer visits, complaints, and warranty claims. Additional customer contact may be required for additional information. These are not easy assignments, but usually the individuals handling them perform well because they realize the significance of the assignment.

During the workshop, these individuals present their data to the rest of the team and lead the discussion to modify their component until they reach a consensus.

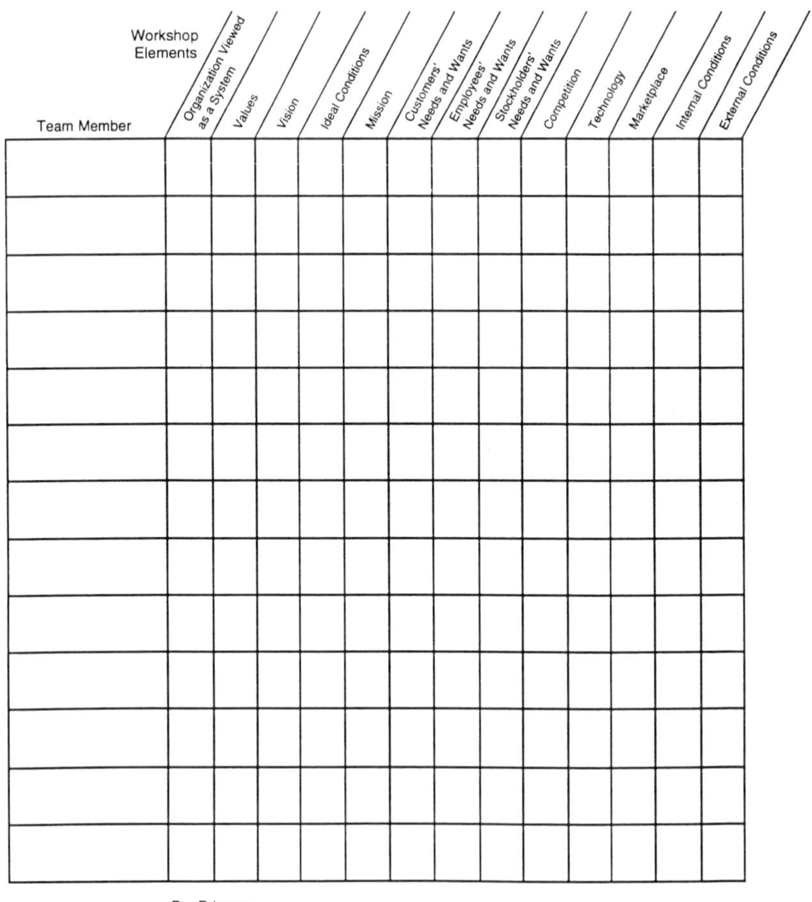

FIGURE 15.2. Strategy Plan Assignments.

The top executive should retain the primary responsibility for drafting a vision statement and for diagramming the enterprise viewed as a system (see Figure 15.3).

The chapter on Deming examined his simple diagram of an enterprise viewed as a system. The diagram starts with suppliers of materials and equipment on the left hand side and ends with

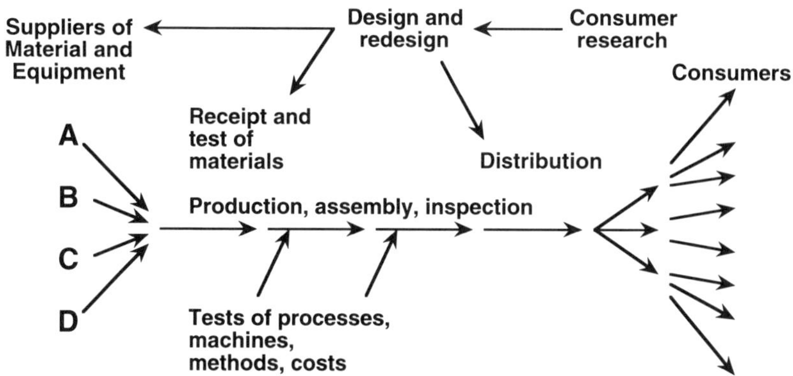

FIGURE 15.3. Enterprise Viewed as a System. (Reprinted from *Out of Crisis* by W. Edwards Deming by permission of MIT and W. Edwards Deming. Published by MIT, Center for Advanced Engineering Study, Cambridge MA 02139. Copyright 1986 by W. Edwards Deming.)

the consumers on the right. This very useful diagram shows who the internal customers and suppliers are, direct and indirect contributions, and how the system is viewed by the product or service itself. Usually, the top executive draws the diagram, since he or she is responsible for optimizing the system. It might be useful for the executive to begin at the loading dock, or some other point of supply entry to the organization and draw the operation while walking through it. Another way would be to start with a customer order and follow it through the organization until it reaches the consumer. The executive should talk with employees along the way, asking if anything has been omitted or does not function as drawn in the chart. The objective of this exercise is to get everyone focused on the organization as a system, unencumbered by rigid departmental or functional boundaries.

The workshop opens with the executive presenting the diagram and leading a discussion to achieve a consensus. The top executive's flowchart helps everyone understand the company as a system. Managers, and even top executives, may struggle with the flowchart, because everyone has a different notion of how the organization works; but the discussion should lead to consensus. The flowchart may be refined during the workshop.

After consensus is reached on the view of the organization as a system, the executive asks each member of the planning team to come forward individually to respond to the following nine questions:

- What is my job?
- Where do I fit in the system?
- Who is my internal customer?
- When did we last get together to define quality?
- What prevents me from delivering quality to my customers?
- How do I measure and track quality as understood by the customer?
- Who is my internal supplier?
- When did I last talk to the supplier about quality?
- Is my supplier able to deliver quality?

Managers may find it embarrassing to answer the questions out loud in front of other managers. The intent, however, is to get everyone thinking on the same plane about what is really important, how they interact with internal suppliers, and what might be done to improve the process between them.

Later, they will develop a one-page Strategy Profile and generate the information to support the profile.

The Strategy Profile

Dr. Shelia Sheinberg of the Center for Life Cycle Sciences in Port Orchard, Washington, tells a story about her five-year-old son, Jonathan, who received a puzzle for Christmas. Jonathan sought help from mom and dad in putting the puzzle together. They could find no box and no picture of what the puzzle was supposed to look like. Faced with the child's pleading, they took three days trying to figure out the puzzle without success. When Dr. Sheinberg was putting out the trash, however, she noticed the word *puzzle* written on something. Jonathan had taken the puzzle out of its box without fully unwrapping it and consequently had not been able to tell his parents where the picture was. Without the picture, the puzzle remained just that, a puzzle. With the picture, they put the puzzle together in three hours.

The moral of the story is that leaders need a picture of what they intend to achieve, in business and other organizations as much as they do in putting together a jigsaw puzzle.

Leaders begin with basic questions. What are the needs and wants of the customers? What about our employees? Stockholders? Not just what they want or need today but tomorrow as well. All these needs and wants must be carefully considered and listed in the Strategy Profile so the strategy can be understood as it moves from management into the daily processes of the organization (see Figure 15.4). Everyone will then be encouraged to move forward together. The Strategy Profile has been also called *strategy mural* or *strategy plan*, but the components remain much the same: short statements spelling out the organization's understanding of customer's, employee's, and stockholder's needs and wants, the strategies and this year's major actions, the organization's guiding values, vision, mission, and ideal conditions.

Customers

Deming often said the customer's expectations are shaped by what companies lead them to believe they can get. If a company is not out in front giving them more than they asked for, competitors might do so and raise their expectations. A company should always be working to delight its customers and creating a situation where they enthusiastically boast about the benefits of doing business with the company. In identifying the customer's needs and wants,* a company must gather actual data from them and, possibly, even from their customers. This needs to be augmented by what research shows might be available tomorrow. The customers' needs and wants should be based on data, plus a prediction of the future. Then a company can provide that extra something that creates enthusiasm in the relationship.

* *Wants* are expectations established by a company and its competitors; *needs* are more than that, so both must be examined.

Needs

Customers' Needs/Wants

- Results
- Total customer satisfaction
- More behavior related training
- A partnership
- Knowledge of field
- Do it quick
- Positioned for long-term

Employees' Needs/Wants

- Learning culture
- Respect
- Viable strategic direction
- Capable management
- Fair compensation
- Professional development

Stockholders' Needs/Wants

- Improve revenue
- Employee ownership
- Market leadership
- Customer orientation
- Improve profitability

Method

Strategic Initiatives

- Achieve revenue growth
- Focus on customers' results
- Create products from services
- Leverage our intellectual capital

Quality Policy

PMI provides products and services to help our customers improve their performance. We continually improve and innovate our processes to exceed our customers' needs and increase the quality of work life of our employees. We assess our processes and procedures against international standards, as well as our own high standards.

Values

We believe…

- that respect for both individual aspirations and collaborative interactions are the cornerstone for building a trustful community of invested employees
- that serving our customers is not simply a business strategy, but an ethical imperative
- that continuous learning, improvement, and innovation is basic to whom and what we are
- that personal integrity, openness, and commitment are essential to our lasting success
- in recognizing and acting upon opportunities to give back to and sustain our natural environment and community
- that organization change and individual change are a system; they need and support each other
- that the wisdom and applicability of Deming's teachings are the core inspiration and catalyst for our work

Aim

Vision

The bridge to never-ending learning, improvement, and innovation

Ideal Conditions

- Mutual trust and respect throughout the organization
- An ample business base of enthusiastic customers
- A community of integrated and aligned associates
- A financially secure organization

Mission

Provide products, services and knowledge that guide our customers to…

- Understand and use principles and methods of process management;
- Focus on customers;
- Promote collaborative approaches; and
- Foster organizational alignment, strategically, culturally, and systemically.

FIGURE 15.4. Strategy Outline.

Employees

The same is true for employees. A company wants them to not only be satisfied with what is provided today, but to make them enthusiastic about the future of the enterprise. Managers must obtain information about the employees' feelings so they can know what is important to the employees. What do they enjoy in their work? Do they feel they are doing something worthwhile? Do they feel the job offers them opportunities for growth? Once they have these and other questions answered, managers can predict of what provides the intrinsic motivation which, Deming noted, is the strongest motivation of all. (For more information, see Chapter 17.)

Stockholders

Stockholders needs and wants also should be based on research. They, too, deserve ample communication on what management intends for the long-term growth of the organization. Obviously, stockholders need to know they will get a return on their financial investment, but they should also be viewed as part of the team. Management must take them into confidence to make them feel part of the long-term aim.

Values

Values drive many of the other items in the strategic plan. They are the ethics, principles, and philosophy of the organization that provide guidance to the people on how to act when they get into difficult situations. They are the basic tenets of the organization.

Vision

When a farmer opens a field, it is important to his pride that the first pass across the field be straight. Subsequent passes are then based on the first one. After all, the results of his efforts are apparent to all his neighbors. He does this by picking a point on the horizon and following the line as closely as possible by gazing steadfastly at the point in the distance without distractions.

Managers may do the same thing, pick a point lying in the future and focus everyone's attention on it to ensure they head in the same direction. With that sort of constancy of purpose, the organization should achieve its vision. Deming recommended creating and publishing to all employees a statement of the aims and purposes of the organization. Management must demonstrate an unwavering commitment to this statement. An effective vision statement should satisfy the following seven criteria:

- It is memorable. It can be recited by every employee without hesitation. If the statement is too long or does not satisfy the other criteria, it probably is not worth remembering.
- It is inspirational. It unites all the employees to achieve the aim. The employees should be sufficiently inspired to voluntarily enlist in a crusade to achieve the vision.
- It satisfies the individuals. It is a force to bring alignments of goals of individuals and the organization.
- It depicts a picture of the future that the employees can visualize or feel. It must be compatible to them and their beliefs.
- It creates excitement. It provides pride and fulfillment at being part of such a worthwhile endeavor.
- It provides guidance. It offers clarity in the unforeseen decision that must be made in today's fast-changing and complex world.
- It is compelling. It must demand and achieve action by each of the employees. Without action there is no gain.

Developing a strong vision may be one of management's most important challenges. As Bishop Paul Washburn of Chicago told the Minnesota United Methodist Conference in June 1972, "We need to be led by a vision of the future as opposed to being pushed by the problems of the present."

Ideal Conditions

The vision must be strong enough to pull the employees toward it. If they do not buy in, there is very little management can do to push them toward the vision. One way of achieving this is for the employees to be able to visualize what their life would be like if the enterprise achieved the vision. What would be the ideal conditions? Financial security? More customers in a certain industry? A different corporate culture? Companies all have notions about ideal conditions. Once listed, they help to focus the vision.

Mission Statement

The mission statement defines the purpose of the organization: what it does, why it is needed, and what makes it unique. It is longer than a vision statement and explains why the organization aspires to the vision. Individuals also may have mission statements (see Chapter 17).

Analysis of Strengths, Weaknesses, Opportunities, Threats and Competition

Strategy becomes clearer with an analysis of the internal and external factors impacting the organization. The analysis should include the following points, taking into consideration the future direction of products and services, government regulations and trade agreements, technology, markets, customers, and the economy.

Strengths. The organization's competencies, capabilities, and other resources used to fulfill the needs of customers. Advantages this organization has over its competitors, resources it has to fulfill the needs of customers, or to contribute to society, unique characteristics that appeal to customers, perceived benefits of this organization to its customers

Weaknesses. A list of vulnerable characteristics that the competition might exploit; reasons, real or perceived, for customers not to avail themselves of the organization's products or services

Opportunities. Significant opportunities for the organization to exploit their strengths through new markets and product or service offerings

Threats. Areas of vulnerability in the marketplace, encompassing the economy and environment trends, legislation, competitive actions, possible market obsolescence or change.

Competition. The major strategies and thrusts of the competition should be studied to understand where they are going and why. This information can be obtained through trade and industries studies and publications, annual or 10-K reports, listening to customers, surveys, and, conversation. Understanding why they are taking certain actions is very important. From this information counteractions can be determined—including development of opportunities, leapfrogging, or opposing action

Strategic Initiatives

Once managers reach a consensus on these items, they can begin to identify the short-term actions to put them on the path to achieving their vision long-term. Normally, there should be no more than six short-term actions, which can be termed *Strategic Initiatives*. Strong leadership is usually essential in achieving a consensus for prioritizing to identify the short-term Strategic Initiatives. These are normally defined in terms of a verb and an object. The top executive should facilitate this discussion and assume responsibility for achieving these actions in a given time frame—normally the fiscal year or other period normally used for strategic planning.

The next activity of the group in starting to identify preliminary strategic initiatives is to compare threats to weaknesses on a matrix chart, as shown in Figure 15.5. When a strong correlation appears between a threat and a weakness, a strategic initiative must be developed to counteract it. This is a defensive action to shore up the weak area.

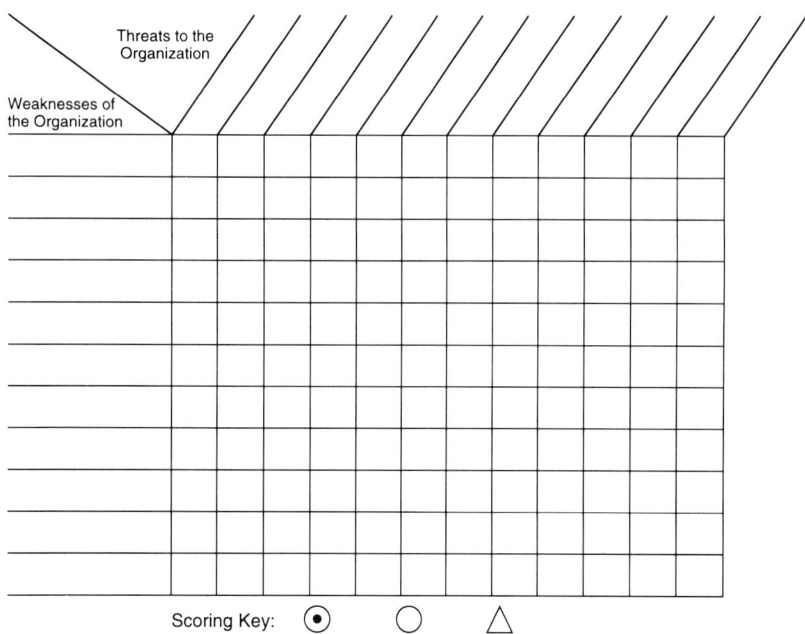

FIGURE 15.5. Weaknesses/Threats Correlation Matrix.

Next, managers should prepare another matrix analysis of opportunities to strengths, as shown in Figure 15.6. Where there is a strong relationship between the two, more preliminary initiatives can be developed to take advantage of opportunities where the organization has the matching strength to capitalize on it. This is offensive action.

Competitive threats and environmental factors could be either threats or opportunities and as such must be examined for other preliminary strategic initiatives.

Having done all this, an organization typically has identified ten or twenty preliminary strategic initiatives, clearly too many to address at one time without losing focus on the most important. As Juran said, there must be focus on the important few and not the trivial many. Fortunately, a tool is available to help identify the critical strategic initiatives and to marshal the resources of the

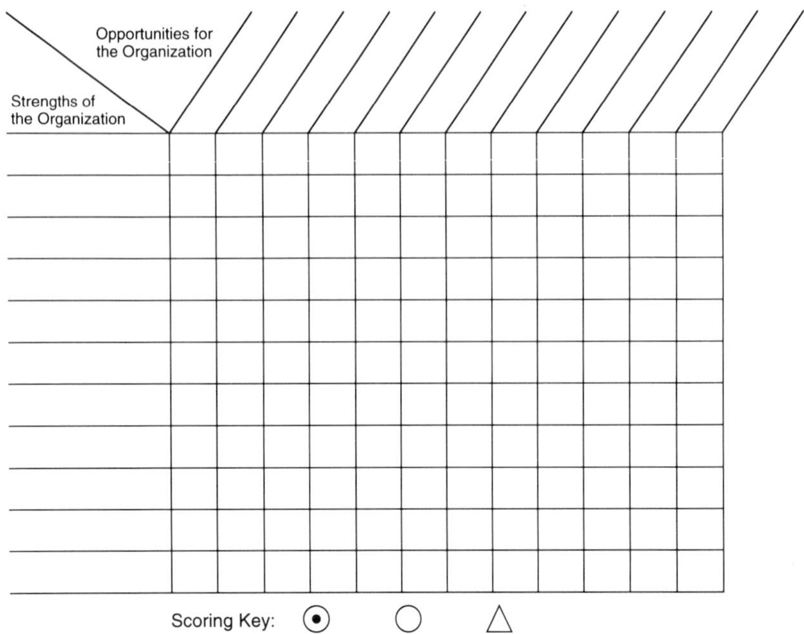

FIGURE 15.6. Strengths/Opportunities Correlation Matrix.

organization to pursue. The House of Strategy, shown in Figure 15.7, is that tool.

The House of Strategy prioritizes preliminary strategic initiatives based on the strength or impact of their relationship to customer, employee, and stockholder needs and wants. When priorities have been established, the team should select no more than one to six of the highest ranking initiatives. These are the initiatives the organization should pursue and behind which all available resources aligned.

The first step in completing this form is to list the preliminary strategic initiatives in the columns across the top row as signified by "6." This can be weighted in row No. 5 if the group feels some preliminary initiatives have more impact than others. A simple system like scoring each a 5, 3, or 1 could be used. For example, an initiative for increasing revenue might be weighted as a 5, while

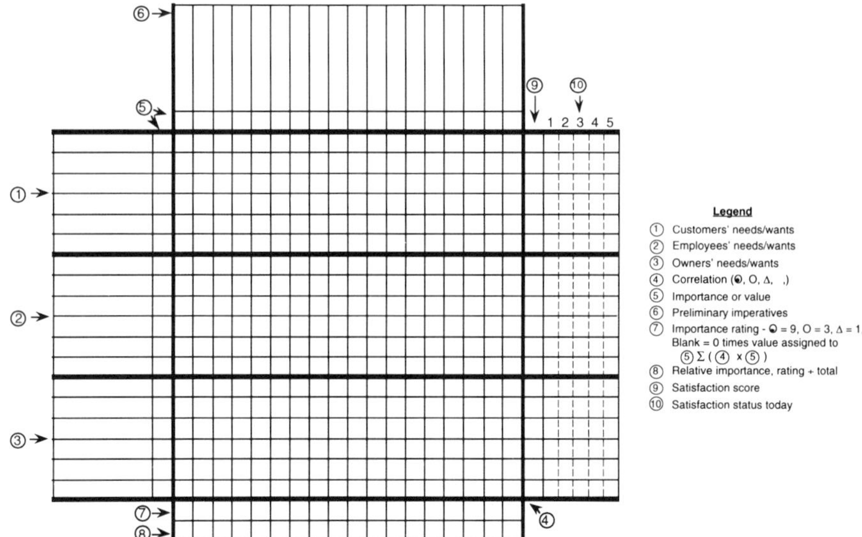

FIGURE 15.7. House of Strategy.

repaving the parking lot might be a 1. Under different circumstances, the weighting could be the other way around.

The next step is to list customer, employee, and stockholder needs and wants on rows found at the left of the matrix as signified by 1, 2, and 3. The team then compares each strategic initiative to each need and want. If there is a very strong relationship between the two, a symbol, such as a "⊙," goes in the common grid. A "○" represents a medium relationship, and a "△" would stand for a weak relationship. Leaving the grid blank indicates no relationship between the two variables.

After this task is completed, tabulation of results can begin. Assign nine points to a "⊙," three points for a "○," one point to a "△," and zero points for a blank. Add the total points for each preliminary initiative, multiply that sum times the weighting factor in row 5, and place the result in row 7. The total number of points in row 7 can be divided into each preliminary strategic initiative in row 7 to determine the percent of the total for row 8.

There is normally some natural break points between the vital few and the trivial many to determine the strategic initiatives for the organization to pursue. As stated previously, this number should be somewhere between one and six. Some people may feel the organization should try to focus on only one or two initiatives at a time. Others feel the number should be in the range of four to six. Most agree the organization should not attempt to focus on more than six or their efforts will become too diffused and may not achieve any initiatives.

The next stop is to communicate the process and outcome of the workshop to all the employees so they can understand and align their efforts with the organization's direction.

There is little point in developing a strategy if employees do not understand and support it. Some organizations, fearing employees will defect to competitors, do not try to share company strategy with employees. One has to ask how employees could be expected to invest their efforts to achieve a plan if managers do not trust them and share the strategy with them. Publishing the Strategy Outline itself can provide employees with a readily understandable, inspiring missive that they can keep as a handy reminder. This is usually done on attractive, heavy paper, suitable for framing so the employees can post it in their work areas. One customer printed it in fine print on a colorful plastic sheet the size of their employees' badges to be worn with the badges.

Publishing the organization's goals and plans, clearly written and discussed in briefing sessions, with ample time for debate and discussion, helps employees join the mobilization effort. A town hall type meeting, presided over by senior managers, is often a good idea. Employees may challenge parts of the plan. Such comments provide managers with opportunities to hear what employees think and to understand the employees' view of the organization.

There are many other ways, of course, to communicate with employees, including memos, one-to-one conversations, audio/videotapes, and staff presentations. There are a couple of important points: Anything put in writing should be very clear, and any briefing session should allow ample time for debate and discussions to ensure no misunderstandings. Employees should be cautioned that the Strategic Initiatives provided by management probably do not include everything that needs to be done. Employees inevitably see opportunities for improvement in their own areas and should feel encouraged to take their own initiatives. Junji Noguchi, executive director of the Union of Japanese Scientists and Engineers, says he believes 80% of improvements come from individual efforts.

Japanese business people call this overall communication process *catch ball* or dualization, meaning the conversation goes on until true consensus is reached. It might be thought useful to propose an American term that would capture the idea of *catch ball*, but quite frankly, the term conjures such a vivid and apt image that it is difficult to improve on.

STRATEGY DEPLOYMENT

Once the strategic plan has been developed and communicated, and employees are enthusiastic about it, it is time to make it happen. Unfortunately, this is where many organizations stumble. Having put the very best people to work developing an excellent plan, organizations allow a return to work as before, causing the plan to lapse. Japanese experts, perceiving this problem in their own companies, devised a method called *hoshin kanri*, which translates as *managing by policy*. *Hoshin kanri* deploys the strategic plan throughout the organization and provides a follow-up system called the *Presidential Audit* to review progress (see Phase IV, below). In what follows hoshin kanri is applied, in "westernized" form, to Deployment, and Phase IV, Diagnosis, of the Rings of Management model.

High Impact Process Opportunities

The House of Strategy exercise determines which strategic initiatives have the highest impact on the needs/wants of customers, employees, and owners or stockholders. Then attention must be focused on the initiatives with the highest potential for impact. This can be done through cross-functional teams using Process Management techniques identified in Figure 15.8. Note the vari-

	Improvement	Innovation
Product/Service	Value Engineering Fault Tree Analysis FMEA (Failure Mode Effect Analysis) Measuring Customer Satisfaction	Quality Function Deployment Market Research Strategic Planning Quality of Design Paradigm Prism
Process	Statistical Quality Tools Process Improvement Teams Experimental Design Process Mapping Value Analysis Work Simplification Personal Management Process Control Table	Process Reengineering Benchmarking Just-In-Time Work Redesign Self-Managed Work Clusters The Seven Management and Planning Tools Value Chain Analysis

FIGURE 15.8. Process Management Tools.

ous tools available to both improve and innovate products/services and processes. Deming insists that organizations must create new processes as well as improve products and services. Juran speaks of the need for breakthroughs. Various ideas have arisen to guide organizations in meeting these needs. A popular one in recent years is business process reengineering (BPR), but this only addresses one part of the equation—process innovation. The term PI^2 is useful to remind us to address *both* improvement *and* innovation when looking at the high impact opportunities.

Key Processes

The cross-functional teams assigned to address the high impact opportunities should first address key processes necessary to accomplish the fulfillment of the initiative. Identifying and listing the key processes provides a basis for evaluating the criticality and effectiveness of the various processes, which should be weighted to establish priorities. Some processes may not currently exist, or do not function very well. Managers should look for processes that relate to several of the critical success factors, particularly ones that do not exist or may not be functioning well. Focusing its attention on these, management can begin to define the processes to create or improve. Ultimately, management will determine some milestones to reach in those processes.

The teams should be chartered carefully for proper alignment, including leadership, process owners, and employees committed to championing certain concepts. A good set of guidelines helps them know what to do and how long to take doing it. Having moved into the area of overlap between Strategy Management and Process Management, they are ready for training in use of the Process Management tools.

The Process Action Chart

An effort to tap the brainpower of the organization must run parallel to the high impact opportunity teams. Once the planning process ends, with strategic initiatives developed, employees may begin to learn develop the details of plan.

This effort also starts with the top executive, who employs the Process Action Worksheet, shown in Figure 15.9, to help define specific actions to help achieve the strategic initiatives.

The Process Action Chart includes action items and specific quality criteria—how one knows if the company is performing well on an action item and what the plan is for improvement. The top executive again is the role model leading the action. He or she has a personal Process Action Chart defining the actions that must be taken to achieve the strategic initiatives. The top executive and executive staff share their Process Action Charts, providing one another with feedback for improvement.

These initiatives are listed in the top of the columns. Down the first column are reminders of dimensions of actions to consider—cost, quality, delivery or time, morale, and safety. Each individual is asked to identify one or two actions to be taken for each initiative by each dimension. When completed, more actions are identified than time or resources could probably allow. Again, the vital few must be identified and marked for action. In this case, simply scanning all the possible actions in a column reveals one or two

Div/Dept: ____________
Date: ____________
Author: ____________

Areas for Improvement / Strategic Initiatives						
Quality						
Cost/Revenue						
Time/Delivery						
Safety						
Service						
Morale						
Process Actions						

FIGURE 15.9. Process Action Worksheet.

Div/Dept: ______

Date: ______

Author: ______

Strategic Initiatives	Process Actions	Quality Criteria (Measurement)	Plan to Improve the Process			
			What	How	When	Who

FIGURE 15.10. Process Action Chart.

actions that stand out as being most important. Those are listed in the bottom row.

They are next carried forward to the Process Action Chart in Figure 15.10 and listed in the first column under Action Items.

The second column on the Process Action Chart identifies the method of measurement to determine progress, sometimes called the *Quality Criteria*. The next columns identify what will be done, how will it be done, when will it be completed, and who is responsible.

After reviewing all of the individual team goals, management checks to make sure individual departments have not suboptimized themselves or each other. Each department lists their goals on a Team Process Action Chart just like the Corporate Process Action Chart. They identify their team's goals and objectives and the action items required to achieve them—what are they going to do, when are they going to do it, how are they going to do it, and who is going to do it?

This brings the next game of catchball, bouncing the action plan up, down and across the department or other business unit to achieve true consensus.

Gradually, action items for each employee become clear, thus deploying the strategy down through the ranks. Line managers can develop means for regular progress reporting, perhaps by reviewing and posting a department Quality Journal (see Chapter 16).

Process Action Review

The Japanese have a system of follow-up (see Chapter 13) which they call the *Presidential Audit*. In this book it is called the Process Action Review *Managerial Diagnosis*, because audit implies something in North America—checking up on people—that it does not imply in Japan. Whatever the name, the intent is not to control people but to review the problems people have in completing their action items, what barriers they encounter, and what management can do to remove those barriers.

Top executives perform the managerial diagnosis annually or semi-annually. Team leaders or department managers should do a monthly diagnosis to check employees' progress in improving processes. The diagnoses involve clarifying present problems, checking the process with current data, and using the problem-solving tools discussed in Chapter 16, "Process Management."

The Managerial Review differs from the old-fashioned quality audit, which checks the process against some sort of standard criteria or specification—the old quality assurance perspective. The Process Action Review is used to analyze the process to find problems or make recommendations for improving the process or system. It's not a pass-fail situation.

Managers ask many questions during the diagnosis, and it is vital that employees do not perceive the managers as Big Brother checking up on them. It is important to remember the spirit of win-win, respect, cooperation, and finding ways to improve. In many books about Presidential Audits, Japanese observe: "Admonish managers not to lose their tempers." Employees must feel free to speak the truth or the managerial diagnosis serves no true purpose.

The following are some sample questions for managers to ask as the strategy is deployed:

- What are the important problems?
- Have the goals been deployed to all employees?
- Are the employees making progress toward improvement?
- Can management help them?
- Has PDSA (Plan, Do, Study, Act) been practiced throughout the procedures?
- Is strategy management carried out as it's supposed to be?
- Is the policy checked to see that it's achieving the goals?
- Are the team leaders checking monthly with employees?
- How are they progressing on individual action items?
- Are processes being revised?
- Are we capturing some of the inputs so we can improve the system?
- Are the methods standardized throughout the organization?
- Are we using data?
- Are records being kept?
- Are plans being revised, if necessary?
- Is there a better way to achieve the goals?

- Are we keeping information/communication channels open?
- Are people throughout the organization aware of what's going on and helping to apply the new knowledge?
- Have we looked at the cost—are we really making time and money available to accomplish these action items?
- Are the plans specific, not vague and lofty?
- Have the team leaders made a thorough study of the problems carried over from last year? Have they made any changes?
- Have there been changes in the business climate? Have they specified their goals in concrete terms?
- Do we have agreement throughout the operation on what is important?

This is a lengthy list, originally developed for a company implementing strategy management. That organization chose to ask some of the questions at each of its monthly meetings, passing through all of them in the course of a year.

Follow-Up

The diagnostic meetings produce certain results or indications for new actions. Top managers should send a recommendation paper to each business team or department within a month after the diagnosis. Within another two months, the business team should develop an action plan covering the recommendations from the diagnosis. Following up the action plans from the diagnostic feedback should be a major topic of the next managerial diagnosis. An integrated flowchart, as shown in Figure 15.11, helps people understand the Strategy Management Process better.

Conclusion

Occasionally, someone confuses Strategy Management with Management by Objectives. They are quite different. In its more common form, Management by Objectives lays a heavy emphasis on results. To summarize the differences, Strategy Management:

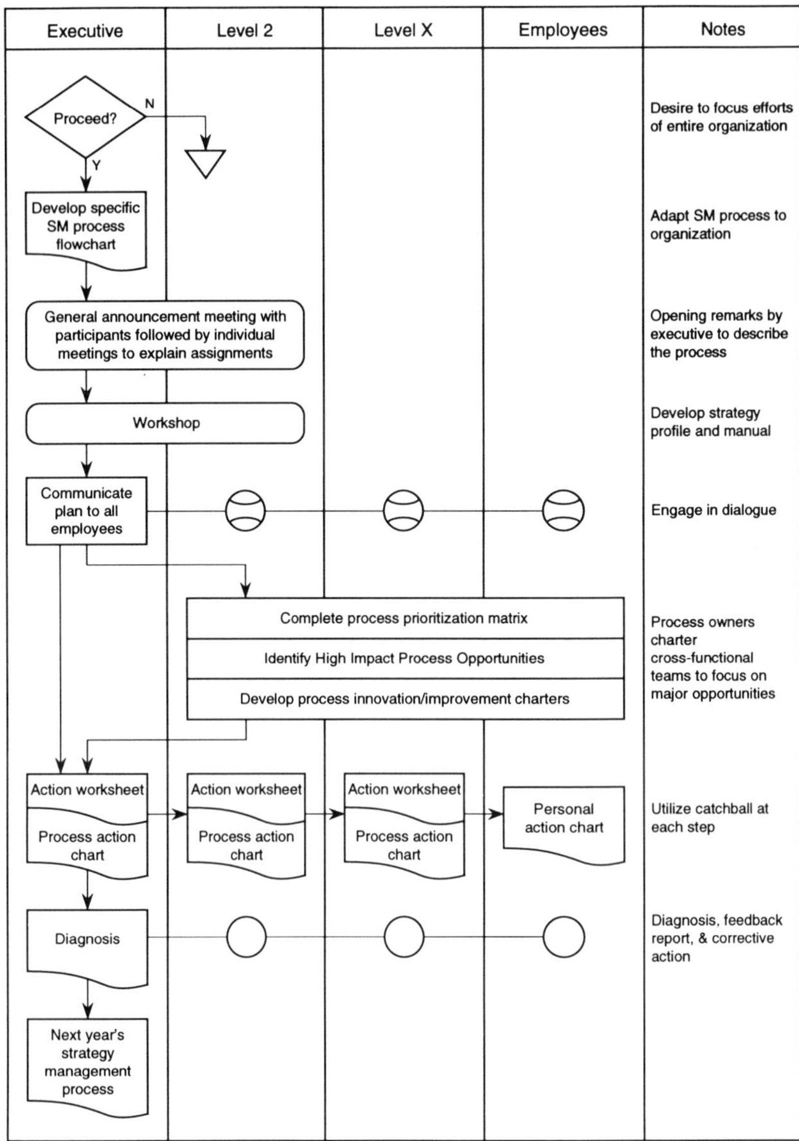

FIGURE 15.11. Strategy Management Cycle.

- Is quality oriented
- Emphasizes both process and results
- Deploys objectives throughout the organization
- Is based on the PDSA cycle
- Provides employees with means
- Includes a follow-up diagnosis with the intent of helping employees.

Whereas, Management by Objectives:

- Is personnel oriented
- Emphasizes results only
- Provides objectives between a manager and subordinates
- Is based on motivation
- Leaves the employees to "go do it"
- Relies only on final inspection, without follow-up.

Strategy Management can be seen as a three-dimensional Plan-Do-Study-Act activity. The vision, the purpose, the mission, the value, the imperatives, and the goals comprise planning. The *do* is the deployment and the identification of the action items as well as working on them. The *study* is the managerial diagnosis; from the feedback provided by this, departments develop action items to *act* or correct any problems and move forward.

One may envision this cycle as a revolving cone (see Figure 15.12). It starts with strategic planning to determine the organization's critical objectives and imperatives that reflect the organization's vision, purpose, values, and goals. The strategic plan is executed by deploying it through the organization where action items is determined and progress on the action items are followed up during the Managerial Diagnosis. During the managerial diagnosis, new problems or opportunities will surface. This is inevitable and desirable; it is a sign of growth. Then the cycle revolves again.

Strategy Management is partly a technique for identifying and staying focused on the processes and techniques that achieve success. It also keeps everyone focused on the organization's values, aim and mission. Once they know each other's needs and wants,

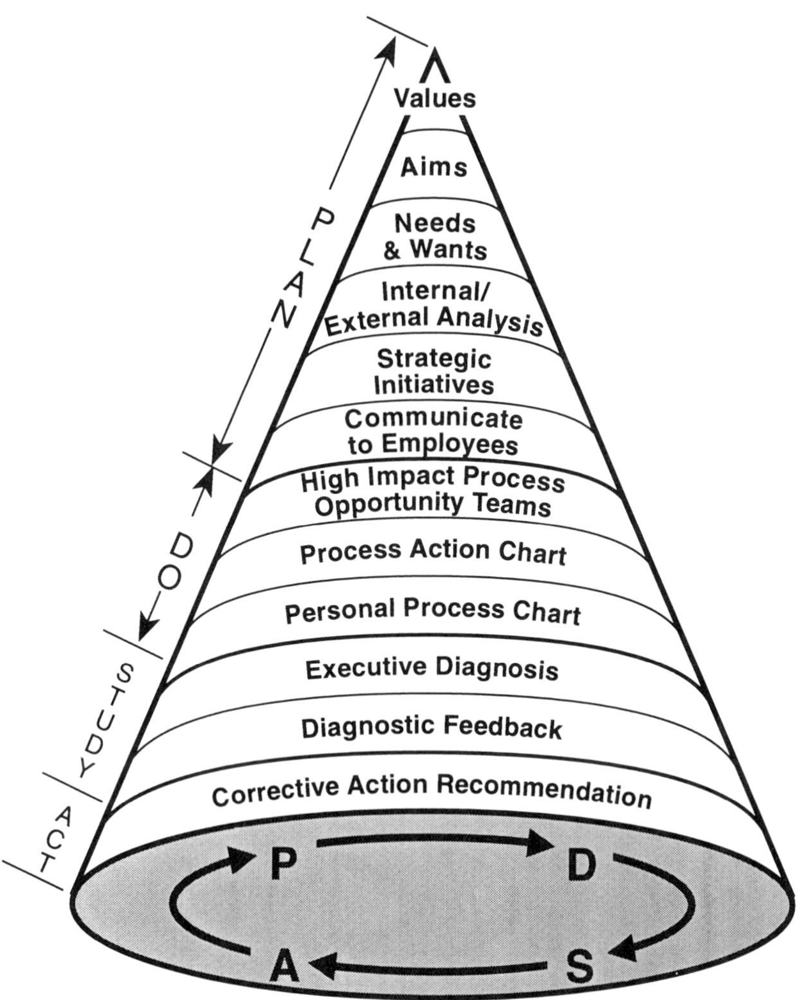

FIGURE 15.12. Plan, Do, Study, and Act Cycle.

the stakeholders can begin to move in the same direction. Strategy Management shows them that direction and how to get there.

Equipped with a powerful tool to identify strategic initiatives, high-impact opportunities, and key processes with an aim to satisfying the needs and wants of those who drive the enterprise, management may find other areas of interest. Improving and innovating (or reengineering) key processes leads naturally to an opportunity to restructure the organization around these processes. Instead of functional departments (or fiefdoms), with their traditional barriers to full communication and collaboration, management can reorganize the enterprise as a *system*, with the structure based on a natural flow of work.

Some refer to this type of organizational structure as *horizontal*, but it is better called a *systems-based* organization, with the top executive leading by applying systemic thinking. The effort results in a leaner, flatter organization requiring fewer levels of management to coordinate and allocate resources. All personnel become members of the key process teams working to satisfy customers. The new global marketplace, with its intense competition, requires such innovative organizational structure for companies wishing to compete and succeed.

16
Process Management

A student gets on the school bus each day. Is the student early, late or just in time? Whichever, there is a process involved in getting to the bus stop. If the student is late, the process needs improvement.

Every activity involves a process and indeed is a process. What is a process? A process is a collection of cause factors, including people, materials, equipment, methods, and environment that interact to produce a given output. Cause factors are often referred to as input, because each of them contribute to the output. Customers' needs are always changing, and processes must improve to keep up with the customers' needs and to anticipate future needs.

Every process has an owner. The process owner, that is, the executive, manager, or supervisor, is accountable for what comes out of the process and for authorizing the people who work in it to make changes or to innovate. For instance, the student is the owner of the getting-to-the-bus-on-time process.

The Ring of Process Management focuses on the improvement and innovation of processes, products, and services. It calls on management, armed with statistical information and the insights of employees, to identify, analyze, improve, and innovate processes, whether in manufacturing or services.

Traditionally, quality efforts focused on inspection, finding defects after they are produced. Process Management focuses on checking, analyzing and changing processes to eliminate defects before the product reaches the delivery stage. This is supported by management's commitment to change and to continual improvement, as seen in the early stages of Environment Management.

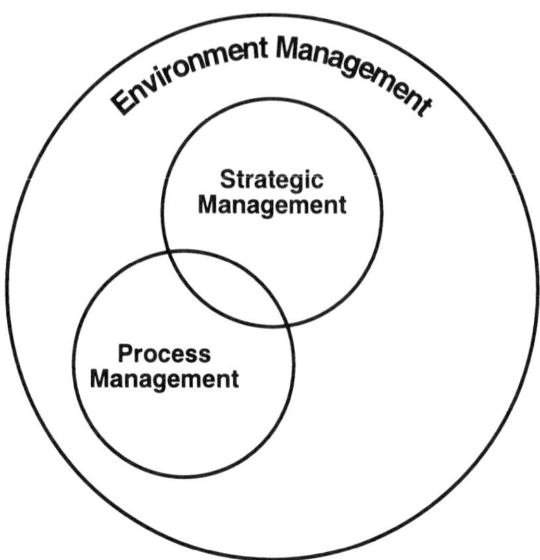

FIGURE 16.1. Process Management.

Statistical tools provide information about the manufacturing or service system throughout the organization.

Led by the techniques proffered by Shewhart, Deming, Ishikawa, and others, Japanese experts developed a process management method, which they call the *Quality Control* (QC) *Story*. The QC Story was developed as a method to consistently apply the quality tools properly and to solve problems or improve processes in the correct sequence. In addition to applying the tools consistently and optimally, using a QC Story produces a sound benefit: communication. By posting the QC Story in the work area, anyone walking by can see the data, offer suggestions, or learn something they might apply in their area. In Japan, management sometimes posts QC stories in the lobby so that suppliers may view them and become involved in solving problems.

The Quality Journal is a westernized version of the QC Story (see Figure 16.2). Before and after flowcharts have been added. One of management's responsibilities is to ensure that employees are trained in simple statistical methods to be used to obtain information about their work processes. With training, employees and

QUALITY JOURNAL

SUBJECT: AUTHOR: DATE:

Process Flowchart Before Improvement

1. Define the Problem a) Statement

b) Data Display

2. Observe the Problem

3. Analyze the Causes a) Setting the Hypothesis

b) Testing the Hypothesis

4. Act On the Causes

5. Study the Results

6. Standardize the Changes

7. Draw Conclusions

Process Flowchart After Improvement

Flowchart Symbols

Action Stop Decision

Involvement Meeting

FIGURE 16.2. Quality Journal.

managers also begin to understand what they see in other departments' Quality Journals. Many of the same statistical techniques may be used throughout the organization, and the Quality Journal is a means of educating everyone about the processes.

It also enables top managers to understand the concepts of stable and unstable processes and thereby know when they must act to improve the system. Everyone must realize there is no quick solution. A successful quality transformation may take five or six years, though there may be positive results in the early stages. It is essential to remember that no work is complete until a system is in place to improve it, both in management and technical areas. The cycle never ends, with continuous improvement becoming a way of life.

The manager must know the aim of the process, how it works, and what it is capable of. Knowledge (i.e., competence) allows the manager to gauge the process performance against customer requirements and to make comparisons and set priorities for improvement.

This may begin within departments but eventually expand to the entire top management team for the coordination of cross-functional processes. Managers must have a thorough understanding of flowcharts, the PDSA cycle, and other tools of process improvement. Often management begins by identifying problems that are "low-hanging fruit," that is, the problems that are most easily solved. After empowering a team or individual to tackle the problem, they determine which statistical or other tools would best monitor the improvement. To ensure success, management finds and removes any barriers, recognizes the effort by the team or individual, provides resources, and, following Deming's edict against tampering, makes certain to help without interfering.

THE SEVEN PROCESS IMPROVEMENT TECHNIQUES

There are seven most-often used process improvement techniques, most of them invented or further developed by the quality masters covered in this book. These techniques are covered in the following sections.

Flowcharts

Flowcharts help visualize sequential steps of a process. People often try to solve a problem without first having a clear picture of how the process works. Flowcharts identify what a process does and what it should do. It is hard to say who first used flowcharts to depict organizational processes, but certainly Allan Mogensen is among the earliest and most prominent to advocate their use.

Flowcharting is not one of the seven basic tools used in Japan. When asked why not, one Japanese business person responded incredulously that, "We just assume you know what is going on in the process before you make any attempt to change it." This is not a safe assumption in most other parts of the world.

There are many types of flowcharts, but this discussion is limited to linear and integrated charts (see Figures 16.3 and 16.4). It's important to determine what kind of information is appropriate before beginning to construct a flowchart. For instance, an integrated flowchart is right for viewing the flow of the process from one organizational unit to another. Linear flowcharts are the simplest, providing a picture of overall flow or details of flow and creating a foundation for other charts. An integrated flowchart provides another dimension to the linear flowchart. It depicts the flow as it imparts organizational units involved. Each organizational unit in the process is assigned to a separate column.

Guidelines for constructing a flowchart include:

- Labeling the chart to identify the process, activity, preparer, and date
- Using symbols to depict the steps or events
- Ensuring that the time sequence of the step follows from top to bottom
- Drawing only one line from each symbol, unless the symbol indicates a decision or cooperation between the units
- Consistently directing the arrows for yes/no decisions
- Using only vertical and horizontal lines

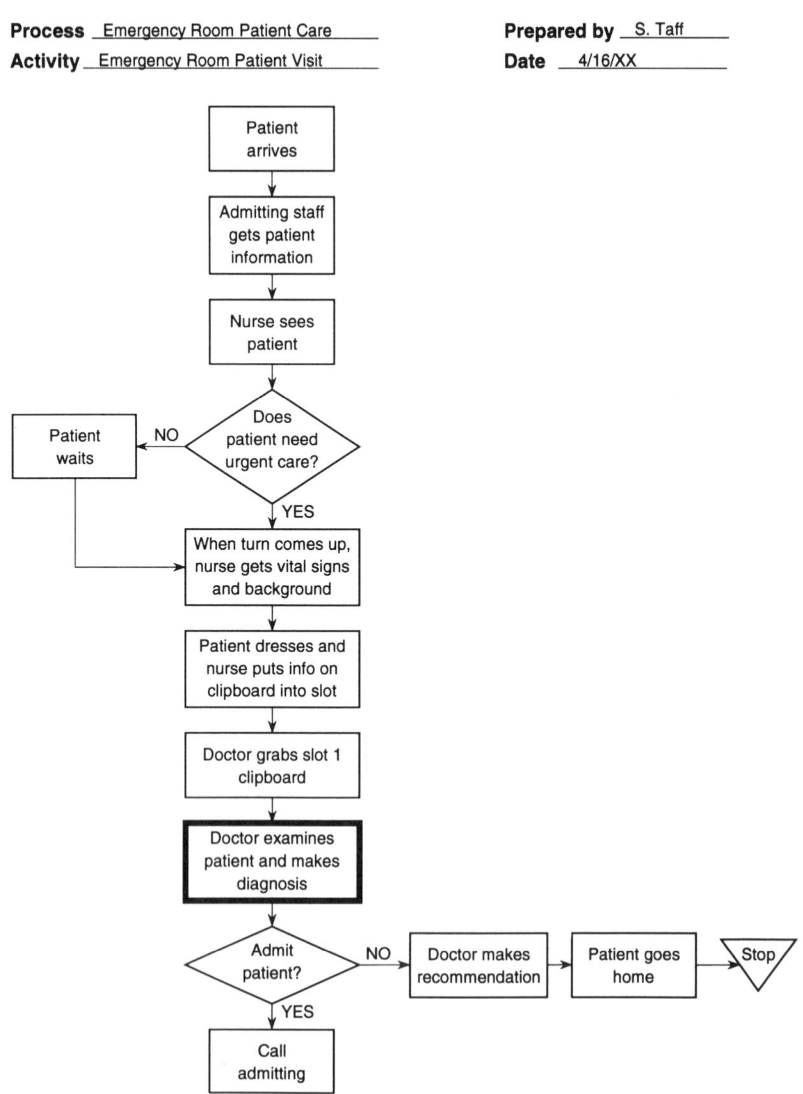

FIGURE 16.3. Linear Flowchart.

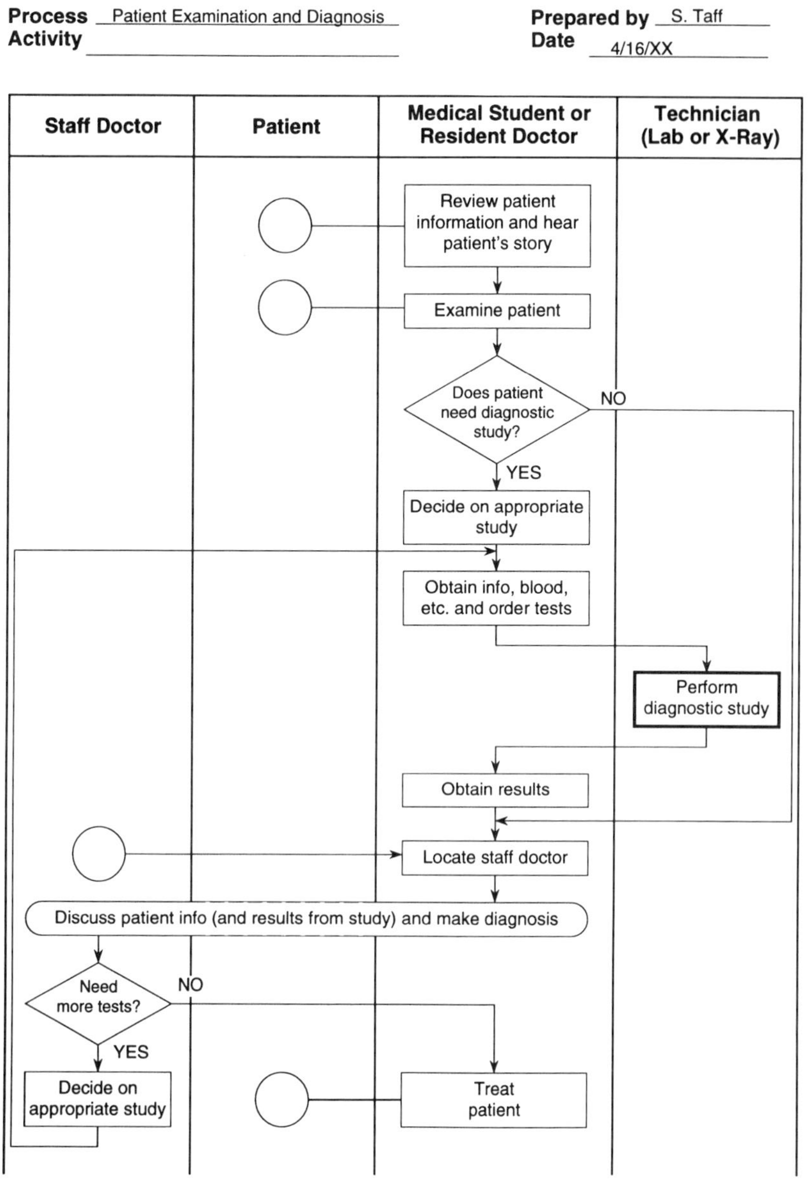

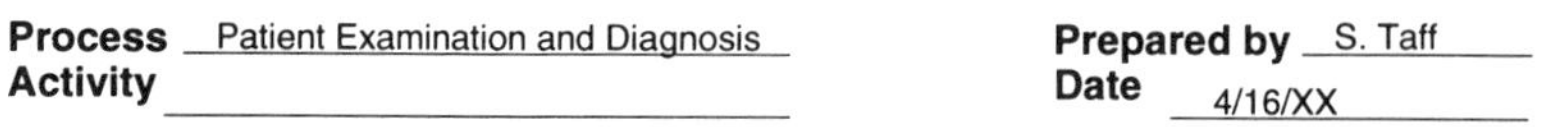

Process Patient Examination and Diagnosis **Prepared by** S. Taff
Activity **Date** 4/16/XX

Staff Doctor	Patient	Medical Student or Resident Doctor	Technician (Lab or X-Ray)

Review patient information and hear patient's story

Examine patient

Does patient need diagnostic study?

NO

YES

Decide on appropriate study

Obtain info, blood, etc. and order tests

Perform diagnostic study

Obtain results

Locate staff doctor

Discuss patient info (and results from study) and make diagnosis

Need more tests?

NO

YES

Decide on appropriate study

Treat patient

FIGURE 16.4. Integrated Flowchart.

Cause and Effect Diagrams

The purpose of a cause and effect diagram is to capture ideas on possible causes for a problem (see Figure 16.5). Developed by Kaoru Ishikawa, the cause and effect diagram often has been referred to as an Ishikawa diagram or as a fishbone diagram, because of its resemblance to a fish skeleton. (In Japan, some who use it are fond of showing it inside a drawing of a fish.) The fishbone diagram is useful to supervisors gathering input from the people closest to the problem or a manager seeking to document everyone's ideas.

Cause and effect diagrams should be used to sort and organize causes of problems, track which causes have been investigated and eliminated, inform others of the team's scope of work, and to guide discussion.

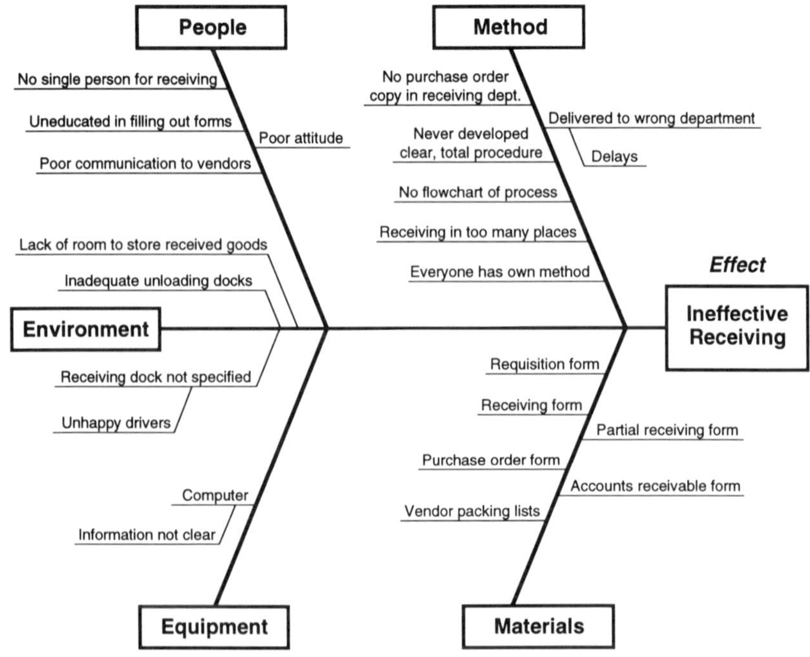

FIGURE 16.5. Cause and Effect Diagram.

Guidelines for constructing a cause and effect diagram include clearly defining the problem, defining major categories that make sense for the specific situation, following rules for brainstorming, and focusing on causes which the team can control. The meaning of each idea should be clarified and the list condensed if possible. Then, each idea can be ranked according to its importance. The team may develop action items for investigating by collecting more data.

The benefits include improving the knowledge and understanding of everyone who participates, guiding discussion, using a systematic procedure for identifying causes, finding causes which may be supported by additional data, learning a systematic approach to solving almost any problem, revealing complex elements, and team building.

The rules of brainstorming include:

- Encourage spontaneous responses.
- Do not discuss each other's ideas.
- Cultivate a supportive atmosphere.
- Emphasize quantity, not quality.
- Build on each other's ideas.
- Write everything down.
- Seek total participation from the group.
- Discourage negative nonverbal responses to ideas.

The brainstorming rules should be strictly enforced, and no one should be allowed to change or interpret anyone else's words. Each person should identify where their ideas fit on the diagram.

Pareto Diagrams

In 1897, Italian economist Vilfredo Pareto developed what he termed the *80/20 principle* to explain that 80% of the wealth in Italy was held by 20% of the people. Pareto's principle showed that only a few important elements account for the vast majority of an outcome. This idea was refined for quality study purposes by Joseph M. Juran, who, as was discussed earlier, called it the *vital few and trivial many*. Juran named it the *Pareto Analysis*.

A Pareto diagram is a bar chart that categorizes items needing improvement and organizes them in order of decreasing frequency (see Figure 16.6). Each bar represents one category, with the vertical axis showing the frequency of occurrence. The total frequency for each item is shown by the height of its bar.

Constructing a Pareto diagram requires the following steps:

- Determining the categories
- Collecting the data
- Selecting the appropriate scales
- Ranking the cause categories
- Labeling the axes
- Plotting the bars on the graph

Pareto diagrams are a graphic method to prioritize issues, enable people to see an issue similarly, help to separate the vital few from the trivial many, provide a means of viewing issues from different perspectives, assist in monitoring effectiveness of improvement efforts over time, and help to rank the order of problems.

Histograms

Histograms display the distribution of a set of data by means of vertical bar graphing (see Figure 16.7). Steps for constructing a histogram include:

- Determining an approximate number of classes
- Establishing class width and boundaries
- Tallying to observations
- Plotting the histogram

Histograms help give an idea of the shape, center, and spread of an output characteristic for a process; monitor the effectiveness of improvement efforts; indicate when more than one process is present; help people see issues clearly; and indicate when sorting or rework have occurred. Histograms only provide historical information. They indicate what has happened in the past but cannot necessarily be used to predict the future, unless the process is stable.

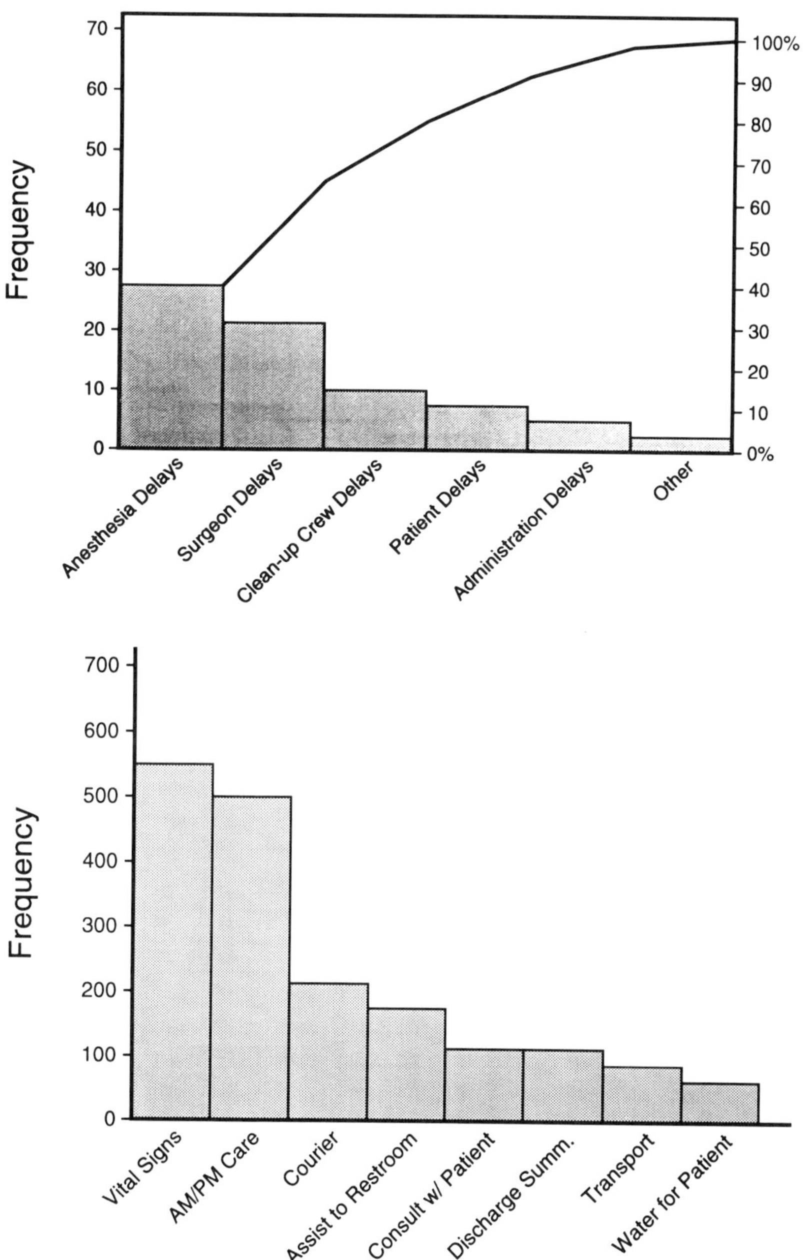

FIGURE 16.6. Pareto Diagram.

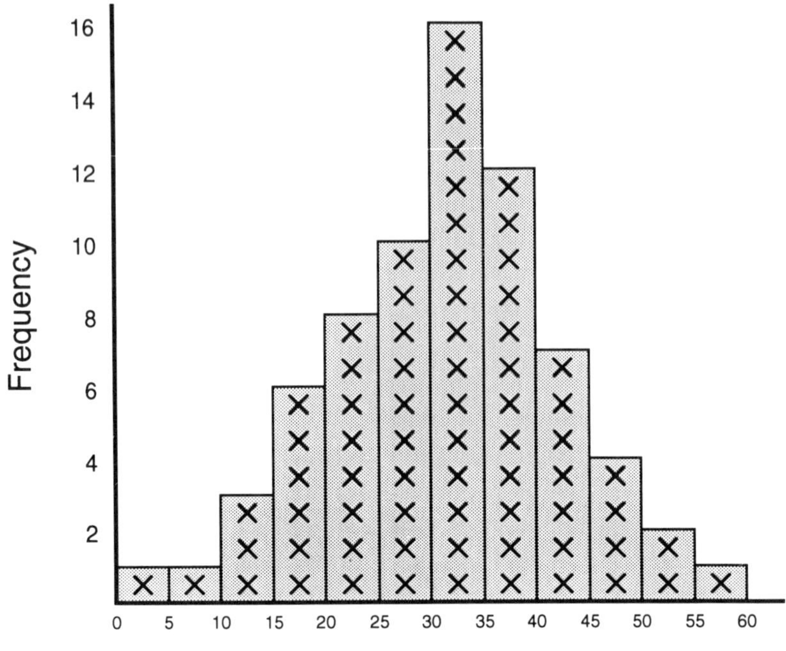

FIGURE 16.7. Histogram.

Control Charts

Control charts, as developed by Walter Shewhart, represent the beginning of the modern quality movement. Control charts tell what a process is capable of doing. They show the variation of the process and help separate common causes due to variation of the system from special causes due to intervention. (See Figure 16.8.) There are several types of control charts, but all have a few common features. Hitoshi Kume, writing in his 1987 book, *Statistical Methods for Quality Improvement*, says control charts all "have a central line, a pair of control limits, one each, allocated above the below the central line, and characteristic values plotted on the chart which represent the state of a process. When all the values are plotted within the control limits without any particular ten-

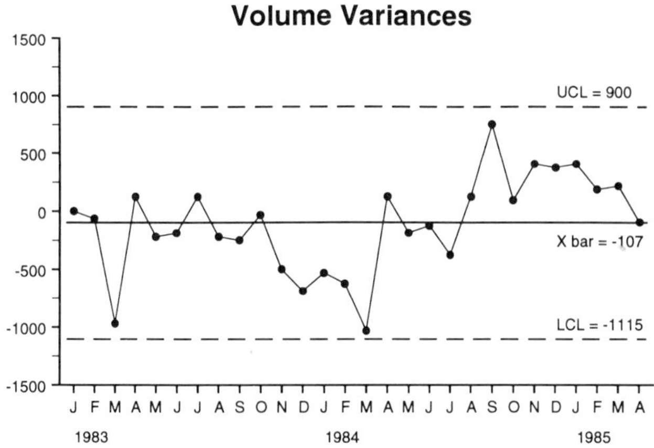

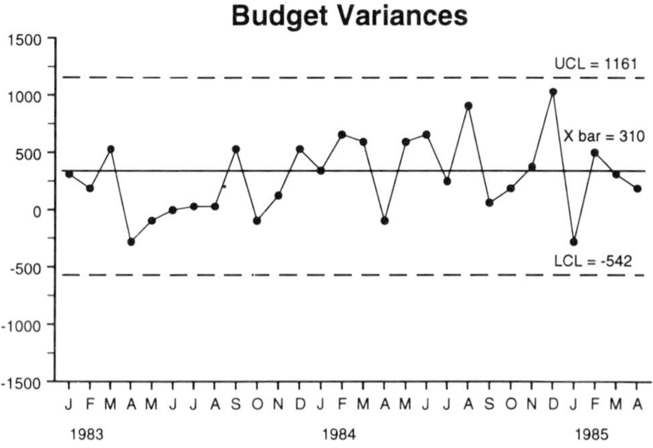

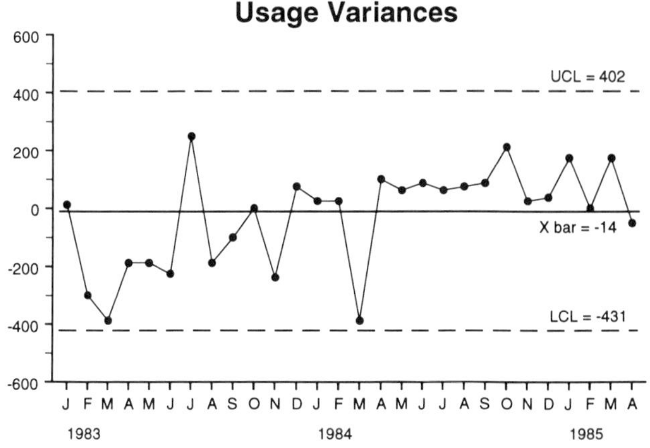

FIGURE 16.8. Control Charts.

dency, the process is regarded as being in the controlled state. If they fall outside the control limits, or show a peculiar pattern, the process is judged to be out of control."[1] In any type of control chart, Kume says, the control limit is calculated by the formula:

$$(\text{average value}) \pm 3 \times (\text{standard deviation})$$

where the standard deviation is that of the variation due to chance causes.

Run Charts

Run charts show characteristics of a process and preserve the time order of the data (see Figure 16.9). This may help in detecting data trends, shifts, cycles, or other patterns over time. Examples of their use include volume orders for each day, the number of

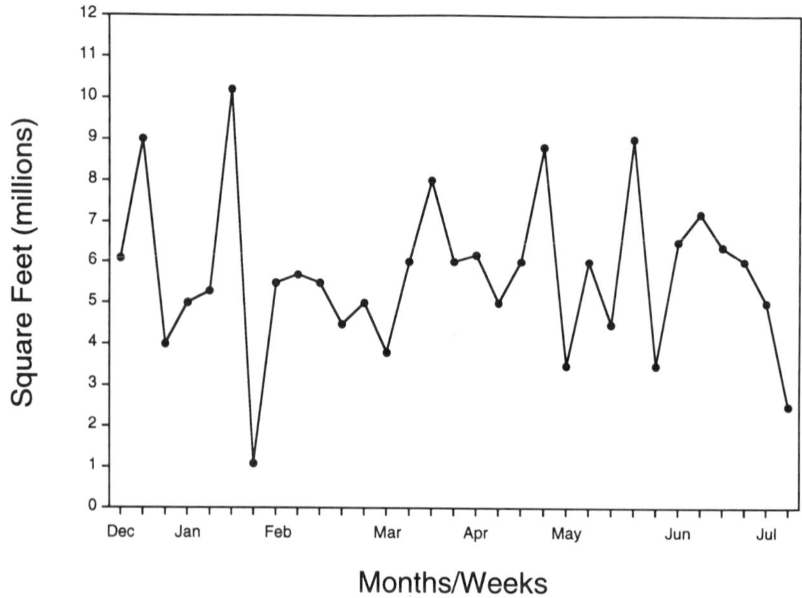

FIGURE 16.9. Run Chart.

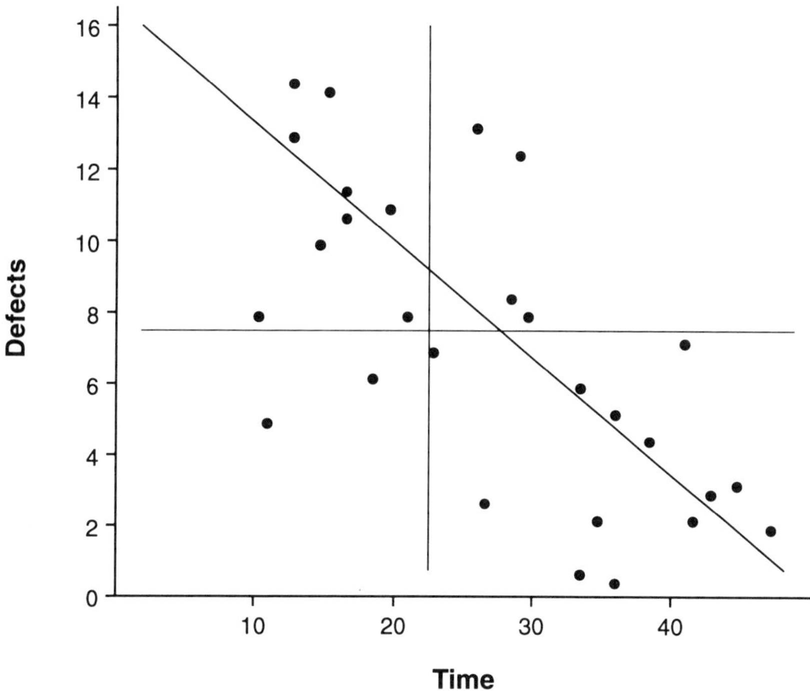

FIGURE 16.10. Scatter Diagram.

telephone calls received per hour, number of errors per shift, or monthly management figures. They can be used to identify upward or downward trends, locate unusual patterns, and obtain clues for what might be causing them and monitor improvement efforts.

Steps to constructing a run chart include:

- Drawing horizontal and vertical axes
- Labeling the horizontal axis to reflect time order of the data
- Labeling the vertical axis with a characteristic of the process
- Labeling "tick marks" to identify the respective units of measurement
- While collecting data, drawing points at the intersection of the time measurement and the characteristic measurement
- Connecting the points after all data has been collected

Scatter Diagrams

Scatter diagrams, also pioneered by Shewhart, provide a picture of the relationship between two variables (see Figure 16.10). They cannot, however, prove that a causal relationship exists between the two variables. Only subject matter knowledge can substantiate a causal relationship. Steps to construct a scatter diagram include:

- Selecting two variables
- Collecting the data
- Selecting the appropriate scales, i.e., increments of 10 pounds
- Labeling the axes and their units of measurement
- Plotting the points at the intersection of the respective variables.

Scatter diagrams help to depict and view the relationship between the two variables and to indicate the type of relationship (i.e., correlation) between the two variables.

There are still other managerial tools managers should understand, including Taguchi's Loss Function diagram, generally restricted to particular manufacturing operations. The others, however, may be widely applied. For instance, the student catching the school bus might use a run chart to show average waiting time. The student might use a control chart to tell when the process of preparing was out of control and he could develop a flowchart for examining the processes that lead up to getting to school on time. Put together in a Quality Journal, the tools represent a turning of the PDSA wheel and the route to process improvement.

17
Personal Management

Fredrick Taylor once wrote, "Hardly a competent workman can be found who does not devote considerable time to seeing just how slowly he can go and still convince his employer he is going at a good pace. Under our system a worker is told just what he is to do and how he is to do it. Any improvement he makes upon the orders is fatal to his success."

That observation is hardly an affirmation of human beings. Later in his life, Taylor regretted what the application of his theories had come to mean for workers. It seems likely that Taylor was espousing a belief common in his time: Workers did the work and the bosses did the thinking. The impact of that attitude was to tell workers to leave their brains at the door and "just do as you are told." The same attitude prevails in many organizations today.

Virtually every quality theorist debunks this thinking, but no one does so as thoroughly as Deming, who, in his 14 Principles, instructs management to institute leadership, with the aim of helping "people and machines and gadgets do a better job." There is much that management must do to optimize the individual's ability to do a better job—providing open communications, training, encouragement, a good atmosphere, the right work tools, and an understanding of psychology. These things, among others, provide the work situation that allow the worker to do a good job and take pride in it.

"The Western system in which management creates standards to be blindly followed does not contribute to good quality products," says Mizuno. "Workers who reluctantly do only what they are told within their allotted time cannot produce good quality

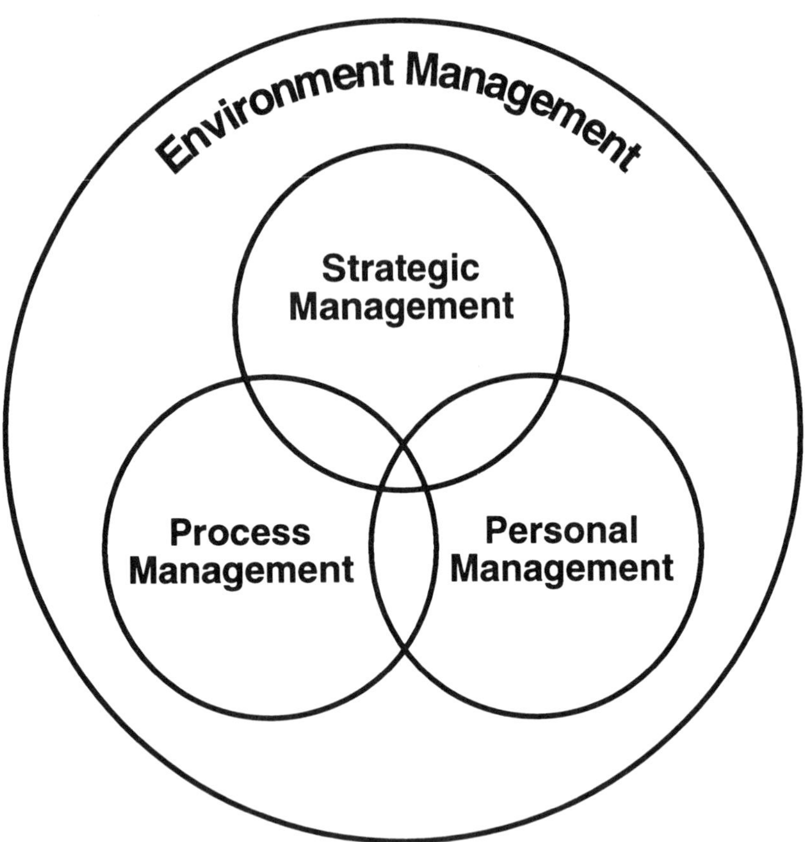

FIGURE 17.1. Personal Management.

products. Good quality products are produced only when every one is willing to put his all into his work."[1]

This is where the concept of personal management comes in: using practical steps to help the individual perform better in his own corner of the organization. The Personal Management philosophy and the tools that accompany it provide a means for continuous improvement of an individual's own processes and systems. It also gives the person a language common with those around for describing their respective functions in terms of tasks, objectives, suppliers, and customers, to name a few.

The new management thinking takes the view that people want to do a good job at work and to take pride in their work, their organizations, and, most of all, themselves. The ability to do good work is dependent upon their work processes, methods, and training. In a mature quality endeavor, the largest gains are made by individuals working to improve their own work processes. Managers seeking to infuse an organization with a zest for quality must replace doubt in the minds of employees with clear expectations. Employees can then turn to the Quality Journal as a tool to help them improve their individual processes.

Regular meetings with group leaders and peers become especially important, because they may be used to make small adjustments in processes, refine supplier-customer relationships, review progress, and share accomplishments. Sharing progress regularly helps to focus effort on important functions, provides constructive feedback from associates, and identifies areas for further measurement and improvement. Involvement by the individual in a team setting and assistance from peers in improving important processes fosters recognition and positive reinforcement. Traditional evaluations become unnecessary, because the individual and the team review the process with an aim to continual improvement.

All managers know there are people under them who have leadership ability, though those people may not have been promoted or otherwise rewarded. Leadership does not require a title; it requires exemplifying certain traits and attitudes as described by Environment Management.

Teams, or small peer groups, provide an opportunity for leadership to evolve. Kano comments about the Japanese *kanji* in quality control circles that the *kanji* learn leadership skills in the circles.[2] Groups like having a leader to coach and encourage them, and see good leadership as a key to success.

THE PERSONAL MANAGEMENT PROCESS

The Personal Management Process is a means to focus and guide people toward improving their work processes. Attendees at Deming seminars readily agreed with the shortcomings of typical performance appraisals but want to know what to use in its place. Most feel that they need some type of communication vehicle to discuss and provide feedback about work with employees, peers, and supervisors. The Personal Management process was developed to fill that need. The process treats people as leaders of their own areas of responsibility and work processes. Everyone is a potential leader, because leadership exists at every level. In the case of an executive, the leader's area may be an entire organization. For the leader's assistant, it may be only that person's immediate work area, which is referred to as a *unit*. Each person should complete a statement of vision for what the area or process will look like in five or ten years, just as the organization did in Strategy Management. The individual should repeat the process as explained in Chapter 16 apply each part of it, state the purpose of the unit, its values and principles, and make sure they align with those of the organization. Once the two are in harmony, the individual can begin to work in the same direction as the organization. A mission statement, spelling out four or five reasons for the individual's activities, also helps to focus individual behavior and work decisions. What about ideal conditions? All have ideal conditions envisioned for work or workplace, though they may not have been expressed.

An Example

Following is a step by step example using an educational training firm. First, a vision statement is written by answering the question, "What can we (the company) be?" An exemplary reply from the product development department might be:

> *to be recognized as the highest quality source for courses and materials in the education industry.*

Second, a purpose statement is written by answering the question, "Why do we (the firm) exist?" One answer is:

> *to provide research, design, development, and production services to produce company course materials and related products addressing the needs of organizations involved in educational improvement.*

Next, a mission statement is created by answering the question, "How will the company move toward its vision?" The product development department has answered:

> *The mission is to plan for and execute the development, production, and distribution of the finest educational products and services in the field. These educational products and services will enable clients and consultants to learn and practice the latest theories and techniques. The department will cooperatively pursue this mission and provide the tools needed to successfully meet work challenges and achieve pride of accomplishment.*

The Leader Performance Matrix

The real exercises of Personal Management is filling out the Leader Performance Matrix and the Personal Process Chart, which focus the individual's efforts on the highest priority functions. A Leader Performance Matrix (see Figure 17.2) could be filled out by:

- Listing the functional responsibilities of the work unit on the horizontal axis of the matrix.
- Listing the major activities (processes) of the leader on the left side of the matrix. First listed are the leader's major

LEADER PERFORMANCE MATRIX

Leader:
Date:

Functional Responsibilities of the Unit

LEGEND: ○ Important ⊙ Very Important

Major Activities (Processes) of the Individual								

FIGURE 17.2. Leader Performance Matrix.

daily activities or processes to identify what is currently being done. Then, the activities are stated in the form of a verb and an object statement and as specific as possible. Examples of major activities might include: provide methods and materials to workers, remove obstacles to performance, and improve systems.

- Drawing a circle at intersections where a major activity is important to achieving a functional responsibility. A dot added inside a circle indicates that the relationship between the leader's activity and the work unit's responsibilities is very important. A triangle indicates a mild relationship, and a blank signifies no real relationship.
- Analyzing what is currently being done and how well each activity supports each functional responsibility. To determine where attention should be initially directed, the relationship between each activity and responsibility should be studied for priorities, additions, or deletions.
- Transferring the six most important leadership activities to the next matrix, the Personal Process Chart, which can identify specific opportunities for improvements in the leader's processes.

The Personal Process Chart

Activities identified in the previous matrix are work processes, and each employee is charged with a continuing search for ways to improve these processes. This is where the Personal Process Chart helps by allowing to identify opportunities which exist within each activity (see Figure 17.3). The complete discovery process for each job activity proceeds as follows:

- *Defining leadership activities* operationally so everyone can understand the meaning.
- *Listing specific tasks associated with each leadership activity*, along with the most important actions necessary to accomplish them.

PERSONAL PROCESS CHART

Major Activities (Processes) of the Individual	Specific Tasks	Objectives of Each Task	Internal/External Suppliers	Internal/External Customers	Quality Indicators	Opportunities for Improvement of the Process
A.	1. 2. 3. 4. 5.	1. 2. 3. 4. 5.				
B.	1. 2. 3. 4. 5.	1. 2. 3. 4. 5.				
C.	1. 2. 3. 4. 5.	1. 2. 3. 4. 5.				
D.	1. 2. 3. 4. 5.	1. 2. 3. 4. 5.				
E.	1. 2. 3. 4. 5.	1. 2. 3. 4. 5.				
F.	1. 2. 3. 4. 5.	1. 2. 3. 4. 5.				
REVIEW DATE:		SUPERVISOR:			LEADER:	

FIGURE 17.3. Personal Process Chart.

- *Identifying one or two objectives* (short- and/or long-term) related to each task.
- *Identifying suppliers* and what can be done to help them become excellent suppliers. Suppliers provide the information, material, methods, environment, and equipment necessary to perform the company's process. Productive relationships here are critical to continuous improvement of processes. Two-way communication between customers and suppliers is a must. Typically, suppliers can provide help with innovation.
- *Identifying customers and their requirements.* This is the first step in devising methods which improve the output, product, or service of the work process. Customers should be asked about what they feel constitutes quality output. Typically, customers can help with continuous improvement.
- *Determining the quality indicators* or critical factors that identify quality performance. Performance measures that can plot progress toward improving the quality indicators should be included. For example, data can be used for comparisons to determine process improvement on such items as competitor's prices, delivery schedule, safety records, and customer satisfaction.
- *Listing several opportunities to improve each job activity.* Identifying areas for improvement should simplify processes, making them more efficient while eliminating waste and rework.

Now that the Personal Process Chart is complete, the results of the discovery process should be shared with the immediate supervisor, seeking to reach agreement on the most important processes. Any necessary revisions are made and then the plan is shared with subordinates, who are asked for their feedback and asked to begin the process themselves. A leader should establish the expectation that group members will share their progress at monthly meetings.

The next step is to complete the Quality Journal, which provides a systematic approach to improving key processes (Figure

17.4). The gap between the current position on an activity and the desired destination is the problem or opportunity for improvement, which is addressed in the Quality Journal. The journal provides the discipline and the consistency necessary for problem-solving processes. It enables employees to show their progress which everyone can understand. The Quality Journal is completed in the following seven steps:

- *Clearly defining the problem* by using facts to demonstrate its extent and how it impacts the total system. The process may also be flowcharted.
- *Observing the problem* by examining it from every point of view, using statistical or other quality tools.
- *Determining the main causes* of the problem, perhaps using a cause-and-effect diagram.
- *Taking action to eliminate* the root causes.
- *Studying the effectiveness* of actions taken, again using quality tools.
- *Standardizing the solution* after desired results are achieved.
- *Reviewing the problem-solving procedure* and identifying what was learned.

Additional meetings with supervisors and subordinates review and verify the findings of the Quality Journal. The leader should then help subordinates do their own Personal Management exercises, thereby cascading the concept throughout the department.

Checking for Consistency

It is always important to check for consistent application when undertaking any quality improvement initiative. Dr. Myron Tribus, whose theories are outlined in Chapter 9, suggested including the following questions in any such review:

- Why were the key processes selected as key processes?
- What will constitute "excellence" in improving this process? How was the definition arrived at?
- What will be used to measure the work of improvement

QUALITY JOURNAL

SUBJECT: AUTHOR: DATE:

Process Flowchart Before Improvement

1. Define the Problem a) Statement

b) Data Display

2. Observe the Problem

3. Analyze the Causes a) Setting the Hypothesis

b) Testing the Hypothesis

4. Act On the Causes

5. Study the Results

6. Standardize the Changes

7. Draw Conclusions

Process Flowchart After Improvement

Flowchart Symbols

Action Stop Decision

Involvement Meeting

FIGURE 17.4. Quality Journal.

progresses? How will progress be identified before the end of this particular effort?

- How will progress be checked and communicated?

In this way the PDSA cycle is applied back to the quality improvement process itself, thus rounding out the effort and raising new opportunities and challenges.

A fine illustration of the Personal Management process in the case of the educational training firm is provided by its 19-year-old receptionist. Jessica K. wanted to improve the time it took to answer the telephone. She believed that as a member of a quality educational organization, she should ensure that the telephone is answered on the first ring. Using a Quality Journal, she did a flowchart of her processes as they existed. This was followed, in sequence, by a histogram, a cause-and-effect diagram, explanations and suggestions, additional checking and, finally, another flowchart showing an improved process. Jessica succeeded in improving the time for answering the telephone on the first ring from 83% to 98%.

Too often people and processes languish in organizations because of a lack of instructions from "on high." There is really no reason to wait. Anyone can begin on their own, with the ultimate result of improved performance and greater pride and satisfaction. As Deming always said, "It doesn't matter when you start, as long as you start now."

18
Conclusion

Learning about quality has been a long process in Western nations. Although begun in the cross-fertilization of ideas between the United States and the United Kingdom in the early part of the century, quality seemed not to catch the attention of Western businesses until the 1980s. Perhaps in its early form, the study of quality seemed too abstract and academic for many managers. The idea of studying work processes by pausing from doing them, taking a step back, and collecting statistical and other data, seemed like an excessive effort.

The Japanese got a head start by being willing to take a leap of faith at a time when they had nothing left to lose. Western businesses, flush with product orders from all over the world, declined to do the same. The chasm between theory and practice seemed too large. If that wasn't daunting enough, the Western business managers learned, there were a variety of theories about how quality might be achieved.

That is why the idea for this book was born. Organizations need a way to span the gap between theory and application. Deming said that there must be theory for learning to happen. The theory must be applied to achieve results. The Japanese developed some wonderful application techniques and the results are obvious.

The task today, then, is to understand the theories of the quality masters and to apply them with the help of the techniques developed and nurtured by Japanese practitioners and now modified to fit U.S. organizations.

Dr. Noriaki Kano said that quality is a tough and sweaty job. He wishes it were easy, but unfortunately he knows no other way than rolling up one's sleeves and doing the sweaty work. Learning a new way of thinking is part of that work.

Everything, ultimately, moves in a circle—the seasons of the year, planets in orbit, and business cycles. All are systems in motion. Progress stops when a company begins to believe it operates in a straight line and may or have, arrived at the end. That end is only a precipice from which there is rarely a retreat. To survive, to thrive, and grow, it is necessary to understand the natural cycles of the universe—including those of the human institutions.

As observed in the introduction, Western organizations traditionally view their operations from a sequential view, focusing on the concrete steps that seem to take them in as straight a line as possible. Learning to think systematically is a large leap. It requires an exercise in the abstract that does not fit usual notions of sequence. Something must help make the gap to holistic thinking, that is, seeing operations as never-ending cycles. By showing how the quality masters progressed from studies of statistics into understanding human beings and theory of knowledge, this book attempts to cross that chasm. By the PDSA cycle and seeing management as interconnecting rings, we demonstrate that organizations operate naturally in cycles that must be understood to be managed properly. That, and a vision of where these continuous revolutions will lead, are the keys, not just to survival, but to growth, profitability and fulfilling dreams.

Notes

Introduction: The Roots of Quality

1. "The Quality Imperative," *Business Week* (October 25, 1991), 15.

Chapter 1: Walter A. Shewhart

1. *AT&T Technical Journal* (March–April 1986), 11.
2. W. Edwards Deming, "A Tribute to Walter Shewhart," *Industrial Quality Control* (August 1967): 112.
3. Walter A. Shewhart, *Economic Control of Quality of Manufactured Product* (New York: D. Van Nostrand, 1931), 53.
4. Shewhart, *Economic Control*, 53.
5. Shewhart, *Economic Control*, 69.
6. Shewhart, *Economic Control*, 71.
7. Donald J. Wheeler, "In Defense of Shewhart's Charts," presented to the *4th Annual Continual Improvement Conference* (Minneapolis, 1993).
8. Walter A. Shewhart, *Statistical Method from the Viewpoint of Quality Control* (New York: Dover, 1986), 45.
9. W. Edwards Deming, "A Tribute to Walter Shewhart," *Industrial Quality Control* (August 1967): 112.
10. Deming, 112.
11. Deming, 113.
12. Leslie E. Simon, "Tribute to Shewhart," *Industrial Quality Control* (August 1967): 121.
13. John Karlin, "Tribute to Shewhart," *Industrial Quality Control* (August 1967): 116.

Chapter 2: W. Edwards Deming

1. Cecilia S. Kilian, *The World of W. Edwards Deming* (Knoxville, TN: SPC Press, 1992), 34.
2. Kilian, 28.
3. Mary Walton, *The Deming Management Method* (New York: Dodd, Mead, 1986), 7.
4. Kilian, 23.
5. Personal letter from W. Edwards Deming to Louis E. Schultz, 1992.

6. Kilian, 78.
7. Walton, 14.
8. Deming *Four-Day Seminar* (Minneapolis, 1991) Chapter 2, 11.
9. W. Edwards Deming, *The New Economics* (Cambridge, MA: MIT/CAES, 1993), 60.
10. Deming Four-Day Seminar, Minneapolis, 1991.
11. Deming, *The New Economics*, 106.
12. Author's notes from a seminar by W. Edwards Deming, Bloomington, MN. August 24, 1987.
13. Author's notes on Deming Seminar in Atlanta, GA, Sept. 1, 1992.
14. W. Edwards Deming, "Foundation for Management of Quality in the Western World" (Prepared for the Institute of Management Sciences, Osaka, Japan, 1989, republished by Process Management International, Minneapolis), 9.
15. Deming, *The New Economics*, 56.
16. Author's notes on Deming Seminar in Atlanta, 1992.
17. Author's notes on Deming Seminar in Minneapolis, 1988.
18. Author's notes on Deming Seminar in Washington, D.C., 1987.
19. Deming, "Foundation for Management," 12.
20. Deming, "Foundation for Management," 15.
21. Deming, *The New Economics*, 110.
22. Author's notes on Deming Seminar, Minneapolis, 1988.
23. Author's notes on Deming Seminar Satellite downlink, Eden Prairie, MN, 1993.
24. Author's notes on Deming Seminar, San Diego, 1988.
25. Clare Crawford-Mason (Presentation to the 4th Annual Continual Improvement Conference, Minneapolis, 1993).
26. W. Edwards Deming, "Foundation for Management of Quality in the Western World," presented to the Institute of Management Sciences, Osaka, Japan, 1989.
27. Author's notes on Deming Seminar, Minneapolis, 1991.
28. Deming, *The New Economics*, 95.
29. Author's notes on Deming Seminar, San Diego, 1988.
30. W. Edwards Deming, *Out Of The Crisis* (Cambridge, MA: MIT/CAE, 1982), 35.
31. Author's notes on Deming Seminar, Minneapolis, 1991.
32. Author's notes on Deming Seminar, Minneapolis, 1989.
33. Author's notes on Deming Seminar, Atlanta, 1992.
34. Author's notes on Deming Seminar, Minneapolis, 1987.
35. Author's notes on Deming Seminar, Minneapolis, 1991.
36. Author's notes on Deming Seminar, Minneapolis, 1991.
37. Walton, 90.
38. Andrea Gabor, *The Man Who Discovered Quality* (New York: Random House, 1990), 27.
39. Author's notes on Deming Seminar, Jacksonville, FL, 1986.

40. Howard S. Gitlow, *Planning for Quality, Productivity, and Competitive Position* (Homewood, IL: Dow Jones-Irwin, 1990), 44.
41. Author's notes on Deming Seminar via satellite downlink in Eden Prairie, MN, 1993.
42. Deming, *Out of the Crisis*, 97.
43. Author's notes, Deming Seminar, San Diego, 1985.
44. San Diego, 1985.
45. San Diego, 1985.
46. An observation of the author.
47. Author's notes on Deming Seminar, Jacksonville, FL, 1986.
48. Author's notes on Deming Seminar, San Diego, 1985.
49. Author's notes on Deming Seminar satellite downlink, Eden Prairie, MN, 1993.
50. Author's notes on Deming Seminar, Washington, D.C., 1987.
51. Washington, D.C., 1987.
52. Author's notes on Deming Seminar, Minneapolis, 1989.
53. Minneapolis, 1989.
54. Author's notes on Deming Seminar, Minneapolis, 1991.
55. Author's notes on Deming Seminar in Bloomington, MN, 1987.
56. Author's notes on Deming Seminar, Minneapolis, 1988.
57. Author's notes on Deming Seminar satellite downlink, Eden Prairie, MN, 1993.
58. Author's notes on Deming Seminar, Minneapolis, 1991.
59. Interview by Anna Maravelas with W. Edwards Deming, 1991.
60. Author's recollections from Deming Seminars, 1985 through 1993.

Chapter 3: Joseph M. Juran

1. Joseph M. Juran, "A Tale of the Twentieth Century," *The Juran Report*, 10 (Autumn 1989), 5.
2. "A Tale of the Twentieth Century," 7.
3. "A Tale of the Twentieth Century," 7.
4. "A Tale of the Twentieth Century," 10.
5. "A Tale of the Twentieth Century," 10.
6. Joseph M. Juran, *Juran On Quality By Design* (New York: Free Press, 1992), 2.
7. *Quality By Design*, 334.
8. *Quality By Design*, 335.
9. *Quality By Design*, 23.
10. *Quality By Design*, 317.
11. *Quality By Design*, 11.
12. *Quality By Design*, 301.
13. *Quality By Design*, 301.
14. *Quality By Design*, 302.

15. *Quality By Design*, 14.
16. *Quality By Design*, 21.
17. *Quality By Design*, 70.
18. *Quality By Design*, 63.
19. *Quality By Design*, 219.
20. *Quality By Design*, 271.
21. *Quality By Design*, 281.
22. *Quality By Design*, 131.

Chapter 4: Homer Sarasohn

1. Sarasohn's personal files.
2. From an interview with the author.
3. From a presentation given to the Minnesota ASQC, 1992.
4. Minnesota ASQC, 1992.
5. From an interview with the author.
6. Interview with author.
7. From an interview with Myron Tribus.
8. From an interview with the author.

Chapter 5: Allan Mogensen

1. Allan H. Mogensen with Rosario Rausa, *Mogy, An Autobiography* (Chesapeake, VA: Idea Associates, 1989), 124–5.
2. p. 124.
3. p. 22.
4. p. 23.
5. p. 24.
6. p. 25.
7. p. 23.
8. p. 23.
9. p. 38.
10. p. 120.
11. p. 120.
12. p. 80.
13. p. 119.
14. p. 40.
15. p. 40.
16. p. 80.
17. p. 78.
18. p. 78.
19. p. 78.

Chapter 6: Armand Feigenbaum

1. Armand V. Feigenbaum, *Total Quality Control*, 3rd ed. (New York: McGraw-Hill, 1983), 6.
2. *Design News*, February 12, 1990, 107.
3. *Design News*, 107.
4. Feigenbaum, 11.
5. *Design News*, 107.
6. *Design News*, 107.
7. Feigenbaum, 73.
8. Feigenbaum, 44.
9. Feigenbaum, 13.
10. Feigenbaum, 13.
11. Feigenbaum, 85.
12. Feigenbaum, 86.

Chapter 7: Philip B. Crosby

1. Philip B. Crosby, *Quality Is Free: The Art of Making Quality Certain* (New York: McGraw-Hill, 1979).
2. James F. Halpin, *Zero Defects: A New Dimension in Quality Assurance* (New York: McGraw-Hill, 1966), 13–16.
3. Philip B. Crosby, *Quality Without Tears: The Art of Hassle-Free Management* (New York: McGraw-Hill, 1984).
4. Crosby, *Quality Is Free*, 22–23.
5. Crosby, *Quality Is Free*, 23.
6. Crosby, *Quality Is Free*, 23.
7. Crosby, *Quality Is Free*, 25.
8. Crosby, *Quality Is Free*, 218.
9. Crosby, *Quality Is Free*, Introduction.

Chapter 8: Myron Tribus

1. Myron Tribus, "When the Enterprise Opts for Quality, What is the CEO Supposed to Do?" (unpublished paper, 1992), 18.
2. Myron Tribus, "Quality Management in Education," (Unpublished paper, 1992), 19.
3. Tribus, "When the Enterprise Opts," 18.
4. Tribus, "When the Enterprise Opts," 18.
5. Tribus, "When the Enterprise Opts," 19.
6. Myron Tribus, "The Three Systems of Quality," (Paper delivered at Drexel University, Philadelphia, 1991), 1.

7. Tribus, "The Three Systems," 5.
8. Tribus, "The Three Systems," 3.
9. Tribus, "The Three Systems," 1.
10. Myron Tribus, "Deming's Way" (Paper published by National Institute for Engineering Management and Systems, 1992), 4.
11. Tribus, "Deming's Way," 5.
12. Tribus, "Deming's Way," 1.
13. Tribus, "Deming's Way," 1.

Chapter 9: Kaoru Ishikawa

1. Kaoru Ishikawa, *Introduction to Quality Control* (Tokyo: 3A Corp., 1990), 7; distributed exclusively in the U.S. by Quality Resources, White Plains, NY.
2. Ishikawa, *Introduction*, 7.
3. Ishikawa, *Introduction*, 16.
4. Ishikawa, *Introduction*, 17.
5. Ishikawa, *Introduction*, 55.
6. Ishikawa, *Introduction*, 429.
7. Ishikawa, *Introduction*, 429.
8. Ishikawa, *Introduction*, 430.
9. Ishikawa, *Introduction*, 78.
10. Ishikawa, *Introduction*, 78.
11. Another of the Japanese quality experts, Noriaki Kano, notes that this last principle reflects the Confucian belief in the innate goodness of man that permeates Japanese education. This view maintains that everyone has hidden potential that teachers and managers should help to develop.
12. Ishikawa, *Introduction*, 98.
13. Hitashi Kume, *Statistical Methods for Quality Improvement* (Tokyo: Association for Overseas Technical Scholarship, 1985), 26; distributed exclusively in the U.S. by Quality Resources, White Plains, NY.
14. Ishikawa, *Introduction*, 402.
15. Ishikawa, *Introduction*, 403.

Chapter 10: Shigeru Mizuno

1. Shigeru Mizuno, *Company-Wide Total Quality Control* (Tokyo: Asian Productivity Organization, 1989), i; distributed exclusively in the U.S. by Quality Resources, White Plains, NY.
2. Mizuno, 4.
3. Mizuno, 3.
4. Mizuno, 3.
5. Mizuno, 17.

6. Mizuno, 28.
7. Mizuno, 41.
8. Mizuno, 49.
9. Mizuno, 111.
10. Mizuno, 114.
11. Mizuno, 114.
12. Mizuno, 129.
13. Mizuno, 130.
14. Mizuno, 133.
15. Mizuno, 133.
16. Mizuno, 148.
17. Mizuno, 13.

Chapter 11: Yogi Akao

1. Yogi Akao, *Quality Function Deployment: Integrating Customer Requirements in Product Design* (Cambridge, MA: Productivity Press, 1990), 4.
2. Akao, 27.
3. Akao, 53.
4. Akao, 56.
5. Akao, 239.

Chapter 12: Genichi Taguchi

1. Lawrence P. Sullivan, "The Power of Taguchi Methods," *Quality Progress* (June 1987), 77.
2. Genichi Taguchi, "Robust Quality," *Harvard Business Review* (January–February 1990), 75.
3. Taguchi, "Robust Quality," 75.
4. Taguchi, "Robust Quality," 65.
5. Lance Ealey, "Taguchi Basics," *Quality* (November 1988), 32.
6. Ealey, 32.
7. Taguchi, 70.
8. Taguchi, 71.
9. Taguchi, 65.
10. Taguchi, 65.
11. Taguchi, 69.
12. Phillip J. Ross, *Taguchi Techniques for Quality Engineering* (New York: McGraw-Hill, 1988), 168.
13. Ross, 168.
14. Sullivan, 77.
15. Sullivan, 78.
16. Sullivan, 78.

17. Sullivan, 77.
18. Taguchi, 68.
19. Taguchi, 67.
20. Taguchi, 65.
21. Taguchi, 68.
22. Taguchi, 66.
23. Taguchi, 68.
24. Sullivan, 77.
25. Sullivan, 77.
26. Taguchi, 26.
27. Sullivan, 79.

Chapter 13: Noriaki Kano

1. Noriaki Kano, "The Right Way to Quality" (Paper presented to the 1993 World Quality Congress), 3.
2. Noriaki Kano, "A Perspective on Quality in American Firms," *California Management Review* (Spring 1993), 12.
3. Kano, "The Right Way," 5.
4. Comments by Noriaki Kano to the author and others in conjunction with the presentation of Kano's paper, "Development of Quality Control Seen Through Companies Awarded The Deming Prize," *Statistical Application Research*, JUSE Volume 37, No. 1-2 (1990-91) 79-105.
5. Kano, "The Right Way," 7.
6. Kano, "The Right Way," 7.
7. Kano, "A Perspective," 20.
8. Kano, "A Perspective," 20.
9. Kano, "Development of Quality Control," 92.
10. Kano, "A Perspective," 20.
11. Paul Lillrank and Noriaki Kano, *Continuous Improvement: Quality Control Circles in Japanese Industry* (Ann Arbor, MI: University of Michigan/Center for Japanese Studies, 1989), 49.
12. Lillrank and Kano, 108.

Chapter 14: Environment Management

1. James M. Kouzes and Barry Z. Posner, *The Leadership Challenge* (San Francisco: Jossey-Bass, 1987), 16–17.
2. Author's interview with Ron Wiley, Ph.D. and subsequent facsimile transmission of Wiley's findings, April 19, 1994.
3. Author's notes on Deming Seminar, Atlanta, 1992.
4. Deming Library Video, No. 19–20.

5. Author's notes from a presentation by Noriaki Kano at a meeting of Deming-based consultants in Minneapolis, 1991.
6. Myron Tribus, "Quality Management in Education" (Unpublished paper, 1992), 11.
7. Shigeru Mizuno, *Company-Wide Total Quality Control* (Tokyo: Asian Productivity Organization, 1989), 16; distributed exclusively in the U.S. by Quality Resources, White Plains, NY.
8. Kaoru Ishikawa, *Introduction to Quality Control* (Tokyo: 3A Corp., 1990), 44; distributed exclusively in the U.S. by Quality Resources, White Plains, NY.
9. Ishikawa, 45.
10. Richard Bawden, "Learning To Create A Quality Culture" (Unpublished paper, University of Western Sydney, 1991), Overhead presented with paper.
11. Ishikawa, *Introduction to Quality Control*, 45.
12. Allan H. Mogensen with Rosario Rausa, *Mogy, An Autobiography* (Chesapeake, VA: Idea Associates, 1989), 125.
13. Author's notes on Deming Seminar, Minneapolis, 1988.
14. Ishikawa, *Introduction to Quality Control*, 67.
15. Allan M. Mohrman, Jr., "Deming Versus Performance Appraisal: Is There A Resolution?" Theory-to-Practice Monograph (University of Minnesota, 1990), 10.
16. Mohrman, 16.
17. W. Edwards Deming, "Foundation for Management of Quality in the Western World" (Prepared for the Institute of Management Sciences, Osaka, Japan, 1989, republished by Process Management International, Minneapolis), 11.
18. Author's notes on Deming Seminar, satellite downlink, Eden Prairie, MN, 1993.

Chapter 16: Process Management

1. Hitoshi Kume, *Statistical Methods for Quality Improvement* (Tokyo: Association for Overseas Technical Scholarship, 1985), 92; distributed exclusively in the U.S. by Quality Resources, White Plains, NY.

Chapter 17: Personal Management

1. Shigeru Mizuno, *Company-Wide Total Quality Control* (Tokyo: Asian Productivity Organization, 1989), 23; distributed exclusively in the U.S. by Quality Resources, White Plains, NY.
2. Paul Lillrank and Noriaki Kano, *Continuous Improvement: Quality Control Circles in Japanese Industry* (Ann Arbor, MI: University of Michigan/ Center for Japanese Studies, 1989), 82.

INDEX